ESSAYS ON TIBETAN CULTURAL HERITAGE

ESSAYS ON TIBETAN CULTURAL HERITAGE

Edited by
KARUBAKI DATTA
Centre for Himalayan Studies
University of North Bengal
Darjeeling, West Bengal

SERIALS PUBLICATIONS
NEW DELHI

First Published - *2008*

ISBN : 978-81-8387-127-3

Published by

SERIALS PUBLICATIONS
4830/24, Prahlad Street, Ansari Road
Darya Ganj, New Delhi-110002 (India)
Phone : 23245225. Fax : 91-11-23272135
E-mail: serials@satyam.net.in

CONTENTS

PREFACE

The Centre for Himalayan Studies is an Area Studies Centre for researches on the Eastern Himalayas which include Tibet, Bhutan, Sikkim, Arunachal Pradesh and Darjeeling. Since its establishment in 1978 the Centre has been organizing lectures and seminars and also bringing out publications on different aspects of religion, society, economy and polity of the region.

The present volume is a compilation of some such articles by both outside scholars and faculty members of the Centre. The theme is the Tibetan culture and religious institutions in the Eastern Himalayas. There are altogether eleven articles in this volume.

The first article is by A.C. Bannerjee which was delivered as special lecture in 1982. It gives a detailed history of the spread of Mahayana Buddhism in Tibet The religion as it developed in Tibet was divided into four major sects each of which in its own turn became subdivided into many more subsects. The theme of this paper is important for a religious history of Tibet as well as for the students of the Himalayan societies which is greatly influenced by religion.

Lopen Pamala's article also delivered as a special lecture in the Centre is a history of Buddhism in Bhutan. It is a detailed account based on Bhutanese sources, of the spread of the religion and the contribution of the various personalities in this.

The theme of the third paper by Pabitra Kumar Roy is Buddhist art. This too had been delivered as a special lecture in 1983. The author discusses Tibetan art in all its aspects and points out its orientation towards religion and religious presuppositions. This discussion is carried on in the context of Buddhist art of India in general and that of

Sarnath and Ajanta in particular. He also gives occasional references to the artistic tradition of Sikkim, Bhutan, Ladakh and Nepal . He concludes that Tibetan heritage actually survives in these places along the frontiers of Tibet.

The next three papers deal with the history and characteristics of Tibetan language and literature. The first of these is by Ratna Basu . The paper was presented in the national seminar on Status of Himalayan Languages with Special References to Tibetan and Nepali in February 1998. This paper is in fact a history of the academic, literary and cultural interrelation between India and Tibet. She discusses how some original Sanskrit works on Buddhist logic and commentaries as well as some pieces of creative literature, lost and destroyed in India can be rediscovered and collected from Tibet in translation. In addition Tibetan canonical literature is actually a part of Indian literature. The number of people speaking Tibetan and its dialects are many in India and one has to adopt an attitude of sympathy and understanding towards them because they bear the same cultural heritage.

Thubten Tsering too had presented his article in the above mentioned national seminar in 1998. After giving the history and origin of the Tibetan language he mentions the different types of Tibetan scripts and points out why a familiarity with the Tibetan language is necessary for a proper understanding of Buddhist literature and culture.

Narendra Kumari Dash's article' originally a special lecture in the Centre in 2003 deals with the same theme but in more details. He too gives an account of the early intercourse between India and Tibet as a result of which a written script was introduced in Tibetan and extensive translation works were undertaken specially under the leadership of Thonmi Sambhota. He also deals with the history of the Dalai Lamas of Tibet.

Rachel Guidoni in her article on the relics in the Tibetan tradition discusses one little known aspect of Tibetan culture. This is the religious practice of preserving some corporal remains of some distinguished lamas. She has discussed different aspects of the practice including those who can let relics, the characteristics of relics and also about how the tradition is gradually becoming rare among the refugee community of the Tibetans. This was presented as a special lecture in 2001.

There are three articles on Buddhist monasteries of Sikkim and Darjeeling all published as occasional papers by the members of the Centre itself. The first article is the Monasteries of Sikkim with Specific Reference to the Economic Structure by Ranju R. Dhamala (1993) Sikkim received its Buddhism from Tibet in mid 17th century. As in Tibet, Buddhist monasteries are numerous in Sikkim too. Of these, five premier monasteries enjoyed a special status and Royal favour in Sikkim. One aspect of this status was the possession of extensive landed properties. The author highlights this economic aspect of the monasteries and explains the management of these landed properties. In course of time the monasteries lost much of what they used to own previously.

D.P. Boot in his article Monasteries in Sikkim: A Geographical Study highlights the history of the foundation , organization and regional distribution of the monasteries from a geographer's point of view. It was published in 1997.

Sikkim, prior to its merger with India used to be a Buddhist state where the Buddhist monarchy extended considerable patronage towards these monasteries. At present too the Ecclesiastical Department of the Sikkim Government takes care of the needs of the monasteries and the monks thereof. There are many Buddhist communities in adjoining Darjeeling too but those monasteries do not receive any such governmental patronage. The Buddhist Monasteries of Darjeeling Hills by Karubaki Datta (2001) is an attempt to trace the history and the resources of the monasteries of the different communities as well as of those established by the refugee monk communities of Tibet.

The last article is The Buddhist Tribes of Arunachal Pradesh is by Hasibul Rahaman. Arunachal, which is a part of the Eastern Himalayas is the homeland of numerous tribes most of whom practice animism. However,some tribes are Buddhist specially those around the region of Tawang which itself used to be a part of Tibet. Some tribes on the other hand practice Theravada Buddhism . Buddhism as practiced by these tribes is mixed with animistic rituals and practices and on the whole it has developed some peculiar characteristics. The article gives a description of these communities and their religious practices.

In the compilation of this volume I have received help and encouragement from different sources. I take this opportunity to thank them all.

Special lectures and National seminars were organized and Occasional papers were published with U.G.C. grant. I express my thanks to the Commission because without their assistance these programmes would not have been possible.

I express my gratitude to Prof P.K. Saha, Vice Chancellor of North Bengal University for his constant encouragement and interest in the academic programmes of the Centre. I am equally grateful to Dr. T.K. Chatterjee for permission to bring out this volume.

I thank Sri Hasibul Rahaman and Dr. D.P. Boot of the Centre. for Himalayan Studies. In addition to contributing an article for the a volume. Sri Rahaman has helped in proof reading and in preparation of the manuscript. Dr. D.P. Boot has helped in locating some of the old articles and gave some valuable suggestions.

Finally I owe a special debt of gratitude to all of my colleagues in the Centre including the office staff and the staff of the Documentation Cell who always stand by me with suggestions and co operation.

CONTRIBUTORS

A.C. Bannerjee; Formerly Director, Sikkim Research Institute of Tibetology and other Buddhist Studies, Gangtok, Sikkim.

Lopen Pemala; Formerly Director of the National Library, Thimpu, Bhutan.

Pabitra Kumar Roy; Formerly Reader, Department of Philosophy, North Bengal University.

Ratna Basu; Professor, Department of Sanskrit, Calcutta University.

Thubten Tsering; Teacher, TNA Academy, Gangtok, Sikkim.

Narendra K. Dash; Formerly Head, Department of Indo Tibetan Studies, Visva Bharati, Santiniketan.

Rachel Guidoni; Doctoral Fellow, University of Paris, France.

Ranju R. Dhamala; Formerly Reader, Centre for Himalayan Studies, North Bengal University.

D.P. Boot; Cartographer, Centre for Himalayan Studies, North Bengal University.

Karubaki Datta; Reader and Director, Centre for Himalayan Studies, North Bengal University.

Hasibul Rahaman; Project Assistant, Centre for Himalayan Studies, North Bengal University.

BUDDHIST SECTS IN TIBET

A.C. Bannerjee

BUDDHIST SECTS IN SIKKIM

A hundred years after Buddha's *Mahaparinirvana* dissension arose among the monks in regard to the actual words of the Master and their interpretations, which ultimately led to the origin of sects in Indian Buddhism, all claiming to have preserved His original teachings. And within a few hundred years after the demise of the Great Teacher as many as twenty Sects or more cane into existence–although a few of them disappeared shortly after their appearance. But in regard to the origin of the sects in Tibet the case has been quite different and about ten sects came into being there in course of time. The Tibetan sects came into existence with a view to preserving the purity of the Buddhist teachings and doing away with the degrading practices, superstitions, beliefs and the like than prevalent prior to the Buddhist doctrines. Wadell (1959, pp. 74-75) writes that the sects "arose in revolt against the depraved Lamaism then prevalent, which was little also than a priestly mixture of demonolatry and witchcraft. Abandoning the grosser charlatanism, the new sects returned to celibacy and many of the purer "Mahayana rules". "Buddhist religion", observed by S.C. Das (1882) "progressed more and more, so as to branch out into numerous different sects as a result of the extra-ordinary growth. This, like the eighteen divisions of the Vaibhasika School of ancient India were designated after the manes of respective teachers and places of origin. Some of the Tibetan Lamas who had devised their religious knowledge from Indian *Pandits*; feeling great veneration for the theories themselves, named their respective sects after them. They did not follow the Indian patriarchies in their nomenclature, for all the Indian Buddhist Schools were designated after the general sense of their philosophies". Indeed, it was through the efforts of these sects, Buddhism was widely spread and occupied the position it did in Tibet. There were no sects in Tibet prior to the eleventh century A.D. Buddhism, as already observed, suffered a violent set-back for the time being because of the kind Glam dar-ma's ruthless persecution. Thus came the great disaster to Buddhism. It was virtually annihilated in Tibet. Prosecution of the doctrine is one of the darkest in the whole history of Tibet". In the 11th century A.D. King Ye-ses-hod who was one of the pious kings of Tibet and to whom Buddhist renaissance owed much invited Atisa (Dipankarasrijnana) to come to Tibet from India to propagate Buddhism there. Since Atisa came to Tibet he corrected, rectified and systematised the Buddhist teachings then prevalent. He reformed the Sangha in Tibet and brought a great renaissance in the religion. With his reformation originated the Kadam-pa sect, the first sect of Tibetan Buddhism as against the unreformed type of Buddhism called Nin-ma-pa "the old ones' founded by Padma-sambhava, better known as Guru Rinpoche. T.W.D. Shakabpa (1967, pp. 59-60). writes that "the teachings of Atisha were subjected to a reformation movement by Drom and, as a result, a new school of Buddhism came into being in Tibet. To distinguish themselves from the unreformed followers Padmasanbhava, the followers of Atisha and Drom were called Katam-pa (one of the doctrine) while the unreformed monks were called Nying-ma-pa (one of the old". Thus Tibetan Buddhism developed into various sects from the time of Atisa. In other words, Tibetan sects traced their heritage to the great acharya Dipankara Srijnana late sometime in the latter part of the 11th century A.D. "All contemporaneous and latter sects without exception were influenced by the teachings of the Bkah-dam-pa sect". "No sects", observes Waddell, "appear to have existed prior to Lan-Darma's persecution, not till more than a century and a half later. The sectarial movement seems to date from the Reformation started by the Indian Buddhist monk

Atisa"(1959, p. 54). Tibetan Buddhism, as we have seen, developed into various sects later on. Most of them are now extant. Only few of them still survive. We have, however, few details about them. The following are the different sects with their subdivisions that came into existence:

1. The Nying-ma-pa (Nin-ma-pa)–was founded by Guru Padmasambhava during the reign of King Khri-sron-lde-bstan in the 8th century A.D. Padmasambhava organised the Tibetan Sangha (order of monks) and introduced certain elements of Tantricism into the existing religion. With him thus originated the new sect called Nying-ma-pa (lit. the old one) sect. Waddell (1959, p. 56) writes that "The residue who remained wholly unreformed and weakened by the loss of "old ones", as they adhered to the old practices. And now, to legitimise many of their unorthodox practices which had crept into use, and to admit of further laxity, the Nin-ma-pa resorted to the fiction of Ter-ma of hidden revelation". He further adds that "several Min-ma Lamas now began to discover new gospels, in caves and elsewhere, which they alleged were hidden gospels of the Gurum Saint Patma" (1959, p. 72-73). This sect claims to have preserved fully the teachings of Padmasambhava. It pays special worship to Guru Padmasambhava–"in a variety of forms, both divine and demonical, expressive of his different moods at different times". Manifold traces of Bon, the primitive religion of Tibet, are still found in the creed of this sect. The followers of this sect are said to have kept necromancy of the Old Tibetan religion more fully than any of the reformed sects that arose later on. They rarely observe celibacy and abstinence in their monasteries. They show greater laxity in living. Thus it may be pointed that Lamas of this sect 'need not necessarily be celebrates and can openly marry if they choose or keep a woman'. "This sect" observes Schlagintweit, (1968 p. 72-3) "adheres strictly to the ancient rites and ceremonies, in the manner probably taught by the earliest Chinese priests, and possesses some peculiar symbolical works which have not been embodied in the large compilations of the Kanjur and Tanjur works".

The Nying-ma-pa sect is also called the 'Red Cap' sect from the peculiar red cap work by the Lamas. It is further known as the old "Translation" sect as its fundamental teachings are selected from the texts translated by Guru Padmasambhava or Acharya Santaraksita, Mahapandita Vimalamitra of Kashmir and others. It principal teachings are thus 'based on these translated texts. It divided itself into several revelation'. Prominent among them are : Dorje-tak-pa (rdo-rje-brag-pa), Min-dol-lin-pa (smin-grol-glin-pa), Kar-tok-pa (bkah-rtog-pa) and Na-dak-pa (mNas-bdag-pa). They are so called after the names of their respective founders of the monasteries or present monastery. But their differences are very slight. The Dorje-tak-pa takes its name from the Dorje-tak monastery close to Sam-ye monastery, the first monastery founded in Tibet. It adopts the revelation of rGod-Idem and has also some branches. The Mindol-lin-pa is nemaed after the Non-dol-lin, its principal monastery. It follows the revelation of bDag-lin-pa. It has also a few brahches. The Kar-tok-pa which is called after Lama Kar-tok follows the revelation of Klon-ch'en Rab-hbyun. It has chief monasteries in two places, east of Tibet. The Na-dag-pa is named after Nah-dag, its founder. It is mainly a branch of Dorje-tak-pa. The Lamas of several monasteries of Sikkim belong to this sect. Thus the origin of so many sub-sects accounts for its most popularity and importance in Tibetan Buddhism.

The Nying-ma-pa sect divides the entire Buddhadharma (Buddhist doctrine) from the Sutra to the Tantra into nine Yanas, which are three Hetulaksanayanas (Yanas of Cause) and six Phala-vajrayanas (Vajrayana of result). The three Hetulaksanayanas are Sravakayana, Pratyakabuddhayana and Bodhisattvayana. The six Phalavajrayanas are:

> The three outer Tantras and three inner Tantras. The three other Tantras are: Mahayoga, Anuyoga and Atiyoga (Mahasampannayoga).

The Sravakayana (Hinayana)–its adherents observe any one of the eight (seven) Pratimoksavows of moral discipline and accept the view of Pudgalanairatma (non-existence of self) and not Dharmanairatma (non-existence of all things of the world). By the practice of Samatha meditation they make both the body and mind relaxed. They concentrate on the Vipassana meditation of the four truths with their sixteen aspects and do present the four paths–Sambhogagamarga, Prayogamarga, Darsanamarga and Bhavanamarga and attain peace and happiness for themselves. By the practice of the sect Paramsasamadha they further attain the four stages of sanctification-sotapatti (stream-entry), sakadagami (once-returner), anagami (never-returner) and arhat (the final stage).

Pratyekabudhayana (Hinayana)–its followers observe any one of the Pratimoksavows as do the Sravakayanists. They assert the selflessness (Mairatma) of objects but they maintain the view that the minutest one of the consciousness in time. They concentrate on the Samatha meditation, the four noble truths will their sixteen aspects and twelve links of the Pratetysamutpada (Dependent origination). Arhatship could be attained by one's own effort.

Boddhisattvayana (Mahayana)–the followers of this Yana believe in Pudgalanairatma–all the existent are without self or true. They practise boddicitta (thought of enlightenment) to achieve Buddhahood for the benefit of other beings– bodhicitta being one of the special features of Mahayana. They practise the six parameters and four aspects of collecting and serving disciples (bsDu-ba-bZhi-Duwa-Zhi). They train themselves in the four paths (margas) and thirty-seven Bodhipaksiyadharmas. After practising for there asamkhyakalpas (countless aeons) they will attain Mahaparinirvana. Then until the samsara becomes empty they will appear for the service of the beings in two forms sambhogakaya and nirmanakaya, because of the pranidhana (aspiration) at the time of their practice. The goal of all the yanas is the same but the way of practice is varied. In lower yanas the adherents avoid the defilements or they use the antidotes to do away with the defilements or they use the antidotes to do away with the defilements. But in Tantrayana they transform or practise to perceive all the appearances of the world and Nirvana as same as pure and perfect. It is indeed a skilful means to attain Buddhahood.

Let us now discuss the six Pharavajrayanas, the three outer Tantras, as already mentioned, are:

> Kriayoga: its followers keep the three doors–mind, speech and body –clean. They live on vegetables, sweets and dairy products. They assert that from the point of view of the Parmarthasatya (absolute truth) all things are equal but from that of the Samvrtisatya (relative truth) the divinity is the lord (master) and the devotee the servant. A devotee visualises the divinity in front of him and makes offerings and recites the mantras and prayers. He concentrates on the body, speech and mind of the divinity and by receiving rays from him obtains the blessings again and again. After seven or sixteen lives he attains the Trikulavajradhara state.

Carayoga (also called Upayayoga)–the viewpoint of this yana is the same as that of the Yogatantra and its carya (activity) is also like that of the Kriyayoga. The difference is, among others, that a devotee visualises the divinity in front of him as a friend or a brother and practises and samadhi.

Yogatantra : its adherents assert that in Paramarthasatya all the existent are free from any sign of conceptualisation. In the Samvrtisatya all the appearances are regarded as the mandalas of the divinities. They do not pay much attention to clean the body.

We have also seen before that the three inner Tantras are Mahayoga (Pitryoga–Fatheryoga), Anuyoga (Matryoga–motheryoga) and Atiyoga (Mahasampanna or Mahasandhiyoga).

Mahayoga–its followers enjoy everything without any attachment to it. To accept all the things as the essence of the mind (mindness) and the Dharmakaya) is the Parmarthasatya. Its manifestations, thoughts and as the Three H Doors of the divinities is the Samvrtisatya. The adherents are enjoined to purify all the existent as divinities or the non-duality of bliss, clarity and non-thought. They thus achieve supreme attainment in this very life.

Anuyoga–it has herein less visualisation of development (utpannakrama) but has more perfection (sampannakrama) of bliss, clearly and no-thought through the yogas or vein, semen and energy. Its followers assert that all the appearances are of three mandalas:

Spontaneous, Emptiness and Great bliss. They attain Buddhahood in the very life.

Agiyoga–its adherents assert that all the appearances are the illusion of the deluded mind. They are false because in reality their nature is non-existent. In nature all the existent are same as pure in the Dharmakaya. In practice there is neither acceptance nor rejection but to practise or accept all the existent as manifestations of the nature, Dharmata. In Atiyoga teachings there are three aspects : Cittavarga (semssde), Abhyantaravarga (Klong-sde) and Upadesavarga (man-nag-sde). These teachings are instructions to introduce to the nature of the mind or the nature of the existent, the Dharmata and the awareness by innermost direct method of practice. After receiving the instruction to the nature one obtains the practice to make clear and stabilise the state and to perfect the freedom from worldly defilements for ever. When perfected all the existent will dissolve into the vast expanse of Dharmata, Dharmakayahood. The Atiyoga is the highest teaching of the Nying-ma-pa sect and this is exclusively the Nying-ma-pa sect and this is exclusively the Nying-ma-pa teaching and practice.

Lastly, it may be pointed out here that in the Outer Tantras the followers make distinction between the two truths, do not take meats and do not visualise the divinity with the female consort. They cannot get the result in the very life. In the inner Tantras, however, the adherences advocate inseparability of the two truths; equality of all the things, taking five kinds of meats and visualising the divinity with the consort. They attain the result in the very life. The truths of the three Yogas are the special doctrines of the Nying-ma-pa.

Many of the Sutra texts of both the Hinayana and Mahayana and Tantras of the Kanjur collection as also many commentaries and works of the Tanjur collection, which were translated into Tibetan in the earlier spread of the dharma (Buddhism) form the scriptures of the Nying-ma-pa sect. Those apart, the Nying-ma-rGud a'Bum (Nying-ma-Gyud-Bum, collection of ancient Tantras) of twenty-five volumes with about four hundred forty treatises.(reprinted from Delhi), also the bKa'-Ma'i mChhos-khag bchu gsum (the thirteen texts of Kama or canon), the gTer-Chhos or gTer-ma of the great hundred or Ter-sTons (treasure discoverers). Man-NgagolTa-a 'Phreng (Darsanamal-supadesa), and g Sang-sNags Lam-Rim (Tantrapathakrama) by Guru Padmasambhava and the works of Vimalamitra and Vaiva cana are also regarded as the most important scriptures. The works of Rong-Zom-Chhos-kyi-bZang-po (10th century); Kun-mKhyen Klong–Chhen Rab-a 'Jams (Longchen Rabjam = 1308-1363; dPal–sPrul Rin-po-Chhe (1808); Mi-Pham Rin-po-che (1846-1912), the 3rd rDo-Grub-Chhen Rin-po g Zhan-d Ha' (Khenpo Zhenga) are further a few of the scholarly works of the Nying-ma-pa sect. They throw much light on the different aspects of this sect.

There are about a thousand monasteries of the Nying-ma-pa sect in Tibet. From the point of view of the history or the size the most important ones are: bSam-yes (Sarmye), monastery built by Guru Padmasambhava and Santaraksita in the 9th century A.D. But it has been under the control of the Sakys-pa sect for the last few years.

G Tsug-lag-Khang (Tsuglak Khang) is the main temple of Lhasa built by kind Srong-tsan-sgam-pa in the 7th century A.D. There are other temples of the Nying-ma-pa sect too. But they are under the control of the Gelug-pa sect.

Lastly, mention may be made here of some of the important monasterics of the present time. They are as follows:

> sMing-Grol-Gling (Mintrol Ling) constructed by g Ter-Chhen a 'Gyar-Med-rdo-rJe (Terchen Gyurmed Dorje) in 1676 A.D., rDo-rJe-Brag (Dojetrag) by Rig-s'Dzin Ngag-Gi d Bang-po (Rigzin Ngagi Wangpo) in 1659 – both of them are in Central Tibet. bDe gshegs (Kadam-pa Desheg) in 1159, dpal-yul (Peyu) by Rig-a'DZin Kun b-Zeng-She s-rab (Rig-DZin Kunzang Sherab in 1665, rDZogs-Chhen (dZogchen by Padma Rig-a'Dzin (Padma Rig Zin) in 1685, Zhe-Chhen by 2nd Rab-s'Byams, a'Gyur-Med Kun=bZang-rNam-rGal (Rabjam Gyurmed Kun Zand Namgyal in 1735 and a 'Khor-gDong (Khordong) they are also situated in Kham. The Dodrup Cham built by the 2nd Bodrup Chen Rinpoche; the Tathang built by Lhatul

> Rinpoche, the Turug-kar of Se-ra, the Rong-Wo-Srib-Gon of Re-kong and Kong-Wo-Nying-Gon of Re-Kong–all are in Golok and Amdo provinces.

There are also a number of Nying-ma-pa monasteries in Bhutan, Sikkim, Ladhak and some parts of Nepal. It may be noted here in this context that now there are many centres and temples of this sect in Europe and America and fortunately, their numbers are growing rapidly.

2. The Kadampa (bKah-gdams-pa)–is one of the sects of Buddhism in Tibet. In Tibetan, the word bKah means 'word, speech' and gdams 'doctrine'. Kadam-pa means that the words are to realise as precepts or instructions. "It is called bka '-gdams, because it conveys the preachings of the Buddha, word for word, without omitting any word". It thus explicitly 'means all the words uttered by the Buddha which form the Tripitaka, i.e., sutra, vinaya and abhidharma and which are also included in "stages of the three purusas" as taught and propagated by Atisa". Atisa's chief disciple Hbrom-ston-pa once remarked:

> "The rare words of the Buddha which form the Tripitaka are embodied in the solemn tenets of the three purusa, like golden treasury and pearl heads; Whoever counts them gets profit".

With one reformation started by Atisa originated the Kadam-pa sect based on his interpretation of Buddhism. "The first of the reformed sects" writes Waddell, ((1959, p. 54) "and the one with which Atisa most intimately identified himself was called the Kha-dam-pa". It is the first sect of Tibetan Buddhism closely related with the name of Atisa. This sect was expanded by Hbrom-ston-pa (Ston-pa Rinpo-che), one of his renowned disciples. "Atisa's reformed teachings, based upon the Yogacara traditions founded my Maitreya and Asanga, led to the establishment of the Pkah-gdams-pa school by his Tibetan discipline Hbrom-ston". Along with other disciples Hbrom-ston built the Rwa-sgren monastery at Hdam-pa for the propagation of Buddhism. "It was the first lamasery of the new sect, though the monastery of T'o-din, in Purang, built in 1025, is considered to have become a Kah-dam-pa

"Institution of Atisa's residence therein". It became the source of the Kadam-pa-teachings. This sect puts more emphasis on the quality of the adherents rather than on the quantity. Phu-chun-ba Gshon-nurgyalmtshan, Po-to-ba Rin-chen-gsal, and Spyan-sna-ba Tshal-Khrims hber known as 'the three brothers' widely propagated the teachings of this sect. Kham-luns-pa Sakya yon-tan was further added to this sect. They are usually known as the 'four great disciples'. Glan-ri-than-pa, S'a-ra-oa, Bya-yul-pa and others made its further expansion to the various parts of Tibet. In fact, the teachings of the Bkah dam-pa sect spread all over Tibet.

The doctrine of the Kadam-pa sect is based chiefly on the well-known works, such as, the Mjo-sdehirgyan-pa (Sutralamkara); Byan-chub-sems-dpahi-spyod-pa. (Siksa-samuccaya), Byan-chub-sams-spahi-spyoda hug-pa (Bodhisattvacaryayatara), Skyespahi-rab-s-kyi-rgyud (Jatakamala) and Ched-du-br-od-pahi-tshoms (Udanavarga). Of them Byan-chub-sems-dpahi-spyed-pa and the Byanchub-sems-dpahi-spyod-pa-la-h jug-pa explain the philosophy and the course of conduct while the others remaining point out the character of the Bodhisattva. These works are known as the "Six Basic Texts of the bka "gdama-pas"(Roerich, p. 810) "The special characteristic of the Brah-gdams-pa sect is that it includes all Buddhist sutras within the scope . Its teachings are simple, mostly in local dialects, but deep and full of meaning and inspiring. Its teachers always strict to the faults of the disciples. Lastly, "it took a synthetic view of the teachings of the Hinayana and Mahayana, enforced celibacy upon the monks and discouraged magic practices". The adherents of the Kadam-pa themselves assert that their doctrine is the confluence of the teachings of bKa' (Kadam-pa) and Phyag Rgya-Chen-po (Mahamudra).

The Kadam-pa branched into three sub-sects. They are as follows:

(a) The Canon sub-sect–it originated with Po-to-ba. It advocates the through study of all the sutras and s'astras, which leads to the attainment of Buddhahood. Its teachings are thus directly based on the Canonical Works.

(b) The Instruction sub-sect–it traced its origin to SpyaM-sna ba. It lays much emphasis on the cultivation of right views and right conduct. The scriptures of Mahayana in general and the works of Nagarjuna and Santideva in particular form the basis of its teachings.

(c) The Discipline sub-sect–it was based on the teachings of Atisa which were subsequently passed on to several others. It enjoins on its adherents to fix one's mind on the five-fold meditation : Sakyamuni, Avalokitesvara, Green sgroima and Mi-gye-be – the four saints along with the Tripitaka are known as the "The Seven Jewels of the Bkah-gdams-pa sect".

The Kadam-pa sect became the most widely spread sect in Tibet. According to its followers its doctrine is the confluence of Maha-mudra (Tantra) and Kadam-pa. Indeed its teachings highly influenced all contemporaneous and later sects. "Everyone among the intellectuals who either built up monasteries for preaching or maintained the correct doctrine of the Buddha was influenced by the teachings of the Bkah-gdams-pa sect". It may be noted in passing that this sect three and a half centuries later, developed into dGelug-pa sect, the most powerful sect under the leadership of Tsong-kha-pa.

3. The Kargyud-pa (bKah-rgud-pa)–is one of the important sects in Tibet. In Tibetan, bKab-rgved means "the transmission of teachings". In other words, it means the tradition of instructions orally transmitted through a continual series of teachers and disciples.

That is why it is called a "School of Successive Order". It may also be called "Oral Traditionalism". Its followers believe in the succession of precepts handed down through a galaxy of teachers. It traces its origin to Marpa (11th century A.D.), native of Lhodrag who visited India and Tibet and studied extensively the Tantric texts with a number of eminent teachers there. On his return to Tibet, he founded this sect on the basis of the teaching of his teacher Naropa, the great Indian Siddacarya (master of mysticism).

The Kagyud-pa (bKra-brgyud-pa) has two main schools : the Shangs-pa bKa' brgud-pa (Shangpa Kagyudpa) and Dvars-pa bKa'-brgyd-pa (Dagpo Kagyudpa).

The Shangpa Kagyudpa–was established by the great Yogi and Siddha Khyung-po-rNal-a Byor (978-1079 A.D.). He spent fifty years in studying Sutra and Tantra texts in India, Nepal and Tibet. Among his teachers were Nigu (the consort of Mahasiddha Naropa), Sukhasiddha and Rahulagupta. He built about a hundred monasteries including his own principal monastery Zhang-Zhong in Shangs Valley and that is why his system is also known as Shangpa Kagyud. He taught for about thirty years and had eighty thousand disciples. His teachings were based on the five Tantras, viz., Samhara, Hevaja, Mahayaya, Guhyasamaja and Vajrabhajrava. He also taught the teachings of Nigu and Sukhasiddha as also the doctrine of Mahamudra. This system is not at present wide-spread as a school.

The Dag-po-bkah-brgyud-pa (Dagpo Kagyudpa)–it means the transmission of the order of Dag-po, which is the name of a great scholar-ascetic who lived in the Dagpo Valley. It spread widely and is one of the four major schools of Tibet. It may be pertinent to note here that now Dagpo Kagyud is the only Kagyud (bKah-rgud), since Shangpa Kagyudpa, the first one is not well known–it is now almost extinct. Marpa (Mar-pa Lo-tse-wa), Chos-kyi-Blo-gros (Chkyi Lodro), is the founder of this school on the 11th century A.D. He studied first with a'Brog-milo-tsa-ba (Drogmi Lotswa) and then visited India thrice and Nepal four times. He received the teachings of Tantras from the renowned teachers such as Naropa and Maitripa. Specially he obtained the absolute realization of Mahamudra mysticism from the teachings of Samvara, Guhyasamaja, Hevajra Mahamaya and other Tantras to his disciples–the most prominent among them being the four chief disciples, so called four pillars, viz., rNgog-, Chhos-sKurDo-rJe (Ngogton Choku Dorje), m Tshur-ston d Bang-Ngo (Tshurten Wang-Ngo), Mes-sTon Tshon-po Meton Tshonpo) and Mi-la Ras-pa (Milarepa), the great hermit-poet of Tibet. This esoteric doctrine was thereafter authoritative historian of Tibet and Tson-kha-pa, the great Tibetan reformer 'in whose hands this tradition gained extensive prevalence and unbroken continuity down to the present time'.

Among the distinguished disciples of Marpa, the famous poet Milarepa was initiated into the mysteries of Tantricism by Marpa himself. In his young age he lost his father and his relation appropriated his property. This hurt him seriously and when he grew up, he learnt the art of magic power. He brought destruction to his relations and destroyed their crops etc. But pangs of repentance overtook him later on and he went to Lho-brag and met Marpa who initiated him into the Tantric Mandala after various kinds of hard labour. He dwelt in caves, living many months on herbs. He wore only a thin cotton cloth in the icy cold winter in Himalayas. Afterwards he took the life of an itinerate preacher and travelled extensively over the various parts of Tibet and converted a large number of populace to his new creed. He died at the age of 84 in 1123 A.D. He had a large number of disciples. Of them Dvags-po-Lha-rje (Dagpo Lhaje) deserves special mention. He left home at the age of twenty six when his wife died. He became a monk and studied the various teachings of the Kadampa sect under the distinguished teachers of this sect. He also received instructions from Milarepa. He wrote a number of books. Of them his Dagpo Thargyan (Dvags-po'I Thar-rGyan) is unique of its kind. It contains the doctrines of both Kadam-pa and Milarepa. Dagpo-Lha-rje died at the age of eighty in 1153 A.D. He had many disciples. Because of him this tradition came to be known as Dagpo Kagyud. Then from this Dagpo Kagyud arose four major sub-sects and eight minor grand sub-sects from one of its sub-sects later on. The four major sub-sects are : Karma Kagyud (Kamtshang Kagyud), I hagtru Kaguud, Tshalpa-Kagyud and Barompa-Kagyud.

Karma Kagyud–was founded in the middle of (Du-sum-Khyanpa). He studied the various doctrines with Dagpo-Lhaje and Rechungpa. He built monasteries at Karma Lha-Ding and in Tshur-phy (Tshu phu) for the grant benefit of the people. He died at the age of eighty. Since Karma Dusum Khyanpo the heads of this subject have been the uninterrupted reincarnations of him till the present time. His next reincarnation Karmapa, Dusum Khyampa is put in the first generation and Pakshi in the second. Pakshi was the first person to be recognized as a Tulku (incarnation, Avatara) of a Lama in Tibet. He also visited the court of the emperor of China and became his guru (preceptor). The emperor 'honoured him with the gold-rimmed black cap. Thence, after Paksi, this sect was also called the Black Cap Sect (Shwa-nag-can). The XVI the Karmapa Rigpa Dorje (Rig Pa 'I rDo-rJe) who used to live in Sikkim, the stronghold of Karmapa. He visited several countries abroad. He has got more than hundred meditation centres in the West. His principal monastery in Tibet is the mTshur-phu in Central Tibet. It should be pointed out here that the Karmapa 'seems to be nearly identical with the Karmaks sect of Nepal.

Phagtru Khyud (Phag-gru-bha-br-gyud) It was founded by Phagmo Trupa Dorje-Gyalpo (Phag-mo-Gru-pa-rDo-rJe rGyal-po) who was born in the southern part of Kham in 1110 A.D. He studied various teachings under different teachers. Afterwards he learnt the Maha-mudra (doctrine of the great symbol) from Dagpo Lhaje at Sgam-po monastery. He constructed a monastery at a place called Pha-mo-gru in South Tibet (now known as Densa-Thil-g-Dan-sa-mThil) to propagate the doctrine and was hence called Phamo-Trupa. He died at the age of sixty one in 1170 A.D. He had a large number of disciples which formed many sub-sects later on.

Tshalpa (Tshal-ba) Kagyud–the founder of this sub-sect was Zhang-Dar mstrog (Zhang Darma Grags) who was born in 1122 A.D. His main preceptor was Wongom Tshuthrim (d bon bsGom Tshul-Phrims S SNying-pa) who was a disciple of Dagpo. Later on he founded the Gung-Thang monastery to popularize the doctrine and to convert the people. He died at the age of seventy one in 1193 A.D.

Barompa-Kagyud (a 'Bab-Rom bKa'–brGud–Darma Wangchug (Dar-Ma-Bang-phyug) was a disciple of Dagpo. He studied all the doctrines both exoteric and esoteric under him and attained all excellent virtues. He built the Barom Monastery in the north and hence his tradition was known as the Barom Kagyud.

We have seen before that the eight minor sub-sects issued from the Bagpo Kagyudpa. But rightly speaking, they originated with the Phagtru Khyud. In other words, they traced their heritage to the disciples of Phagmo Trupa. They are:

(i) **Drikung Kagyud (a 'Bri-Gung bKa brgyud)**–it was founded by Kyurre Rimpoche (Skyu-Re Rin-po-che). He received the teachings of the Kagyud from Phagmo trupa and became an eminent scholar and a fomous monk. His religious discourses were usually attended by a number of his disciples including many monks. He built a monastery in Drinkung Valley in Central Tibet and hence his tradition is known as Drikungpa. He wrote a scholarly series of treatises called Gongchig (dGongs-gchig). Later, in this tradition Rinche Phung shog (Rin-chhen-Phun Tshogs) was a famous scholar and writer of both Nyingmapa and Kagyudpa. In Ladak, there are a large number of Drikung Kagyud followers and many monasteries.

(ii) **Taglong Kagyudpa (sTag-Lung bKa 'brgyud-pa)**–it was founded by Taglung Thangpa Trashipal (sTag-Lung-Thang-pa bKra shis dPal) who was born in 1142 A.D. He became an attendant of Phagmo Trupa who taught him all his doctrines. He built a monastery at Taglung (sTag-Lung) Valley for propagation of Buddhism and so his tradition became known after it. He was well-known for his strict discipline. He also led an ideal life of a monk. He died at the age of sixty nine in 1210 A.D. Sangye Wontragpapal (Sangs-rGyas dBon Grags-pa dPal), a distant nephew of Dagpo, of this tradition, built another monastery called Riwoche in Khams wherein teachings of the various schools of Tibetan Buddhism were imparted.

(iii) **Yamzang Kagyud (gYam-bZang bKa-brgyud)**–it was founded by Ye-She-Sang (Ye-Shes Senge) a disciple of Pnagmo Trupa and a native of Mon-hgar. He got the highest realization just at the sight of his guru (preceptor). His foremost disciple was Yazangpa (gYa-bZang-pa) who built the Yazang monastery where he trained many disciples. Their tradition was named Yazung Kagyudpa.

(iv) **Throphu Kagyudpa (Khro-Phu-bKal-brgyud-pa)**– originated with two brothers (according to some, nephew and uncle), Rinpoche Gyal-thsa and Kunden Ragpe, disciples of Phagmo Trupa. The former built the Throphu monastery. Their nephew was Throphu Lotsava who was ordained as a monk by his uncles and learnt extensively all the teachings from them. He invited many Indian teachers including the great Pandita Sakyasri of Kashmir. He built a temple at Throphu monastery and installed a big image of Maitreya Buddha therein. He also wrote a number of books. Their tradition is thus known as Throphu Kagyud.

(v) **Shugseb Kagyud (Shugs-gSeb bKa brgyud)**–originated with Chokyi Seng (Chos-Kyi-Senge), a disciple of Phagmo Trupa. He built Nyephu Shugseb (SNye-phu-Shugs-gseb) monastery and gave religious discourses to the people. His tradition is known as Shugseb Kagyud.

(vi) **Martshang (sMar-Tshang)**–this tradition was started by Marpa Richen Lodro (sMar-pa Rin-chhen-Blo-Gros).

(vii) **Yapa (Yel-ba) Kagyud**–this tradition was established by yelpa Yeshe Tseg (Yel-Ba-Ye-Shes-Tsegs). Hebuilt shar Dorje Dzong (Shar rDo-rJe rDzong), Lho-Yel-phug (Lho Yel-Phug) and Chang Tana Byang rTa-rNa) monasteries for propagation of his teachings.

(viii) **Drukpa Kagyud (sBrun-pa-bKa 'brgyud)**–this tradition was established by Phagmo Trupta's disciple Lingrepa (Gling-Ras-pa) and his disciple Tsangpa Gyare (gTsang-pa Gya-ras). Later it divided itself into three sub-schools, viz., the Middle Dukpa, Lower Drukpa and upper Dukpa.

(ix) **The Par-Druk (Middle Dukpa Kagyud) (Barys 'Brug)**– Lingrepa Padma rDo-rJe (Gling-Ras-pa-Padma rdo-rJel) was a highly enlightened disciple of Pahgmo Trupa. He built a monastery at Naphur (sNa-Phur). Among his disciples, Tsangpa Gyare (gTsang-pa-rGyur-Ras) was a famous teacher. He discovered the texts of "Six Circles of one Taste" of Rehungpa (Ras-Chhung-pa). He built Longdrol (Klong-rDol) and Ralung

(Ra-lung) monasteries. Then he went to a place called namkyi phu (gNam-Gyi Phu) to build a monastery. Along with his party when he reached there they saw nine Druks (s 'Brug-Dragons) flying into the sky with roars. He took it to be a good omen. And he called the name of the monastery as Druk (a Brug), and Druk Sewa Changchub Gon as also Namdruk (gNam-s Brug). It is that is why his tradition was known as Druk and his followers as Drukpa. This sub-school became very popular in Tibet and his adherents were simple and vigorious a spiritual practitioners. There is a Tibetan proverb which runs as follows:

> "Half of the people are Drukpas Kagyudpas,
> Half of the Drukpa Kagyudpas are beggars,
> And half of the beggars are Drubthobs
> (Siddhas)"

Later, in this tradition appeared many disciples. Among them there was Padma Karpo (Padma dKar-po), also known as Kun Khyens (Kun mKhyen-Sarvajnra) who founded the Sang Ngag Choling (gSang-sNags Chhos-Gling) monastery near the border of Assam (in Tibet) and it became the seat of the Drunk-Chhen incarnations. Tibet apart, this sub-school is very popular in Bhutan. It is because of this Bhutan is Druk (a Brug).

(b) Med-Druk (sMed-s Brug)–Lower Druk–Lorepa Darma Wnagchuk (Lo-Ras-pa Dar-Me dSang-phyug) was a disciple of Tsangpa Gyare and others. He led a very humble and disciplined life. He built Wuri (dbu-Ri) monastery and then made Sang-Ri as his seat (residence). His tradition is known as Med-Druk.

(c) Tod-Druk (sTod-a 'Brug–Upper Druk)–Godtshenpa Gonpo Dorje (rGod-Tshang-pa mGon-po rDo-rJe) was a distinguished disciple of Tsangpa Gyare. He had many disciples. Later, in this tradition Baraba Gyaltshen Palzang (a 'Ba-Re-Be-rGyal mTshan dPal-bZang) wrote numerous works. Ogyenpa Rinchenpal who was a disciple of Godtshangpa was a great Siddha and visited Bodh-Gaya, jalandara, Ordiyana (Ujjain) and China. He wrote among others the famous guide to Odiyana country. Among his disciples were Karmapa Rangchung Dorje (Rang-yung-rDo-rje), Kharchupa (mKhar-Chhu-pa) and Togden Dasens rTogs-Dan-Zla-Seng).

At present among all the Kagyudpa sub schools Karma Kagyud (Karma Kamtshang) is the most widely spread sub-school, then comes Drukpa Kagyud and then the Drikung Kagyudpa.

"All the branches of the EKar-brgyud-pa sect are founded on the common basis of the thought of renunciation of the Sravakayana, the mind for bodhi of the Mahayana and the pure Samaya of the Mantrayana, each sub-sect has its own specific, excellent points, e.g., the Commentary on Tantras of Mar-rong, the austerities and instructions of Mi-la, Sgam-po-ba's discrimination of the substantial Nature, Karmapa's indifferentiation of the Air and the mind. Ela-ma-lam (two methods in the practice of the Great Symbol), the esoteric mantras of Phag-grub, the thirty nine memoirs of Stag-lun-pa, Hbri-gun-pa's principle of Casual Origination and the Universal Taste, Lo-ras and Rgod-tshan's faith in the Truth and renunciation of the world, etc. Each sub-sect, besides the general range of fundamental doctrines that it must include, has specific methods of its own in instructing disciples, in accordance with the particular aspects that it emphasizes in propagation. As a whole, however, all these sub-sects are in conformity with the holy creed of the Bkah-brgyud-pa sect".

Lastly, the Bakyudpa generally follows the tradition of Kadampa on doctrinal matters. But they further practice the four Tantras, viz., Kriya Tantra, Caryatantra, Yogatantra and Anuttaratantra of the New Translation Tantras. Its special teachings are Naro-Chodruk of Mahasiddha Naropa and the Mahamudra teachings of Mahasiddha Maitripa.

The Sakyapa (Sa-sKya pa) sect–was founded by Khem Konchok Gyalpo (a'Khon dKon-mChhog-rGal-po). In 1073 A.D. Sa-sKya means grey earth. Because of the colour of the soil of the place where the monastery was built, this sect took its name Sakya and the followers as Sakyapas.

The predecessors of Khom were noted followers of Nying-ma-pa sect. But he went to Drog-mi (a 'Brog-mi) Sakya Yeshe (Ye-Shes), the great translator of the New Tantra (gSarma) and received teachings and initiation in the New Translated Tantras. Specially he received the teachings of Lamdra (Lam-s' Bras = the path and the result) from Drokmi who received these teachings from Indian scholars Gayadhara and Prajrnendraruchi. Later, Khom's son and Siddha Sachen Kunga Nyingpo (Sa-Chhen Kun-dGa'-sNgin-po) received the Lamdre teachings from Mahasiddha Bairupa himself. The latter came to Sakya monastery by his mystic power and stayed there for one month and imparted teachings to the people. Sachen had four sons and their younger brother's son Kung Gyaltshen (kun-dHe rGyal-mTshan) became the greatest scholar of the Sakya-pa sect. Although he was not the founder of this sect he is respected as its highest authority. He became a monk and wrote numerous scholarly works and hence he is known as Sakya Pandita. He was incited by the Mongolian emperor of China, Gotan, a grandson of Chengiz Khan and became the chief of the Chinese Court. He made the first Mongolian script and grammer – there being no script for the Mongolian language before. The elder son of the young brother of Sakya Pandita, Drogon Chogyal Phagpa (a Gro-mGon-Chhos-rGal Phags-pa) was a distinguished teacher and later became the first Lama ruler of Tibet. After his uncle's death in China he became the supreme teacher of the Chinese Mongolian emperor who offered him the thirteen States of Tibet. On Phagua's second visit to China the emperor again offered him, among others, the three provinces of Tibet. Thus the sovereignty of a great part of Tibet was conferred on him. It was indeed "the laying of a new era of theocratic rule in Tibet". The Sakyapas had since ruled over Tibet for about a century. Afterwards Rongton Mawe Sange (Rong-ston-sMa-bai-Senge) who was a renowned scholar built the Phempo Nalantra monastery, Ngorpa Kungo Zangpo, another great scholar, also built the NGor E-Wam Chhoden monastery and it became the second greatest monastery of Sakyapa sect for centuries past. Gorabjamba sodnam Senge (Go-Rab-a 'Byams-pa bSodnams Seng-ge), one of the disciples of Rongton, called Kun Khyen (Kun-mkhyen-Sarvajna) by the Sakyapa built the Tanag Thumpten Ling (rTa-Nag-Thub = bsTan Gling) monastery in Tsang.

Lamdre (Lam-sBras) is the special and extraordinary teaching of this school. In Lamdre, there are different traditions of the teachings expounded by nine different great Indian Mahasiddhas (most of them from the 84 Mahasiddhas). But the Lamdre teaching expounded by Siddha Bairupa is the main teaching and it is also known as the Earlier Lamdre and the other eight are the Later Lamdre.

Since Khom Konchok Gyalpo the Sakyapa sect has been under the headship of his generations. They are the head of the Sakya monastery too. At present Thri Rin-po-Chhe Kunga Thrinle Wangpo (Khrin Rin-po-Cche Kung-dgd a Phrin Las dBang-po) of Drolma Photrang (Tara-Palace) is the head of the Sakyapa sect.

The Sakyapa sect has many monasteries. Of them most important ones are: The Sakya monastery and Ngor monastery in Tsang, Lhundrop-Tang (Lhun aGrub-sTang) of Dege (sDe-dGe) province and Dzongsar Trashi (rDzongs-gSar-bKrs Shis Lha-Tse) of Kham.

Sakya Pandita Rongton and many others were mainly followers of the Svatantrika Madhyamika and Redewa (Re-mDa-ba) the Prasangika Madhyamika. There were a few other adherents of Dzongchan (of Nyingmapa).

Lastly, it may be noted that "the Sa-sKya-pa was even more closely related with the old Rnin-ma-pa school than the Bkah-rgyud-pa and the monks of this sect were not celeb ate either. They sought a synthesis between the old and the new Tantrism on the basis of Nagarjuna's Madhyamika philosophy and had already developed into powerful hierarchy before the rise of the great Tson-Kha-pa".

The Gelukpa (dGe-lug-pa–the virtuous one)–it traces its heritage to the celebrated monk-scholar Tsongkhapa (Tsong-Kha-pa), Lozang Trakpa (Blo-bZang-Grags-pa) of Amdo, eastern Tibet. He founded the Gaden (dGa'lDen) monastery in 1409 A.D. in

Central Tibet and this sect came to be known first as Gaden and then Gadenpa (dge-lDen-pa) or Ge-lugs-pa (dGe-lugs-pa). "With striking powers of organization and comprehensive intelligence, he set himself to the task".

Tsongkhapa was born in a valley called Tsong-Kha-in Amdo province, and hence he is known by the name of Tsong-kha-pa. He received the precepts first from the third Karmapa, Rolpai Dorje (Rol-pai rDo-rje) and then from Choje Dondrup Rinchen (Chhos-rJe Don-Grub Rin-chen). At the age of sixteen he went to Central Tibet. He took the precepts of a monk in the tradition (lineage) of Sakya-sri of Kasmir. He studied the Madhyamika and Abhidharma with Redwa Zhonu Lodro (Re-mDs-Ba gZhon-nu Blo Gros) of Sakya sect and Tantra with Khyungpo Lhapa (Khyung-po-Lhas-pa), a disciple of Bu-ston at Zha-bu, Redawa and Lhotragpa Namkha Gyaltshen (Lho-Brag-pa Nam-mKka' rGyal-mTshan) and became the greatest scholar of Tibet. He also believed in the traditional practices of the Nadampa. He devoted most of his time in organization. He reformed the corrupt practices of the Sangha. All monks, nuns and mon-Tantrics were only admitted into the Sangha. He wrote a number of works on both Sutra and Tantra. He had hundreds of disciples. He was succeeded by Gyaltshbjey and then Khedrupjey. Since then the senior-most scholars of this scholar have been occupying the throne of Gaden monastery. They thus become the head of the Gelugpa sect. Ling Rincpoche is the present holder of the throne. He is also the senior tutor of the present Dalai Lama and is in India.

There are many big monasteries and training centres for Gelugpas in Tibet. Some of them provide residence for numerous monks. In Mongolia and China also there were Gelugpa monasteries.

The Gelugpas are the followers of the Prasanghaka school of the Madhyamika system. They follow the practices as laid down by Atisa. They further follow the teachings of the four Tantras – Kriysyoga, Caryayoga, Yogatantra and Anuttarayoga of the New Translated Tantras. They lay emphasis on inter-dependent arising to prove everything void and free from conceptualization. They assess that no objects exist by their own nature. All the existent appear conventionally because of the interdependent arising of the causes and conditions. But they are empty since they do not exist by way of their own and there is nothing which functions independently. They study both Sutra and Tantra texts. Of the Sutra texts, mention may be made of the five texts: Nyaya texts of Dignaga and Dharma-Kirti, Prajnaparamita Sutra of Maitreyanatha and Asanga, Madhyamika of Nagarjuna and Chandrakirti, Abhidharma of Vasubandhu and Asinga and Gunaprabha. There are, of course, commentaries on those texts written by Indian and Tibetan scholars. The Guhyasamaja, Sambora, Vajrabhairava, Hevajra, Kalackra and Vajrayogini are the Tantra texts they study seriously.

Zhichedpa (Zhi-byed-pa) are–Zhiched means 'to pacify, to smooth to mitigate'. It is the doctrine which mitigates or stills sufferings. The founder of this sect was Padmapa Sangje (Pha-dam-pa Sangs-rgyas), the great miraculous saint of South India. His father was named brTson 'grus-go-ch's and his mother Rasha. He visited Tibet five times his last visit being in 1112 A.D. He also visited China. His teachings were based on the Prajnaparamita sutra. He followed Nagarjuna's philosophy in interpreting the meanings. He also used to teach that the defilements could be purified by purifying the causes of the sufferings. It has three periods of spread : earlier, intermediate and later–of Zhichedpa according to his discourses on his different visits to Tibet. One of his major teachings practiced in Tibet in a very popular way is Chod (gChod) which means' cut off'. It is a practice for cutting off all the defilements and the fetters of Samsara. It is thus the cutting off the grasping of the self, the root of the Samsara. The followers of the Chod practice six Paramitas (Perfections) by giving away their own bodies and possession without any attachment, fear and doubt.

At present there is no separate sect for this tradition but in all the schools, specially in Kagyudpa and Nyingmapa, Chod transmission and its practices are well-spread.

7. Jonangpa (Jo-nang-pa)–Yumo Mikyod Dorje (Yu-Mo-Mi-bakyod rDor-rJe) a great preacher of Kalacakra tantra in Tibet. He realized the meaning of Emptiness and Zhentong (gZhan-sTong). Later, Kunpang Thugje Tsondru (Kun Spang Thugs-rJe brTsen-A 'Grus) who was born in 1243 A.D. and an ardent advocate of yamo's tradition built a monastery at Jomonang (Jo-MO-Nang). It became the source of Jonangpa teachings and the name of the tradition came to be known as Jonangpa. He wrote many texts on Jortrug (sByor-drug = Six Yogas). Kungpang's grand disciple Dolwo Sherab Gyaltshan (Dol-bo-Sehs-rab-rGyalmTsan) became a very famous scholar at that time. He wrote a number of scholarly works expounding the philosophy of Zhentong (gZang-sTong). Jonangpa school mainly depends on his works for teachings and religious practices, and among the Jonangpas he is known as Kunkhyen (Kun-mKhyen = Sarvajrna. Afterwards Taranatha who was an incarnation of Kunga Trolchog (Kun-dGa' Grol-mChog) and born in 1575 was a great scholar, historian and translator. He wrote numerious books and propagated the Jonang doctrine. He also built a monastery named rTag-brten and filled it with numerous books and images. But soon, in the 17th century A.D.; this sect ceased to function in Central Tibet because of political misfortunes. Shar Dzamthang) monastery in Golok, built by Kashipa Rinchenpal (Kabzhi-pa Rin Chhen-dpal), a grand disciple of Kun Khyen Dolwo, remains till recent time, the centre and source of Jonangpa doctrine. It has thousand of followers with many branches of monasteries in eastern Tibet.

There is no gainsaying that Buddhism was introduced into Tibet in phases and not all at once. The sacred Buddhist books were also brought there at different times by different scholars. Those works offered the same fundamental religion and philosophy, but scholars, however, differed in their interpretations. As a result separate groups developed into distinct organizations or sects with the very same basic tenets. Thus originated several sects in Tibet. "Each of them adheres to all these teachings and of Hinayana and Mahayana including Tantrayana; for Tibetan Buddhists do not separate these teachings, but has equal respect to them all. For moral guidance, they conform to the Vinaya rules which are principally followed by Hinayana, while for more esoteric practices, of every degree of profundity, they use the same methods of the Mahayana and Tantrayana schools".

Of the aforesaid sects the four – the Nyingmapa, Kagyudpa, Sakyapa and Gelugpa along with the pre-Buddhist Bon, have survived till the present time, while the others, Kadampa, Zhichedpa and the like are mainly of importance historically as they have variously influenced and left their mark on the other sects which have survived.

Lastly, the Nyingmapa, Kagyudpa and Sakyapa are designated as the Red hat sects whereas the Gelugpa as the Yellow hat sect. The adherents of the Red sat sects and the Yellow hat sect differ widely in regard to the esoteric and monastic discipline. But the Tibetans regard "all temples and monasteries of different sect are equally holy and good both for congregation and pilgrimage".

NOTES AND REFERENCES

1. Waddell, L.A. *Buddhism of Tibet or Lamaism*, 2nd ed., 1959, p. 74-5.
2. *Journal of the Asiatic Society of Bengal,* 1882, Pt. 2, p. 5
3. Shakabpa, T.W.D., *Tibet : A Political History,* 1961, p. 59-60.
4. *Buddhism of Tibet or Lamaism*, p. 54
5. *Ibid.*, p. 56.
6. *Ibid.*, p. 72-3.
7. Schlagintweit, Emil. *Buddhism in Tibet*, 1968, p. 72-3.
8. Reprinted in Delhi two years back.
9. *The Buddhism of Tibet or Lamaism*, p. 54.
10. Roerich, G N, *tr. Blue annals*. Pt. 2, p. 810.
11. Encyclopaedia of Buddhism, Colombo, Govt. of Srilanka, V. 3, Fascicle I, p. 143-4.
12. The six aspects of instructions of Naropa are : Tumo (Heart-yoga) Gyulo (Mayabody), Milam (Dream) Odsal (Radiant Clarity), Pardo-Bardo (Intermediate stage between death and birth) and Bhowa (Transference).

A SHORT HISTORY OF BUDDHISM IN BHUTAN

Lopen Pemala

Around 653 A.D. i.e. 1534th year after the nirvana of the Buddha, Songtsen Campo, the king of Tibet, constructed the temple of Thrulrang (=Jokhang) at Lhasa in Tibet In Bhutan the Byampe Lhakhang in Bumthang and the Kichu Lhakhang in Paro were constructed during the same period (7th century) and this marks the beginning of the spread of Buddhism in our country.

Later in the 8th century A.D. (807/808), king Sendha of Chakhar, invited Guru Rinpoche (= Padmasambhava) who subdued the Eight classes of Demons (lhasin Degye) and converted the king and his subjects to Buddhism. Then Guru Rinpoche went to Tibet upon invitation from the king Khrisong Detsen. Keeping his former promise, Guru Rinpoche came back to Bhutan accompanied by Denma Tsemangm his scribe. Guru Rinpoche preached teachings such as Dsokpa chenpo selway malong (Clear Mirror of Mahasanti) to the King Sindhu Raja and his subjects. Around 858, exhorted by Muthis Tsenpo, Prince of Tibet, Guru Rinpoche went to Khenpajong in order to expel the King Khikha Rathoe from there no Chitsum in Tang, Bhumthang. This being donem, Guru Rinpoche went to Khenpajong in order to expel the King Khikha Rathoe from there to Chitsum in Tang, Bumthant. This being done, Guru Rinpoche blessed Khenpajong and made it a 'hidden land' (beyul). After this, Guru Rinpoche came back to the Kuje temple in Bumthang to turn the wheel of teaching there. In the same way Guru Rinpoche personally visited and blessed other places like Moenkha Nering, Paro Taktshang, Chumophy (Paro), Celkidra and so forth. He also went to place like Agya and Dromalung in different parts of Bhutan to hide many 'treasures" (ter) there and he blessed the places as "hidden lands". It is said that there was at that time in Bhutanese disciple of Guru Rinpoche named Wemination or Goentson who made brown leather-boxes in which "treasures" were preserved.

In the 11th century A.D., Ngok Choeku Dorji, a disciple of Marpa (1012-1096), came to Choekhor and Tang in Bumthang and propagated Sarma Kagyud. His temple together with its Holy Water (drupchu) which is the soul-lake of Pelden Lhamo can be seen till today.

In the 12th century A.D. Nyang (rel) Nyima Oeser (1124/36-1204), the great tertoen (discoverer of 'treasures') came to Bumthank, where he not only preached his doctrines, but discovered 'treasures' from places like Genedra. Likewise, Terton Guru Choewang came to Kurolong; established the Lugchu Gonpa and preached the precepts of Guhyasama ja. His descents, known as Nyalam Dungyue, exist till today.

During the same century Gyalwa Lhanangpa alias Lama Lhapa Sangye Rinchen alias Zijipal or the Nyoe lineage came to Bhutan and established the Chelkhar Dsong at Paro, the Tokhar Dzong in Bemey and Dongoen Dzong in Thimphu. With the offerings and taxes the collected, the repeatedly made large donations to the Drigung monastery.

At about the same time as Lha (nang) pa, the "percected one" uthoen Sangue, born in the family lineage of Jikten Goenpo, came to Bhutan in order to protect the beings to be converted, as prophesied by Jikten Goenpo. Staying at Dakala in summer and at Tshamdra in winter, the returned the wheel on teachings of the Dringung Kagyupa School. The lineage of the Metem Choeje of Tahamdra are his descendants.

Around 1219, following the prophecy made by Tsangpe Gyarey (1161-1211) and being exhorted by Onrey Darma Senge (1177-

1237), Phajo Drugom Shikpo (1208-1276) arrived in Bhutan. He meditated in the "Four Great Dzongs": 1. Lingshi Jagoe dzong; 2. Yangtsethawo dzong; 3. Tagtshang Singye Samdrup dzong; 4. Dsonggo Choeyung dzong), the "Four Great Caves": 1. Tsedongdophy, 2. Gawaphug, 3. Langthangphu, 4. Sengyephu), and the "Four Great Rocks" (1. Komdra, 2. Thujidra, 3. Chedmdra, 4. Dechendra). He took as his spouse Sonam Poldren, an incarnation of Macik Lapdroen (1055-1145). He performed many miraculous deeds and propagated the teaching of the glorious "Misddle" Drukpa School.

The setting up of the 12 above-mentioned places of retreat or meditation centres marked the beginning of the Drukpa Kargyupa in Bhutan. Phajo Drugom Shikpo then established the Palden Drukpa system, and appointed his 5 miraculous sons–namely, Dampa, Nyima, Wangchuk, Gartoen and Lama–for spiritual and administrative work. It was from these sons that the Palden Drukpa tradition was passed down.

During the same time, the leader of the Lower Druk School Gyalwa Lorepa Drugpa Wangchuk came to Bumthang valley and established the Choejidra and Zhuri monasteries, besides propagating the Lower Druk tradition.

Subsequently, Drupthop Pyikawa or 'The Perfected One' came to Paro valley to spread, for the first time in the country, the teachings of the Upper Drukpa school. He also established the Chilkar monaterry. He as a disciple of Goetshagpa Goenpo Dorji (1189-1258), who introduced the Upper Druk tradition.

After Drupthop Pyikawa, Barawa Gyetshen Pelsang (1310-1391) came to Bhutan, where the extensively propagated the Upper Druk tradition and established the Drangye Goempa. His relics are still preserved there.

In the 13th century, the Nenyingpa School was also introduced in Bhutan. Kashi Rinchen Samten Pelsang of the Nenying monastery received in his dream a clear prophecy from a Khandroma (dakini). He explained it to the "Perfected One' Goenpo Dorji of Byang Taktse in Latoe. Accordingly Goenpo Dorji produced to Paro. There he opened the "gate" of Dsongdra (kha) and found a relic of Sugata (Buddha) as big as an egg of a pigeon. He then built a chorten (stupa) on the cliff which looks like the stretched paw of lion to contain the relic. Thus was founded the monastery of Lzongdrakha. Later when Rinchen Samten Pelsang cane from Nenying, the chorten had moved of its own accord (this is the famous Chorten Karmo gulshe "The White Stupa Which Moves"). Later on Jamyang Rinchen Drupix (1403-1452) of Nenying came to Bhutan and constructed many temples, such as Tsharkhang, Samadzongphy, Gongsarkha (Paro) Tarakha, and Punakha. He preached extensively and profoundly and spread the teaching of the Nenyingpa School.

In the 14th century Jamyang Kunga Singly came to the Paro and Thimphu valleys and established a meditation centre at Duchhending and a monastic order at Changankha. He also visited Dechhenphu at the invitation of Drundung Loden Gwalpo and extensively propagated the Palden Drukpa tradition.

Also in the 14th century, as prophesied by Guru Rinpoche, the Omniscient Longchen Bapjama (1308-1363) came to Bhutan and constructed eight monasteries which are Tharpa, Ling, Samten Ling (both in Chumey, Bumghang), Ogyen Choeling (Tang, Bumthang), Shingkhar Dechen Ling (Ura, Bumthang), Kunsang Ling (Kurtoe), Ngenlung drechaling, Kunzaling (Sha), Rinchen Ling (Khothang) and Samten Ling (Paro). He preached and turned the wheel of the dzokchen (Mahasanti) doctrine extremely which is the supreme Vehicle of all.

The same century produced another great figure in the history of Buddhism in Bhutan, tertoen Dorji Lingpa (1346-1405). He discovered treasures at Jaolhakhang Byakar lhakang, Singphu, Dangchu, Wangdi Gon, Bellangdra and Lingmo terchu and contributed to the diffusion of the Darling Sect of Buddhism in the contrary by propagating Kadue and dzogchen of the Dorling tradition.

In the 15th century Nyagre Gyetshu Drukthop Dendup, disciple of Ngorchen Dorjichang Kunga Zanpo came to the Goen valley in

Bhutan and established the Ritshog, Choeding, and Nebung monasteries, while propagating the Sakyapa tradition. This period also saw the arrival in Bhutan of Thinley Rabyang, who continued the propagation of Sakyapa tradition. The ritual ceremonies of the Sakyapa tradition are still performed at Chishing and Pagar monasteries.

In the same century, Jomo lhari, Jobo dragke and Chungdue invited Drupchen Thangtong Gyalpo, who built 6 iron bridges east to west over rivers and founded the Duntselhakhang in Paro, the Tachogang Bardong near the confluence and the Shar Ciwotakha.

Among the other major religious personalities of the period was Tertoen Sherub Mebar from Kham, who discovered many secret treasures in the Bumthang valley and established monasteries at Bumthang Tangsabji and Paro Pangpisar. When he died, he left his skull as a gift to posterity, and this is still preserved at Pangpisar.

After Tertoen Sherab Mebar came Thruelshig Namkhani Naljor and Gelwang Rje Kuenga Peljor, who propaged their doctrines and established monasteries at Duegoes and Dochorten respectively.

The great tertoen "text-discoverer' Pema Lingpa (1450-1521) was born in Chel in the Tang district of the Bumthang valley. He made many discoveries like the Longsel sangwa nyingcu from Member tsho. He preached for the first time to Lama Rinchen Phel at Dungbithang. He established the Tamshing Lhundrup choeling in Choeling in Choekhor, Kuenzang da, Chel Pemaling, Dechenling, Kurte terbang, Kunzangling and Bamrin Dekiling.

Pema Lingpa turned the wheel of esoteric doctrines for the benefit of all sentient beings. His relics are still preserved at Punakha, the winter residence of the central monastic body.

In 1508 Trulku Soenam Gyeltshen from Katho established the Ugyen Tsumo mastery at Taktshang. The teachings he diffused widely included the 35 volumes of the Nyingmcy gyubum or the 'Collection of Old Tantras'. He also opened the door of the sacred above in Sikkim and composed many Nyingms texts, thus consolidating the Nyingms.

Tertoen Letho Lingpa arrived in Bhutan in the 16th century. He discovered many sacred and esoteric doctrines from various places in Bhutan for the benefit of all sentient beings.

The great Drukpa master Ngawang Chogyal (1465-1540) preached around the same period and founded numerious temples. They are, among others, the Druk Phodrangding at Pangri zampa, the Thrinleygant, the Cilagan, the Dechen choekhor at Pumo and Samted tsemo at Drela, the Drunchoeding at Paro, the Choekhorgang at Pokhar. Thanks to him, the teachings of the Drukpa Schools were widely spread.

His elder son Tenpey Gyeltshen (1506-1538) and especially his younger son Ngaki Wangchuk (1517-1554) travelled extensively in Bhutan establishing the Byakar Lzong and the Tongsa Dzong etc. They contributed also to the diffusion of the doctrine of the Drukpa School.

Mipham Choeki Gyalpo (1543-1606), son of Ngaki Wangchuk, also visited Bhutan several times and greatly benefited the sentient beings.

In the same period Pema Thinley, son of Tenzin Dagpa (the re-incarnation of Tertoen Poma Lingpe) established the Gangte monastery and propagated Tertoen Pema Lingpa's Nyigma doctrine.

Mipham Choeki Gyalpo's son Mipham Tenpey Nyima (1567-1619) visited Mongar, Lungsamkha and Mangde Raphel and extensively preached the doctrine. He lived in Bumthang Chumo Chorten Nyenpo, where he constructed a preacher's seat outside the monastery which can be seen till today.

In 1616, Shabdrung Ngawang Namgyal (1594-1651) arrived in Bhutan and established his seat at Tango to start the monastic order of the Drukpa School. He successively constructed the Cheri monastery (1620), the Sangngak Saptoen Phodrang (Simtokha Dzong) in 1629, the Punakha Dzong (1637), the Wangphodrang Dzong (1638), The Dongoen Dzong (now the Tashichho Pzong) in 1641, and the Rinpung (Paro) Dzong in 1646.

After the establishment of the Paro Dzong, he instructed the 3rd Desi Mijur Tenpa to set up the Chakar Izong in Bumthang, the Lhuntse Dzong in Kurte, the Yangtse and Tashigang Dzongs in Tashigang, the Shongar Dzong in what is now known as Mongar and the Shemgang Dzong. Thus Shabdrung unified and consolidated the Palden Drukpa tradition throughout the country. He also established the Central Monastic body at Punakha.

In 1751, 3 months after the completion of the Daga Dzong, Shandrun appointed Umze Tenzin Drugye as the 4th Desi, before passing away on the 10th day of the 3rd month.

During his life-time, Shabdrung turned the wheel of Dharma which comprised among others, the following precepts: (Yonten kunjung, a text of guruyoga (practice in honour of the lama) composed by Pema Karpo (1527-1592); methods of propitiation for the five deities which are Demachok ngoedrup, Lhenkye Kusali, Phakmo byinlap, Tumpo nupa and Nyenpa choetoe; four essential teachings for the practice such as 'Thargyen composed by Dakpo Lhaje Campope (1079-1153), "Six Doctrines of Naropa"(naro choedruk) etc. In this way, he placed the entire territory of Bhutan under the glorious teaching of the Drukpa School.

At the same time, he invited Rikzin Nyingpo, a descendant of the great tertian Sangyo Lingpa (1340-1396), from Kongpo in the east. Shabdrung received from him the initiation, the oral transmission and the explanation of the precepts of the Nyingmana ("Old") School, such as the Gongdu, the Kegye and the Phurpa. Thereafter Shabdrung started the Gongdu rilpu ceremony (a puja of the Gongdu cycle) at the Paro Dsong and the Phurpey drupchen (a puja of the Phurpa cycle) at the taktshang monastery. He also fixed the ritual of the Gongdu cycle. The tradition of concurrently practicing the teachings of both the Nyigma and Drukpa Schools was thus established.

The great Omniscient of Tsang (Tsang Khenchen) Jamyang Pelden Gyamtsho arrived in Bhutan in Shabdrung's lifetime. At Shabdrung's request, he started the teaching of the Tripitaka (denoc sum : sutra, vinaya and abhidharma) and the five branches of science (rikney nga), mainly the grammer, the poetry, the matrics and the three basic texts of Sanskrit grammar (ka tsan yang sum). In the same period, Lhawang Lodroe, at Shabrung's behest, introduced Bhutanese astrology and the liturgic system.

During the reign of the Second Desi (regent) Tenzin Drukpa's (1607-1667/68, reign. 1656-1667), the shedra (school of Buddhist studies) was maintained without interruption by a staff or monk scholars, such as Lopon Kunshe, versed in logic (tshem), Kacupa (master in ten difficult subjects) Penlop Gyalsang, and Geshe Mipham Wangchuk.

The Third Desi Migyur Tanpa (reign. 1667-1680) invited Lapon Drungrampa Kunga Korsang from the great college Dreyul Ketshol which was the seat of the Omniscient Sangye Phel. Thus the shedra was enlarged and developed. Further, the Government sent at its own expense two intelligent monks, Ngawang Drukpa and Ngawang Sonam, to study the metrics, the three basic texts of Sanskrit grammar etc. under Jamyang Pelden Gyamtsho at Menchunak in Paro.

The Fourth Desi Tensin Papgye (1638-1696, regn. 1680-1695) selected numerous intelligent students from the monk body and put them under the tutorship of Shakya Papgye, great master in metaphysics (tshennyi), Jimpa Lapgye and Choenyi Dorji etc. Recognizing their service, the Desi increased the reward for them and without imposing any restraint, he let them act according to their own initiative. The shoera prospered and became the Tshennyiki de (college specialised in the study of metaphysics), a distinct division in the monk body.

The 9th Desi Ngawang Gyamtsho (reign: 1719-1729) was himself a traditional scholar, and put special emphasis on literary studies. He created a distinct division called Drapey de (college of literary studies). The teaching staff was composed of well-known scholars like Lopon Ngawang Pelden Sangpo, Ngawang Drukpa, Ngawang Sonam and so on. Since then the central monk body comprises 3 distinct divisions: Ngakarey de (tantric studies and practices), Tshennyippey de (metaphysical studies) and the Drapey de.

The 11th Desi Khuwo Peljor further developed the School of Buddhist Studies by recruiting promising students like Kunga Jamtsho, the legendary Yonten Thaye, Tenzin Namgyal and Kunzang Namgyal, all of whom received instruction from the same eminent teachers just mentioned.

In the 19th century, Shabdrung's thugtuel or mind–incarnation Jigme Dagpa, Sherub Gyeltshen, Yonten Gyeltshen, Jigme Norbu and Tenzing Lhendup protected the doctrine. Also eminent students like Sishi Namgyel and Sharap Dorji studied in Bumthang under Geshe Penjor, Gesha, Nyima Dorji and Mindruk, and later promoted the teaching of the Buddha.

Subsequently, numerous scholars have emerged. Some of them who excelled in teaching, debating and composing became the Je Khenpo. Many other, although they didn't become the Je Khenpo, were however knowledgeable, respectable and good-natured.

In the 20th century, Ugyen Wangchuk (1862-1926), the First King of Bhutan (regn. 1907-1926), selected Shudra Tenpa Rinche, Aco Pasang from Tongsa. He sent them to the Dzokchen Shri Singha Mahapandit. After studying the sutras, tantras and other fields of science well, they returned to Bhutan.

During the reign of Jigme Wangchuck (1905-1952), the Second King of Bhutan (reign. 1926-1952), a shedra was established at Tharpaling where Geshe Tenipa Rinchen propagated the doctrine by teaching the "Thirteen Fundamental Texts" (shungchen cusum), lexicography, poetry and grammar. At Nyimalung, Doring Trulku started a shedra and he taught the Vinaya (dulwa) and the Madhyamika (uma) philosophy. At Phajoding, Minyak Kyorpon started a shedra and diffused teachings.

In 1961, Jigme Dorji Wangchuk (reign: 1952-1972), the Third King of Bhutan, and Her Majesty the present queen Mother Ashi Kezang invited Dingo Khyentse Dinpoche (born 1910) to start a shedra at Simtokha which is known as the Simtokha Rigney School. Her Royal Grand mother Ashi Phuntshog Choeden and rJe Khenpo Jamyang Yeshey Singey jointly established a shedra at Tango monastery. In 1979 His Mahesty Jigme Singye Wangchuk established the National Religious Committee under the Chairmanship of the Home Minister. In February 1981, the Religious Committee revived the shedra and drupdra at Phajoding.

In this way, the Government has been taking immense care to restore and promote the teaching of the Buddha in our country. While taking our country forward through planned development, modernisation and greater participation in international affairs, our present King Jigme Singye Wangchuk, who has been on the throne since 1972, has spared no pains in encouraging the preservation and growth of our traditional Buddhist culture and ethos. As a result, the eternal truths of Buddhism still retain the pre-eminent place in our scale of values.

In conclusion I would like to add that, within the brief span of this address, it has not been possible for us to touch upon each and every religious teacher who visited our country in past and propagated Buddhist to teachings. Among the other distinguished religious figures whose names I have thus left out our Tertoen Choewang (1212-1270), Drupchen Melong Dorji (1243-1303), Tertoen Ogyen Lingpa (born 1323), Tshering Dorji (14-15th century), Patna Ligpa (1403-1479), Drimey Lingpa (18th cent.), and Drupchen Lekyi Dorji.

APPENDIX

The doctrinal texts prevalent in the Shedra or the schools of Buddhist Studies is as follows:

Kanjur the precepts of Lord Buddha, or the Tripitak of the Mahayana tradition. It comprises more than a hundred volumes, including:

(i)	Vinayasutra	(13 vols.)
(ii)	Sutra	(30 vols.)
(iii)	Tantra	(20 vols.)
(iv)	Ratnakuta	(6 vols.)
(v)	Maha Sangika Sutra	(6 vols.)

Tenjur the commentaries on the teachings of Buddha by various Buddhist scholars. The Tenjur comprises:

(i) Vinayakarika
(ii) Karika
(iii) Pratimokshassutra
(iv) Mulavimayasutra
(v) Bodhicaryavatra
(vi) Madhyamivatara
(vii) Muladadhyarikarika
(viii) Vigrahavyavartani
(ix) Sunyatasapatatikarika
(x) Yuktisastika
(xi) Vaidalyasutra
(xii) Madhyamika (1-400)
(xiii) Madhyalankara
(xiv) Mahayanasutralankara of Maitripa
(xv) Paramitrasutralankara
(xvi) Madhantavibhanga
(xvii) Dharma-dharmata-vibhanga

(xviii) Uttaratantra
(xix) Abhidharmakosha
(xx) Abhidharmasamuccaya
(xxi) Pramanayuktanidhi
(xxii) Tshema Lighter or the Treasury of Reasoning
(xxiii) Siksasmuccaya
(xxiv) Philology
(xxv) Samketshastra
(xxvi) Dictionary
(xxvii) Grammar
(xxviii) Kavya or Prosody
(xxix) Preparatory texts
(xxx) Astrology
(xxxi) Astronomy
(xxxii) Gyalse Laglen or The 37 Practices of All Buddhas
(xxxiii) Surhllokha
(xxxiv) Gyudtagnyi
(xxxv) Sangwainyingpo
(xxxvi) Pomsum
(xxxvii) Gunakosha
(xxxviii) Ngelsokorsum.

In the Shedra, all these texts have to be thoroughly read and understood.

In the Drupda or meditation college, the prevalent practices can be divided into two progressive categories.

1. Ngondro or Introductory Practices
   (i) Meditation out the difficulty of acquiring a human birth, along with its various implications.
   (ii) Meditation on the impermanence of life.
   (iii) Meditation on the cause of suffering.

(iv) Meditation on Karmic cause and effect.

(v) The changing of Chapdro (refuge formula) one lakh times.

(vi) The chanting of Samkye one lakh times.

(vii) One lakh time of Yigja.

(viii) One lakh time of offering of mandala.

(ix) Five lakh time of Lamai Nelyor.

(x) The taking of initiations and guidance from Guru, Yidam, Khandro (dakini) and Choechong (dharmapala), with the upadesha as support.

These stages are followed by entering into retreat.

2. Ngoezhi

(i) Practise of Tsalung, a type of yogic breathing.

(ii) Narochoedruk, comprising six topics:

(a) the development of the mystic inner heart

(b) the experience of one's body as phantom

(c) the dream

(d) the radiant light

(e) the experience of the state between dream and re-birth

f) the practice of transferring the mind to higher spiritual levels.

(iii) Mahamudra practice

(iv) Taking the guidance of Mahasanti.

RELIGIOUS AND HISTORICAL SOURCES OF VARIOUS LAMAS OF BHUTAN

(All in Bhutanese Manuscript)

1. MANI KABUH (the authorship of which is attributed to Avalokites'vara by rNyin-aa sect)
2. History of King Sendha or Sindhu Raja
3. Tamdin pawo chigpai manngag (Upedesha of Hayagriwa)
4. The Guide to Beyul Khenpa Jhong or Hidden land Khenpo valley.
5. The book on Khenpa Jhong.
6. Thangyig Yidki Munsel (Clear decree of the heart)
7. Ngog-gi Densa genrab-ki Logyud (The story on the seat of Ngog lineage)
8. Jangter Choskorgi Shum
9. The history of Ngadag Nyang and his lineage
10. The story on the seat of various lineage
11. The Lineage of Nyos
12. The History of Drigung Kyop
13. The History of Ngawang Drukpa
14. The History of Phajo Drukgom Zhigpo
15. The History of Ghalwa Lorepa
16. The story on the seat of Chilkar lineage
17. The Barawai Sungbum (The One Hundred Thousand Precepts of Burawa)
18. The Leneage Nenying
19. The History of Jamynag Kunga Sengye
20. The History of Kunkhen Longchen
21. The History of Gyalwangji
22. The History of Dorji Lingpa
23. The History of Ngorchen Dorji Chang
24. The History of Prupchen Thangtong Gyalpo

25. The History of Padma Lingpa
26. The History of Letho Lingpa
27. The History of Ngawang Chogyal
28. The History of Mipham Chogyal
29. The History of Zhadrung Ngawang Namgyal
30. The Lhoi Ghosjung (The religious History of Bhutan)
31. The History of Tenzin Rabgye
32. The History of rJe Kunga Gyamtsho
33. The History of rJe Yonten Thaye.

All the dates and centuries and cycles are based on the historical chronology.

THE PROBLEM OF BUDDHIST ART

Pabitra Kumar Roy

I

The concept of Buddhist art may be understood as the articulation in terms of images (*murti*) through the medium of the visual plastic languages of sculpture and painting the idea of *bodhi*. But *bodhi* is an abstract concept, has no visual properties, though it can find a habitat in a living being. In such one as the Buddha the abstract concept of *bodhi* is said to be come personified properly so-called is the image of *bodhi.*

The Buddha idea has a life story of its own and is not necessarily coeval with the story of the Buddha image, which came into vogue by the middle of the first century of the Christian era. But the imaginative experiences of *bodhi* or *prajna* does not seem to begin to be articulated in any meaningful way before the fourth and fifth centuries. The early images of the Master give us no visual experience of *bodhi* or *Prajna*. Iconographically however, the cross-legged position is manifest as much as the attributes of a *mahapurusa-cakravarti*. But purely mundane terms in a clear mundane sense.

Yet the concept of *bodhi* or *Prajna* was a property of early Buddhist thought and imagination. Under the impact of the Mahayana ideology of the second half of the first and the second century ideology of the Christian era there evolved the concept of Karuna. Nor was Sakyamuni a human teacher any longer, but was an eternal principle that had made itself manifest in human form for the salvation of mankind as a being of a universal love and infinite compassion. Apropos of this ideology, Sakyamuni the Buddha in his apparitional form (nirman kaya) was imagined to exhibit a melting quality in the expression of his face and in the texture of his body. This feature was conceived to be but the outer manifestation of his inner state of experience of Karuna since in his *Prajna* he had realised that the world was full of suffering and on that account his mind and heart were always melting in love and compassion.

Further, by about the third and fourth centuries of the Christian era *yoga* had been evolved as an authentic and effective technique of contemplation and also as a full-fledged system of speculative thought. The *Digha* (sutta no. 22) has a short description of what *yoga* was in visual image. But a more insightful description occurs in the *Bhagavad-Gita* (VI. 10-21). The visual concept of the technique of *dhyanayoga* was not unknown to the early Buddhist, and Mahayana Buddhism did not remain unaffected by the system of thought *yoga* represented. The Yogacara school of Buddhism seems to have been a direct response to the intellectual movement of yogic contemplation of the third and fourth centuries. The point about mentioning all these ideological factors is that finally Sakyamuni was transformed through the centuries into a deified ideal state of being, an incarnation of the ideal concept of *yoga*, shining in the luminosity of and softly melting in *Karuna*. Whatever might have been the reasons - inability of the artist to experience perceptually and imaginatively the concepts of *bodhi* and, of and *yoga* or his technical inadequacy for the realization of the experience in terms of his art and craft, or both-the Buddha idea spelt in terms of the aforementioned ideational terms are skilfully and meaningfully articulated only in the images of Sarnath of the fifth and sixth centuries. Considering the ideological factors influencing the Buddha idea and its translation into the plastic visual image from the first to the sixth centuries one may now put the problem of Buddhist art as follows : how to transmute into concrete visual terms the ideas of *bodhi*, and *yoga*?

The articulation in terms of visual plastic art of anyone or a set of the above concepts was not only a matter of comprehension and perception but also that of execution in terms of a given material. The fullest and deepest response to the ideological as well as the aesthetic challenge came from Sarnath, and meets with almost unbelievable success. There alone is achieved perfect articulation of the illumination of *Prajna of Karuna of yoga* and of blissful experience in concrete form. Here is indeed the fulfillment of the evolved idea of *bodhi* and its embodiment in the Buddha image, which henceforward became the source of inspiration to and the sole term of reference for all later images all over India, and in countries beyond her frontiers. At Sarnath was the end of a quest, and quest further ahead meant vanishing into the world of no image, of formlessness.

II

Transparency, Coomaraswamy said truly, is the most universal element in Indian art. For an achievement painting one has to look at the Ajanta murals. The painting of Ajanta is Buddhist and is marked by Mahayana sensitivity. The Avalokitesvara of Ajanta is an embodiment of the Buddha's mercy and compassion. The figures convey a feeling of the same abstract perfection of form that is seen in the great sculptured images of the Gupta period. It is so rendered as to make it a kind of absolute and abstract symbol of the divine and ineffable anatomy of a supernatural being. It is said that the great Buddhist philosopher Asanga resided for a time at Ajanta. A reflection of Asanga's teaching may perhaps be seen in the composition of the Avalokitesvara in the presence of his *sakti*. The ephemeral, ghostly presence of the Bohisattva with a blue lotus moves with unearthly grace and is tremulous with Karuna and seems to suggest that in Yogacara even the gods are illusions. The portrait of *bodhi* at Ajanta is drawn in terms of a loveliness so refined away from humanity that it becomes a beauty beyond reality, and the fact is valid in a lyric pensive abstraction. Besides the great Bodisattva figure, one should look also for the face of the Buddha in Cave XIX, which is a sixth century creation. The contemporaeity of the Sarnath Buddha, the Bodhisattva with blue lotus, and the Buddha in Cave XIX is hardly an accident. The same ideological motivation informs all of them. The accent on the transcendent render them symbolically illuminative of an ineffable Thatness Apart from the technical problem-solving operations in their respective media, they remain for us our nearest approximations of that has been called the ideas of *bodhi*, or,and *yoga.*

III

In Buddhist thought the notion of 'picture', or 'image' is related to that of the 'concept' or *vikalpa*. The Lankavatara Sutra (III. 77) has it that the being of the world is conceptual (vikalpamatram) without external validity (bahyamartham*na vidyate)*; it is as a concept that it is seen pictorially (*Vikalpam drsyate citram*). The theses of the twin ontology of *vikalpa* and *citra*, together with their correspondence should lend support to the view that the Buddha-idea, spelt in terms of *bodhi*, Karuna and *yoga,* finds a plastic statement in Sarnath images as also in the Ajanta Bodhisattva with blue lotus. There of course is another remarkable instance of plastic transformation of the Buddha-idea. I mean the Buddha in Samadhi at Anuradhapura. This is a Buddhist primitive, dating back to the second century A.D. Since we have been arguing in terms of paradigm cases, we do not mention the case of the Anuradhapura Buddha. Its massive form austere outline and moral grandeur is only a plastic spelling of the idea of Buddha as *yogi, sans Karuna*. It does not show the conscious elegance and suavity of Sarnath types, though it is far ahead of the insincerity and misinterpretation of Gandhara images. Its monumental simplicity of form and volume lacks the expression of the ineffable perfection of the body Sarnath images.

IV

The Tantrik interpretation of Buddhism emerged between the seventh and twelfth centuries, and in its wake i.e. art tended to become more and more hieretic. Although iconographic demands hampered the creation of true art, individual works of a esthetic merit have nonetheless been found. To the Tantrik interpretation of Buddhism we owe the medieval Buddhist art. Historically, the creativity of this period is known as the Palaschool of art, which the Tibetan historian Taranath, denominates as the "Eastern School," What is important to note about this school is its equal facility in handling stone sculpture, architecture, bronzes and paintings. Nalanda was its greatest and most active centre during the ninth and tenth centuries. Iconographically three stages of the Pala Buddhist art can be recognized; an early Mahayana phase with Buddha and Bodhisattva images both in stone and bronze, then Sahajayana images, and finally the Kalacakra ones. The last mentioned derive their inspiration from the Vajrayana (rDo-rje theg-pa) school of later Mahayana thought. Inspite of all this, it would generally be true to say that the medieval Buddhist art, sculpture and painting, are continuations of the achievements at Sarnath and Ajanta. The Sarnath Bodhisattvas are the earliest recognigable personifications of the archangels of the Mahayana pantheon. One such Avalokitesvara bears the attribute of the small figure of Buddha Amitabha in the diadem. The Sarnath Boddhisattva images are the artistic ancestors of the icons of the Pala period.

On taking a closer look at the Pala sculpture one would pass different judgments, on stone sculpture vis-a-vis the bronzes. Let us first consider the case of the Pala bronzes, and compare them with the colossal copper image of Buddha from stone. Sultanganj, in the Birmingham Museum. Stylistically this figure is the equivalent of the Sarnath. Buddhas in stone. The parfection of form and inspiration mark the images of *bodhi* and in two different media. Comparatively, the Pala Buddhas are marked by a loss of monumentality. They are either replicas of famous images or pretty icons, and on both counts, they are at once a prolongation and a degeneration of the Sarnath tradition, But this was inevitable, as we have remarked earlier, owing to the paradigmatic character of the Sarnath achievement. Whatever may the case be, the Pala statuary do not usually touch the highest reaches of Buddhist creative art and the aesthetic aspirations. In almost every case the sense of plastic conception is lost under the intricacy of surface detail, even though the Pala icons are characterized by a great finesse and precision of execution. The austere bareness and purity of conception that had once marked the Sarnath images might seem to have been left centuries behind. Marked as the Pala bronzes are by a certain heiretic formality and lack of vivacity, their innovative character need not be lost sight of. They approximate painting in respect of being guilded; the intricacy of their composition in cases of *Yuganaddha* figures; elaboration and ornamentation of their designs is remarkable. But these are surface features, and can hardly be taken either to touch or improve the aesthetic core of the images.

The Pala stone sculptures are chiseled on hard black stone, and more free than their proto-types in bronzes, perhaps more elegant too. Yet in them one is much more conscious of the precise and sharp definition of the detail of Jewelled ornaments than of the plastic significance of the bodily form that seems to exist as a frame work for these attributes. Consider the sharp Pala masterpiece of the seated Buddha in the Museum of Fine Arts, Boston. The Buddha is represented in the yoga pose and earth-touching gesture of the enlightenments. He wears the crown and jewels of a royal personage, the very worldly attributes discarded at the time of the renunciation. Now this may be explained as part of the process of the Buddha's deification in Mahayana Buddhism. The crown and jewels may be taken to suggest the Buddhist's power as Cakravartin and the state of radiant transformation attained as the supreme moment of Enlightenment. But judges in comparison with the Sarnath Buddha in *dharma-caicra-praartana-Pata*, the elaboration of surface detail in the Buddha militates against the properly sculptured conception of the whole. In it emphases on technical finish and virtuosiy of carving and plastic modelling are not maintained in perfect equilibrium. To put the matter in ideological terms, in the Buddha the idea of Karuna usurps or dislocates those or *bodhi* and *yoga*.

Two further points may be noted about the Pata Buddhist art, First, Buddhism as Vajrayana offered, besided those of the Buddha, images of new gods and goddesses. Of these Manjusri and Tara deserve mentioning as also Hevajra with *sakti*. Images of these divinities were not found in the Gandhara and Gupta schools of sculpture. Wrathful images as those of Hevajra or Yamantaka are of *grotesque* genre, and may have been inspired by the Hindu notion of the avenging deity in man-lion form. Images with many heads and many hands are also a *forte* of the art. One Havajra image found in Bengal is an excellent specimen in this respect. With regard to the Tantrik Buddhist images one might conjecture a connexion between *yuganaddha* icons Sahajayana and Vajrayana inspiration and the like ones of Hindu inspiration at Bhuvaneswar or Konarak and Khajuraho. If such a study were undertaken, it should be evident that the aesthetics of sex under Tantrik Buddhism hardly ever excels a similar achievement at Orissa or Madhya Pradesh. The pulsating absorption or the self-noughting of the mithune or 'sexual mysticism' (in Sri Aurobindo's phrase) is only thinly depicted within the bounds of the hieretic formality and rigidity of the Pala icons. But perhaps the comparison would be inadmissible on grounds of theology.

Secondly, the Pala bronzes were made for pilgrims to take away from the workshops near the sacred Buddhist shrines. Many of them were exported for dedication to far-off countries. There can be no denying the fact that they helped art-communication between India and South-Eastern Asia, Nepal and Tibet.

V

What happened to the 'problem' of Buddhist art in the Pala times? The problem, as we have noted earlier, was one of creating plastic visualizations of the ideas of *bodhi, Karuna* and *yoga*. From that point of view medieval Buddhist art had no new grounds to break. This remark is true at more than one level. Aestherically, there was nothing more to achieve after the perfections attained at Sarnath and Ajanta. Now at Nalanda or Bengal the accent was no longer on the Transcendent, rather the Supernatural. The focal point was no longer directed on the Buddha, but the Tantrik *mandala* and its deities. The Pala Buddhist art was an art of Dhyana-mantras and their meditational aids. The work of art was no longer a *murti* but a *pratima*. And the artist was not to follow his experience but the *pratima-laksanas.* Hence the task of embodying the artist's experience of the ideas of *bodhi*, Karuna, and *yoga* came to be, if not discouraged, at least less encouraged.

The difference between the classic Buddhist art (as at Sarnath and Ajanta) and the medieval Buddhist art can be appreciated in terms of the difference between the concepts of *murti* and *pratima*, 'image' and 'icon'.

If it be conceded that the Buddha images of Sarnath represent the highest peaks of achievement of the quest of Buddhist creativity in the realm of plastic arts, then one could also hazard the opinion that they were images of ideas, *murtis* or forms of a felt experience. An image or is an objective obverse of that which is amunta formless. Or to resort to another terminology, a is what is *Vyakta*, fully articulated form of what is *avyakta* or inarticulated. This terminology not only illumines the connexion between matter and form but also that of idea and image. Now taking the term 'image' in the sanse of murti, it should be possible to appreciate the point that 'image' implies 'idea' while the converse does not hold necessarily in aesthetics. The presupposed argument about the converse non-implication appears similar to Nagarjuna's dictum that one cannot talk about Paramartha without having recourse to samvrti, or what Tagore said to be the case of diving into the sea of forms hoping for the pearl of the formless.

Contrarily with image, an icon is a Pratima, symbol *arcca* an object of cult worship. It is recognized and known by certain specified *laksanas* or attributes, sense and stances, gestures and attitudes. But these are external to the icon and are demanded only by ritualistic requirements. A *murti* is not recognized this way, nor is any mark or attribute external to it. It is governed only by prescriptions of its own, that is the laws and principles that govern its form. A *murti*, therefore, is a product of those laws which regulate the work of concretizing an idea, of giving a body to the bodyless. It is a presence to be felt. A *Pratima* on the other hand, is a symbol, and functions mnemonically as a referent helping a worshipper to think of and concentrate on the original vision of which it is supposed to be a *Pratima*. Further, a *Pratima* need not be an object of art, but always is made according to hieretic prescriptions and meant for worship. As distinguished from a *Pratima* a *murti*, is a vivid, immediate and concrete articulation of a felt experience, offers itself to help others to taste and live through a similar experience. To paraphrase what Ananda Coomaraswamy has said, to see an image of the Buddha is hardly significant, what is important is to see the Buddha in the image. A *murti* is the product of an aesthetic-spiritual experience. So is the view of it.

It should further be noted that an icon or *Pratima*, for the purposes of worship, is required to be presented in full frontality, and is more rigid and formal. Compare an iconic Boddhisattva of the Pala times with the rock-cut image of Bodhisattva at the Kanheri cave no. 3. Standing in front of the latter, one would easily see what a spiritual experience in depth could really mean. Sunk in deepest, most concentrated meditation, this Bodhisattva swells from within itself. A Pala Bodhisattva, in stone or metal, may be technically adequate, even efficient, and have a formal charm and elegance of a sort, even some amount of sophistication. But of the direct experience of *bodhi* and *yoga*, of luminosity and compassion of inners strength dignity there would be but little, and hence, no realization of these qualities in form and expression. The point is that a *murti* is more free and dynamic, inspirited by vivid vibrancy of life. It is characterized by what the *Visnudharmottara* describes as the quality of the stone as if it were breathing. A *murti* never stands apart and aloof as a formal icon does at the sanctum.

From the conceptual distinction between a *murti* and a *pratima*, it does not follow that a *pratima*, can never be an object of art. An icon can also be an object of art. It can be so despite its being an icon.The point is that to be a good icon is its primary consideration, aesthetic consideration being secondary, if not immaterial altogether. Seen in this light, one might doubt there stone sculptures and bronzes of the medieval Buddhist art were meant to articulate the ideas of *bodhi*, Karuna, and *yoga* in aesthetic and ideological terms. Such articulation one meets only in the art of Sarnath and Ajanta. There alone art is the visual concretization of the quintessence of the speculative wisdom of Asanga and Vasubandha. After that paracigmatic achievement, the medieval Buddhist art is only commentarial in nature. To say this is not to deny any value to the creations of the Pala times, they do indeed have a value, but a value of another sort. Great achievements in art always make art all the more difficult for the succeeding generations.

VI

"Brethren, have you ever seen a masterpiece of painting?" "Yea, Lord." "Brethren, that masterpiece of art is designed by the mind. Indeed, brethren, the mind is even more artistic than the masterpiece." Samyutta Nikaya.

Let us begin with the Buddhist notion of 'painting' or the art of painted surface. The Lankavatara Sutra has numerous references to the art. According to it, a painting is discharged, as it were, from a cornucopia behind the painted surface. This cornucopia is the mind. Its contents are poured out of the 'storehouse of consciousness' (alaya vijnana) in to the field of mental vision (dhyana). In that light they are modelled and projected, as if in a shadow play, on to the white surface of attentiveness, which is the ground of printing. This coming forward into visibility from the storehouse of consciousness supports the intellectual structure of the paintings. It may be at once noted that this is a Crocean thesis, and rules out naturalism in art. The Lankavatara Sutra reminds us time and again that the painting is not in colour, neither on the surface, nor in representation. Its essence is to be sought in intuition.

The term used in sanskrit for 'painting' is *citrabhasa* while the term *citra* is reserved for 'sculpture'. It that be so, it would be expected, and it is the case in point of fact, that modeling (vartana) in line and colour, and all other possibilities of shading so as produce the illasion of volume, are employed to give the painted figures the quality of sculpture. Stylistically, the medieval Buddhist painting is connected with its contemporary sculpture in stone and bronzes, in the same banner as Ajanta murals is related to the Gupta sculpture.

Buddhist painting of the Pala times had its roots in the so-called Eastern school of the Gupta painting, and was complementary to the sculpture and bronzes of the age. This school began its carrier in the early decades of the ninth century, and derived much of its charm from the classical plastic modelling of colour at Ajanta. But the history of painting from Ajanta to the time of the is one or devolution and gradual thinning of the context. The story of the medieval Buddhist painting is the story of illuminations of Buddhist manuscripts.

With the rise of Tantrik interpretation of Buddhism such works as *Astasahasrika Prajnaparamita, Pancaraksa Kalacarratantra Dhorn* etc. became religiously important and objects of devotion. Of these the Prajnaparamita manuscripts were highly adored, since they were looked upon as the source of the knowledge about the Tathagata state of being. Among the Mahayana circles of devotees recitation and worship of Prajnaparamita manuscripts were thought as specially, productive of religious merit. Moreovr, the apotheosis of Prajnaparamita as a goddess of the highest wisdom naturally motivated the paintings of the deity. The protective refuge of Tara was sought for, and so her paintings abound the manuscripts. But the works contain painted scenes of the major episodes of the Buddha's life as well. And these are thematically unrelated to the works illuminated. Now the question is: how can this apparent incongruity be explained?

The Pala kings were patrons of Tantrik Buddhism, and encouraged the progagation of their faith in terms of intellectual and visual media. Many therefore were the donors of illuminated manuscripts to the libraries of monasteries, princes as well as pilgrims. Further, Buddhism as Vajrayana was an esoteric doctrine, and set great value on the power of conjuring deities through mystic formulas or vija *mantra*. This could be done once the essencelessness or *nihsvabnavata* of the empirical world was grasped. The Void then could be filled in by the presence of conjured gods and goddesses. Hence it was required that the Tantrik works be approached in a spirit of devotion, and the paintings were no less meditational aids than icons in stone and bronze. The paintings were like rafts believed to take one across the river of the senses to the other shore, and thereby deepen one's feelings for and faith in the path of *nirvana.* It follows then that the paintings were not intended as arbitrary decorations, and did proceed from a conscious avowal of the esoteric doctrines of the Vajrayana version of Buddhism. From the nature of the Prajnaparamita treaties, the paintings might not have been demanded they did enthuse their readers. They created a visual atmosphere that was valuable for the general tenor of Mahayana devotionalism and Vajrayana esotericism. They were devotional paintings, and should be judged in that light. It should be futile to expect of these paintings to have solved the problem of correspondence between Buddhist ideas and their images.

The Tantrik Buddhist paintings are outspokenly iconic, and are more faithful to religious imagination than either sculpture or bronzes. The gods and goddesses of Vajrayana are heiretically prescribed to be conceived as having specific colours, which are of magi co-gnostic significance, besides of course their respective attributes such as seances, stances, gestures and *mudras*. Unless sculptures were painted (as indeed it used to be done) or bronzes gilded it would not be possible to have meditational aids of the required description. But this could be achieved easily in painting as the art of painted surface. A few examples can be adduced Avalokitesvara (Chenresik) is white, Manjusri (Jampeyang) is red, Vajrapani (Chhanadorje) is dark blue, Tara's (Drolma) principal forms are white and Green. The Buddhas Amitayu (*Tshe-pame*) and Amitabha (*O-pame*) are identical figures in red. They are to be distinguished by the fact that the former's hands rest palm uppermost in his lap to support the vase holding the water of immorality. Sakyamuni the temporal manifestation or apparational form (*nirmankaya*) of Adi Buddha, the Tantrik Absolute, called Vajradhara, is painted golden, while the latter is blue.

Buddhist manuscript paintings reveal a linear style, and in course of time the entire conception becomes flat and decorative, even though many a figure preserves something of the sansuous elegance of the Ajanta manner. The drawings gradually become more delicate and nervous in outline, with a loss of plastic modelling. Some critics ascribe the resposnibility of this feature to the influence of the medieval Indian style of painting as exemplified in the Jain manuscripts of Western India. The Jain leitmotif of showing the farther eye outside the facial contour is also to be seen in some of the later Buddhist manuscripts. But that is another story. What is important in this context is that in purity of form and colour, the place of the medieval Buddhist painting in Indian art is similar to that of Byzantine painting in the West. And more than that, these paintings were chiefly the ultimate proto-types of all later paintings in Tibet. Like the Pala bronzes, illuminated manuscripts too were taken away by pilgrims and missionaries. Professor Tucci has reports to have noticed gallaryful of bronzes and large collections of illuminated Sanskrit manuscripts in various Tibetan monasteries.

VII

In the final evaluation of the medieval Buddhist art it should be reckoned that the problem of plastic concretization of the ideas of *bodhi* or Prajna, Karuna and *yoga* had shifted away from the aesthetic focus, and given place to a plethora of supernatural deities of Vajrayana ideology. The Pala works of art in stone sculpture and bronzes have been mainly iconic, yet quite a few of them have indeed been images. The new religious ideology had helped a baroque style and taste to emerge and mature. The Gupta style of the Sarnath Buddhas has often been called mannerist in the sense that it was a mere small alteration of the classical taste. Consider the halo of the Sarnath Buddhas. In the classic sculptures it was entirely plain. The halo of the Ratnagiri Buddha tends to be even oval, the throne highly ornate, with additional decorations. Yet the figure of the Kaster dominates the entire conception. One might say that the Ratnagiri Buddha is done in more mannerist a style than the Sarnath ones. But if one compares the crowned Buddha of the Pala times, one would realize that in point of ideology what a sea-change the Buddha-idea had undergone in course of the centuries. Austerity, purity and transparency had yielded to variety, individualism and ornament. The one who had discarded all the vanities of the world ought to have been devoid of all adornment, and he is shown gorgeously crowned. The idea of depicting the Buddha wearing enormous ear-rings, rich necklaces and anklet would have been preposterous a hundred years earlier. The case of the crowned Buddha is a characteristic piece of evidence for the Pala fashion of the baroque style which, in complete disregard for the ideas *bodhi*, Karuna and *yoga*, is proof of the love of ornamental representation. The sculpture could have been called one of a Bodhisattva, a compromise between the emperor (*cakravartin*) and the monk, except for the gesture of turning the wheel of the Law. But the Pala art is not the lonely heretic in combining a monk's garb with royal decoration. It was a special feature of the Buddhist art at Fondukistan. To this the Pala art might have been looking back.

Since the medieval Buddhist art was an art under a new religious ideology, its apprcciation would demand a new aesthetics. Its peculiarities, ideological and formal, should appear bizarre only if we did not take them granted. The achievements at Sarnath and Ajanta had brought the dialectic of idea and image to a paradigmatic point from where further movement should have been only into formlessness. This *impasse* could be broken by a new ideology alone, and vajrayana came in handy. The new ideology demanded a new art, rather a new Buddhist art. The Buddha idea defined in terms of *bodhi*, Karuna and *yoga*, and the Buddha as the *nirmankaya* of Adi-Buddha or Vajradhara or Samantabhadra are perhaps never equivalent notions. And if they are not so, they would surely inspire different styles and different idioms of aesthetic articulation.

The point henceforth would be to see how far a work of art expresses its own there in an impassioned form, through a definite pattern a motif deeply felt. With this provision we may now turn to the Buddhist art of Tibet.

PRESUPPOSITION OF TIBETAN BUDDHIST ART

I

Vajrayana is the basis of Tibetan Buddhism, and since Tibetan artistic work, in all its aspects, is determined by and oriented towards religion, Tibetan art cannot be intrinsically appreciated without its religious presuppositions. It is Vajrayana, which links the medieval Buddhist art in India with that of in Tibet.

Buddhism is divided into two systems of thought: the Madhyamika and the Yogacara. The importance given by the Yogacara school to *vijnana* and its cultivation gradually led to several esoteric developments in Buddhism. The general name 'Tantrik Buddhism' is given to such aspects of the faith. One of the branches of esoteric Buddhism is Vajrayana. The development of Tantrik tendencies in Buddhism has been consistent and of great antiquity. The Mahasanghikas had their *Dharani-pitaka*. Even the according to some authorities, goes back to the first century A.D. But this much is certain that the Buddhist Tantrik system had crystallized into a definite form by the end of the third century A.D. The famous treatise, the (also called *Guhya-*) is that ancient.

The scriptures of esoteric Buddhism go by the title of 'Tantra' (*rgyud*), and are invariably of a mystic nature. It should be noted that the term *tantra in* Hinduism is used indiscriminately for all sorts of literature. But in the Buddhist context it is exclusively applied to works representing Tantrik principles. The Buddhist Tantras are not only the legitimate heirs of the ways of thought and practice, but the logical outcome of the central thesis of Nagarjuna's interpretation of the yogaccra ways of tough practice but the logical outcome of the central thesis of Nagarjuna's interpretation of the *Pratityasamutpada*. This is so important that it is often said to be the second turning of the wheel of the Law.

What then is Vajrayana and what are its tenets? According to Padma-dkar-po it aims at *bodhicitta* or enlightenment understood as integration of the human being. This is spiritual maturity. It depends on the efforts of the individual and is in itself incommunicable, yet certain preliminary rites are necessary in order to facilitate the process of integration. There are steps for that, one has to take refuge, i.e. resolve to attain enlightenments for the sake of all sentient beings. Then an attitude has to be formed for *bodhicitta*, and consciously begin to oneself and the world around from an intuitive standpoint. This attitude is required to be strengthened through a meditative process. At this stage the recitation of *mantras* plays an important part. A *mantra* is a protection of mind, a formula which prevents the mind from going astray and helps in meditative concentration. One meditates to realize the identity of Reality and Appearance. The analytical methods and techniques of the intellect split up the identity arbitrarily into a number of opposites. Appearance and mind, said the Tibetan saint and poet Milarepa, are born together. If so, then the ultimate in mind, *dharmakaya* the and the ultimate in Appearance are also born together, i.e. are identical. The point of the teaching is that man is not only an intellectual being, but also an emotional one. And does not deny the fact that the emotive meaning of anything whatsoever is of greater importance for shaping the life of an individual than the more intellectual connotation. Therefore one has to refer to the whole of human nature.

II

To look upon the Buddhist Tantrik system is a variant of the Hindu Saktaism would be a category mistake. The symbology of Tibetan art requires this point to be clearly understood. One should guard against arbitrarily transplanting the termini of a theistic system into a non-theistic one.

1. Vajrayana Buddhism is non-theistic, while the Hindu Tantras are theistic. The vajrayana concept of the Adi Buddha is hardly a God. The Adi Buddha is the symbol of the universality, timelessness and all-comprehensive experience of the enlightened mind. It is man's true nature.

2. The Buddhist Tantric system has no concept of *Sakti*, which in the Hindu Tantras forms the focus of interest. The central idea of Tantrik Buddhism is Prajna. Sakti is *maya*, the very power that creates illusion, from which only can liberate us. *Sakti* is the creatrix of the universe, when she is united with *Siva*. The Buddhist does not want unfoldment of the world, but the coming back to the uncreated unformed state of sunyata, from

which all creation proceeds. To become conscious of (stong-pa-nyid) is Prajna (shes-rab). The realization of Prajna in life is enlightenment or *bodhi* (byang-chhub). Hence the iconic 'sexual' metaphor that when Prajna, the passive female principle from which everything proceeds and into which every thing recedes, is united with the dynamic male principle of universal love and compassion which represents the means (Upaya 'thabs' in Tibetan) for the realization of Prajna, then perfect Buddhahood is attained. This process of enlightenments is represented in Tibetan art by the symbol of the union of male and female in sexual embrace. It should be noted in this connection that in the Hindu Tantras the male principle is passive, while the female one is active.

In Buddhist symbolism the knower (Buddha) becomes one with his knowledge (Prajna). This becoming one is the highest happiness, (bde-mchhog). The Tibetan *yuganaddha* (yabyum) is a way of life, its figural representation is meant to be a plastic concretization of the experiences and visions of meditation. Prajna and Upaya are super-individual polarities, their union therefore has nothing that could be called sexual. The state of union is called *mahamudra*, (phyog-rgya-chhen-po) the Great Attitude. It has given its name to one of the most important systems of meditation in Tibet. It is one of the remarkable achievements of Tibetan Buddhist painting to have rendered the entire process of enlightenment in terms of the *yuganaddha* motifs of the Dhyani Buddhas in union with their respective Prajnas. The term dhyani *buddha* means a Buddha seen in meditational vision, or an ideal Buddha, in short. The historical Buddha Sakyamuni (Shakya-thuppa) is never depicted in the *yuganaddha* manner. It should further be noted that the Tibetan 'sexual' symbology is essentially non-erotic. An evidence for this case is to be found in the fact that the so-called sexual polarities of prajna and Upayaand is also depicted in terms of non-anthropomorphic symbols of the bell (gril-bu) and *vajra* (rdo-rje) respectively. A Dhyani Buddha, paired even though he is with his Prajna, is shown, in icons and paintings, holding a bell and a *vajra*. Hence the great importance of these objects in ritual and its art.

THE SOURCES AND FORMATIVE FACTORS OF TIBETAN ART

Art provides an instance of Tibet's dependence on the centres of civilization that were instrumental in her conversion to Buddhism. This dependence was however modified by indigenous influences. Yet it remains largely true that Buddhism came to Tibet not merely as a body of doctrine, but with a highly developed art. The Lhakhang Ckhenmo at Sakya, reports Tucci, held a whole gallery of bronzes from various parts of India, and from the Pala dynasty in particular. The monastery at Toling in West Tibet treasured bronzes from Kashmir, whilst at Samye there were others from the Pala Kingdom and from Central Asia.

Influences in art flowed from four distinct sources into Tibet: Central Asia, where the Gandhara style had enjoyed a prolonged survival, China, Nepal, through her the Pala style penetrated and Kashmir, which influenced Tibet's morals. But distinguishing manners or styles, assigning works of art to periods, schools, etc., are impossible in Tibetan art, except in the oldest period. The reasons for this lie in the nature of Tibetan dependence on the sources of inspiration. This dependence was never mere copying. The different inspirations that meet in it are so well blended that Tibetan art is distinctive. Yet a historical account of the development of the major stylistic trends may be given as follows.

Datable Tibetan history begins from 600-850 A.D. the time of the "Religious Kings". In the north Kucha and Khotan and come under the influence of Buddhism. Kucha followed the Himalayan tradition, while Khotan and adopted Mahayana and had become a centre of the Avatamsaka school of thought which strongly influenced the development of Buddhism in China and Japan. Traces of it are also discernable in the "Old Tradition (Nying-ma) of Tibet.

To the west of Tibet was Ta-zig, probably Iran; still farther to the west was Byzantium, often called Krom/Phrom in Tibetan sources. Iranian influence is apparent in Tibetan art in a certain way to carving beams and the frequent use of lion figures in the porticos of a temple. Other important areas to the west were Gilgit and Kashmir. Hellenistic trends in Tibetan art came from the ancient land of Gandhara. South of Tibet is Nepal. It had considerable influence on the early development of art in Tibet. In India, the kingdom of Kanauj under King Harsa, and Bengal, where Tantrik Buddhist ideas were developed, were two important centres with which the Tibetans had contact. China, at that time under the T'ang dynasty (618-908), had less influence on the early development of art in Tibet. All these various influences are hinted at in early Tibetan sources. Contacts with art centres in India, China, Nepal, Kashmir and Khotan entered a deep influence in Tibet that lasted well into the fifteenth century.

In reaction to and interrelation with the trends in the surrounding countries, Tibet gradually began to develop different art schools of her own which often started from a pre-dominent influence of one of these countries but then developed their own individuality. The earliest such school of artistic trends in painting and sculpture flourished in West Tibet under the kings of Guge. Developed from the style prevailing in Kashmir, it retained its individuality upto the sixteenth/seventeenth centuries in the temples in Sipti, Guge and Purang.

Gyantse in South Tibet developed the Beri or Nepalese style, the most significant style of Tibet painting upto the fifteenth century. In Derge, the most important art centre in East Tibet, the line of development was less uniform. There in the fifteenth century the Meuri School was founded, which incorporated Chinese and Mongal elements in elegant embroideries and tapestries. In the following century the Khyenri school was founded. In this case, too the Chinese influence was evident in the treatment of the background and in the close attention to details. The Khyenri school favoured in the Saskya monasteries, declined in the seventeenth century, and the "New Meuri" School, blending elements of Khyenri, Gadri and late Indian styles, prevailed in Lhasa and Central Tibet up to the twentieth century. The Gadri or Karma Gadri School, which shows the greatest Chinese influence in the use of colours and shading retained its individuality for a long time.

APPRECIATING TIBETAN ART: PAINTING

I

Tibetan religious paintings are well-known in the form of thankas. They are paintings of secred and ceremonial subjects, which are hung up in temples or private chapesls, or rolled up to be carried over the shoulder when travelling. A thanka properly speaking is a painted banner. Aesthetically they are marked by decorativeness, bold colouring and air of naive astonishment. But the real point is their content, the variety of religious themes, the search to express a profoundly complicated mystical world through these figures' symbolic attributes.

Tibetan painting can be appreciated at two distinct levels. First, the purely visual level; where it pleases the eye with vividness and decorative harmony, without regard to the content. Secondly and perhaps more importantly, at the level where it should interest any student of religious experience, and mystic art.

Among the factors that add to the efficacy and define the particularity of Tibetan art are the completeness of its overall conception, the intensity of its grotesque imagery and concomitant serenity of its quiescent modes, and the combination of seemingly divergent emotive forms within the same composition. In these aspects art reflects religion to such an extent that it might well be said that Tibetan art itself is the most direct and eloquent form of expression that Tantric Buddhism has developed. Iconographically and, by definition, visionary, the art of Tibet is also characterized by a peculiar intensity suggestive of psychic departments. This quality typically reflects the impulse of art, but in the Tibetan context it also refers to one of its most direct aims : the creation of models for visualizing meditation. A beautiful, grotesque or moving image may help the meditator to recall the details of a particular form. Therefore, the artist is doubly inspired to create an image that satisfied his own aesthetic requirements and also one that expands the significance of iconographically prescribed forms of the divinities. The inspirational aspect of art then becomes central to the aesthetic endeavor for it is a religious motive that inspires the art of Tibet and a religious goal of transformation that it seeks to achieve.

II

In Tibetan painting, we find a great variety of colours, and a free and seemingly unrestricted use of different colours for one and the same motif. We encounter landscapes and clouds in "possible" but also, from a naturalistic point of view "impossible" colour compositions, in colours feasible perhaps only in a dream or in a vision, so that we are induced to seek the cause which gave rise to an art of this kind. This cause is to be found in the forms of Mahayan and Vijrayana. Important perspectives which influenced the creation of art were : the fundamental realization of the transience of the external world, the relativity of all values, and the transparency of all visible and created manifestations against the invisible but translucent background of the universal void. The world is seen as a manifestation of forms composed of separate transitory elements, forms which are themselves transient and hence illusory. All phenomena are only states of momentary existence in a stream of continuous arising and decay. The world that appears to our eyes can be surveyed by the inner eye in its past, present and future stages. The identity of the void and the manifest, repeatedly emphasized in the extensive literatures Prajnaparmita enables the artist to see the world of phenomena as a vision, as a state yet to be realized, in which form and colour are changed at will in accordance with the intensity of contemplation. The value of the colours is relative and adjusts itself to the aspect of the moment and not to external reality. Similarly, meditations on remote lands of the Buddhas and the celestial realms of the Bodhisattvas open up to the artist a visionary world of divine spheres to be experienced in a supersensual way, spheres which he than tries to depict in transparent colours.

The Mahayana doctrine of Trikaya opens up to him further realms for pictorial art. The artist therefore tries his hand at representing the bodies of the heavenly enjoyment of supreme happiness (Sambhoga Kaya) in which the Bodhisativas reside; he creates the ideal picture of the Buddha in the pure body of his earthly incarnation (nirmana kaya), or else he tries to represent the highest form of the Buddha as the body of the universal law (*dharma kaya*), the nature of the Buddhahood. All these worlds and their illusory forms of the reflections of light-filled forms of higher realizations can be penetrated by the artist with the rays of knowledge as in recommended in the meditation for monks and lay followers. This light-filled character, this dissolution or transparent penetration of material with the rays of enlightenment, makes things appear in the visionary reflection of the five-coloured rays, which in vajrayana mysticism, become the foundation of systematic pictorial meditation. Thus the entire material world is composed, in accordance with Buddhist doctrine, of five elements whose subtle material forms manifest themselves to the inner eye as a five-coloured light.

III

These infinite possibilities open to the artistically creative spirit are constrained however by an ancient and traditional Indian iconography which prescribes a strict hierarchical and creatively ordered pattern within which the representations have to be kept. At an early date the large number of Buddhas, Bodhisattvas, deities and saints was fixed in iconographic textbooks. Their appearance was clearly defined in terms of form, dimension and colour, as well as appropriate symbolism. The member of these pictures with all their variations and special forms runs into thousands. The accepted special symbols of deities, the positions of the hands, the positions of the body, as well as the colours are the familiar identification marks recognizable by those initiated into the mysteries of vajrayana. Only when all these aspects are taken together with their underlying meanings can the entire cognitive content of a picture be understood.

The artist, of course, must be initiated into this normally arcane knowledge before attempting the difficult representation of such symbolic deities. He creates those Buddhas and Bodhisattvas who-raised to a pure, higher sphere on their lotus flowers-radiate in a thousand works of pictorial art. The lotus, in Buddhism, the symbol of purity and also of the meditative unfolding of the heart offered up by the yogi as a symbolic throne for the deities. The lotus is the unfolding centre of the heart upon whose petal throne the germinal syllables (*vij mantra*) issue forth and radiate multicoloured light so that the deities may arise from this light. It is from the heart-lotus that all images and visions originate which then grow into the magnificent pantheon of the Buddha worlds. These worlds are realized by the mystic in his meditations: he experiences them and actualizes their meaning, eventually "returning" them back into the infinite voidness.

The meanings contained in many *mantras* and germinal syllables as crystallization points for the visionary representation of the tantric deities are part of the basic knowledge of the Tibetan artist. He has learned the meditative texts with *mantras* in which the deities are described with all their attributes, *mudras* and colours for the purpose of pictorial meditation. The Tibetan artist, being initiated into the profound teaching of the themes represented, thus creates works which in turn can be, and are designed to be, understood only by the initiated. This is an important factor in the contemplation of Tibetan art, an art frequently so obscurely encoded that access to it often seems barred to a thinking mind. It should be remembered that a sculpture, an iconographic painting, a visionary representation (especially in the *mandalas*) can represent only one of the different levels of the inner path of knowledge. Such pictures may correspond for instance, to the stage of the pure spirit, the pure word or the transfigured body. But the pictures may also refer to the plane of the Buddhas, the esoteric initiation deities, the parasidisical worlds of Amitabha. All these possibilities must be considered in an examination and interpretation of Tibetan art. They prove that this art often has a profound background of many separate levels, frequently transcending the boundaries of what is representable. Anything beyond those boundaries–the spiritual content, the meditative level, the experimental content and the degree of initiation-is expressed as far as possible by symbols of form, implement and colour. Many picture, simultaneously show several levels of internal transformational or several levels of meditation which only the initiated can realize during contemplation. This religious art therefore aims not at laying claims to perfect aesthetics or creative beauty or appeal of form but, by observing a strictly formalized iconography, aims at making visible religious, meditational, purely spiritual and visionary contents so that the initiated may in turn re-live them. To the initate, therefore, the work of art is only an external aid for pictorial meditation. The works of art serve spiritual discipline and realization; they are objects for a ritual of invocation and veneration of the deities and hence fulfil a totally different function from that of decoration or art for arts' sake. The thankas functioned as supports or visualization of the deities whose qualities the initiated strikes to develop within himself.

IV

Art is a technique of visualization or mystic introspection of secret fields of forces, possible ecstatic states-the resulting visions relativize all external laws of image, colour and form. That is why the handling of colour in Tibetan works of art is often preternatural, highly expressive, visionary and fantastic, landscapes, thees, sky and clouds often correspond more to the inner picture of an all-transforming vision than to and external realistic picture of nature. Time and again clouds may appear unreal. The clouds frequently carry the deities as symbolic apparitions. Clouds are the ethereal heavenly or dream-like spheres from which visions energe, they can become the bearers of meditative representations and the transparent source of visions. Often the pictorial representations of the customary earthly and the visionary transcendental spheres move freely, without boundaries and seem to merge with one another. In some pictures the heavenly sphere reaches far down into the earthly world, in others the trees and snowy summits reach up into the realm of Buddhas and Dakinis floating within clouds, and on other pictures cosmic creations of the world appear, between heaven and earth.

Tibet's art is a serious attempt to represent doctrine, symbolism and the ideal image, worldly and transcendental experience, reality and the visionary content of mediation, the courses of the worlds, enlightenment and salvation, things created and things transparent, and finally the nature of the void itself. Just as objects in the world of phenomena are transient and void, so the work of art is likewise void in itself, without real and abiding existence. These are pictures of momentary phenomena meant for meditation, to be filled with life through invocation. These representations are not experienced as definite deities or real figures, but as symbols of a spiritual process which could be perfected and realized only in pure introspection.

V

The field of painting comprised large-scale room decoration and murals at one end of the scale and the form of scrolls, the thankas, within the monasteries. The temples were most lavishly painted. Columns, capitals, friezes and architecture were decorated in colours on a red ground, with sacred symbols, calligraphic lettering, flowers, intertwining leaves and dragon motifs.

According to the various techniques employed the thankas can be classified under four heads:

1. Thankas painted in colour - also from printing blocks;
2. Gold paintings, either on gold ground or red ground with line drawing in gold and colouring;
3. Painting in black ground, monochrome with white or gold, or polychrome with limited use of iconographic decorative colours;
4. Pure embroidery or applique' techniques, sometimes with additional painting. Thankas can also be grouped according to their pictorial content under the following subject headings:
   1. Historical or legendary representations;
   2. Representations of the spiritual succssion and hierarchy;
   3. Representations of meditative contents;
   4. Mandalas and cosmic diagrams;
   5. Visionary representations.

In the first category we find the representatiors froms the life of the Buddha, the saints, the Arhats, the yogis and the Siddhs, and legends of saints or stories of Tibetan Kings.

The second group is frequently found as wall paintings in monasteries as wall as in many thankas. There are the pictures showing the line of gurus, the founders of a sect or doctrinal tradition. They are described as the Golden Rosary of the Gurus. These paintings mirror, as it were, of the spiritual descent or succession the sect or doctrinal tradition represented there. This is why these representations of the succession include not only the teachers but also the specific esoteric divinities and gurdian deities of a particular school.

The third category includes the large number of pictures of meditative content, representing Buddhas, Bodhisattvas, and esoteric deities. The meditational pictures are aids to contemplation of certain aspects of the esoteric teachings and the attributes of the deities, as well as to meditation on the ideals of Mahayana Buddhism generally.

Under the fourth group *mandalas* are represented in a closed (concentric) form. These *mandalas* are esoteric meditation diagrams embodying a particular doctrine or some practical aspect of a doctrine. This doctrine is to be understood through progressive pictorial meditation proceeding from the centre of the picture. The *mandalas* thus serve the inner process of individuation - spiritual contents to be systematically attained through yoga. These contents are contained in the mandalas, coded in a wealth of symbolism, and are intended to achieve a step-by-step purification of consciousness through growing awareness of the spiritual values of the secret doctrine.

The fifth group comprises all paintings of visionary type. The visionary pictures, mostly on black ground, are of a highly asoteric character and most secretly guarded in Tibet against the eyes of the uninitiated. The paintings from the temples of the guardian deities are forms, to this day, the ones whose real significance and inner force remain most hidden from us. The sight of these wrathful representations on a back ground engender psychic process of individuation which demand a thorough preparation and an advanced knowledge of manipulation of the forces and powers of human consciousness.

THE LESSONS OF TIBETAN PAINTING

I

There remain extensive areas in Ladakh, Nepal, Sikkim and Bhutan where Tibetan Buddhist art continues to enjoy that unbroken tradition and viability it once possessed in Tibet. It is in these countries, along the frontiers of Tibet that a good portion of Tibetan heritage survives.

The art of painting in Sikkim and Bhutan has been exposed to the same set of influences and inspirations as that in Tibet. But the metamorphosis in art styles appears to have been carried out in these two Himalayan, countries. If it was possible to speak of 'groups' (*a la* Tucci), on the evidence of shared charactaristics in the case of Tibetan art, it is not even possibile to refer to these groupings of stylistic influences in the art of Sikkim and Bhutan.

Tibetan art in Sikkim and Bhutan exhibit more Indian conventions in landscape painting. For example, since the Shakya-pa period, under the Chinese influence, mountains were depicted in the shape of crags of Dolomites. But in Sikkim as well as Bhutan mountains are drawn in the shape of a cone, which is typically Indian. Besides, there are a lot of locally inspired elements which do not conform to Tibetan rules. Again, the murals of the Punakha chapel in Bhutan are remarkable. They do not depict the legends of the Buddha's life, they narrate the story of the lives of the *siddhas*. And the pictorial composition is essentially Ajantan. It should remind any trained observer of the great Bodhisattva panel. In the Bhutanese panel too the central figures are motionless, and as the scenes spread out, more and more movement is felt.

A mention should be made of the Buddha mural at the Bajo monastery in Bhutan. It is a sixteenth-seventeenth century painting, and is marked by the same lack of modeling in colour as one notices in the Pala manuscript illuminations of a later period. Pure colours such as reds, blues and greens predominate in soft shades, without modeling. They are used as a kind of pattern outlined to form shapes. The entire painting looks as though it were a *mandala* to be meditated upon. Later Buddhist art, under inspiration and persuasion has indeed been an art of the *mandala*.

II

The influence of Tibetan art on recent Indian painting should be a matter of interest as well as curiosity. One of the sources of modern Indian painting has been Buddhist, i.e., the Ajanta murals. But seldom the Tibetan inspirations are mentioned. Nivedita was an admirer of Tibetan religious symbolism, and her services for the cause of modern Indian painting can hardly be profaned. Many of the formal features of Tibetan painting were adapted by Nandalal Bose, the stylizations of drawing in particular. Nicholai Roerich produced many canvases under the inspiration of Tibetan Buddhism. They are Tibetan paintings in respect of theme, composition, colouring and symbolism. But more Buddhist and Tibetan are the paintings by Lama A. Govinda. Recently much interest is being evinced for Tantrik art. Excepting a few of Nirad Mazumdar's works, the trend appears towards fashionableness and novelty. But one could hope that in not too distant a future the artist of kindred sensibility would turn towards Tibetan painting in their search for a new aesthetics. If one of the functions of art be to heighten consciousness, it is Tibetan Buddhism's *forte*. That art can become a *yana* or 'carrier' for man's spiritual integration is decidedly one of the great lessons of Tibetan art.

BIBLIOGRAPHY

1. The Fourth Panchen Lama, *The Practice and Theory of Tibetan Buddhism*, Geshe Lhumdup Sopa and Jeffery Hopkins (tr.), Rider Co. London, 1976.
2. Heinrich Zimmer, *Myths and Symbols of Indian Art and Civilization,* Dover, New Yourk.

3. Benjamin Rowland, *The Art and Architecture of India,* Penguin, London, 1953.

4. H. V. Guenther, *Yuganaddha, the Tantric View of Life,* Chaukhamba, Banaras, 1953.

5. G. Tucci, *Tibet,* Driver (tr.), Oxford & IBH Publishing Co., New J.E.S. Delhi, 1967.

6. A. Coomaraswamy, "The Origin of the Buddha Image" in *Journal of the American Oriental Society,* Vol. 46, 1926.

7. Niharranjan Ray, *Idea and Image in Indian Art,* Munshiram Manoharlal, New Delhi, 1973.

8. Krishna Chaitanya, *The Mural Tradition,* Abhinava Publications, New Delhi, 1976.

9. Charles Fabri, *Discovering Indian Sculpture*, East West Press, New Delhi, 1970.

10. M. Singh, *Himalayan Art*, UNESCO, 1971.

11. K. Peterson, 'Sources of Variation in Tibetan Canons of Iconometry' in *Tibetan Studies,* ed. Aris and Kyi, Vikes, New Delhi, 1980.

12. S.K. Sarasvati, *Pala Yugera Chitrakala* (Bengali) Ananda Publishers, Calcutta, 1978.

13. P. Belikov, *Nicholai Roerich*, Progress Publishers, Moscow, 1979.

14. C. Sivaramamurti, *Indian Painting,* NBT. New Delhi.

15. A. Coomaraswamy, *The Dance of Shiva,* Asia Publishing House, Bombay, 1956.

16. Benoytosh Bhattacharya, *Bouddhadera Devadevi* (Bengali) Visva-Bharati, Calcutta.

THE HISTORICITY OF INDO-TIBETAN RELATIONS AND INDO-TIBETAN LITERATURE

Ratna Basu

About 2 million 10 thousand people of India speak Tibetan as their Mother tongue. This number excludes the Tibetan refugees in India. About 85 thousand in Ladakh, 12 thousand in Leh, Lahul and Spiti, and almost 10 thousand people in Arunachal Pradesh. speak Tibetan. It is to be noted that even the Sikkimese Language itself is an offshoot of Tibetan Language. In Nepal Tibetan people live in about one-third of the total area of the country; their population calculated approximately is to be about 1,00,000. In Pakistan the region of Baluchistan (Soalti) is inhabited by Tibetan people.

The reference of Indo-Tibetan relation can be traced back in the narratives related to the Mythical early age about Tibet. In all the works on the history of Tibet or history of Buddhism in Tibet, history of Buddhism in Mongolia and other related works it is narrated that the first king of Tibet was actually an Indian Prince. This prince was abandoned by his royal parents in the childhood and was brought up by some cowherd-farmer. As a grown up young man he left the country and crossed the Himalayas, because he was too aggrieved to learn the story about his birth and about how he was abandoned by his king father.

The Mahabharata records that a Ksatriya king named Rupati fled to snow clad Tibet during the war of Kuraksetra and the indigenous people over there accepted him as their king. This great epic further narrates that when Rupati perished Tibet was divided into several independent Kingdoms.

The Tibetan historian Bu Ston (1290-1362 A.D.) records that the son of Prasenjit, the King of Kosala went to cross the Himalayas and reached Tibet. This is actually the story narrated above in brief. It is also to be noted that the King who abandoned his son, the child Prince, is mentioned as a King of the Licchabi Clan. It is further to be noted in this context that following V.A. Smith, Suniti Kumar Chatterjee also identified the Licchabi clan as a family of Indo-Mongoloid origin. They were very powerful and dominant in Northern Bihar, as it is referred to in S.K. Chatterjee's *Kirãtajanakrti.*

The First King of Tibet, who came from India was named Gña thri'btsan po, meaning 'the king who was carried on the throne on the shoulders' of people. In the lineage of this king only, the 33rd king was the famous Tibetan King Sroñ btsan Sgam Po (620-649 A.D.). This king married a Nepalse princess who brought the images of Aksobhya Buddha and Maitreya Buddha. The King had also married a Chinese Princess. In Tibetan belief and religious history king *btsan sgam po* is the incarnation of Avalokiteswara and his two wives are incarnations of the Goddesses Green Tara and White. Tara King Sroñ btsan Sgam Po sent his minister Thon mi sam bhota to India to learn the language and script of the holy language of India. The minister learnt the Sanskrit language and vast range of Buddhist literature. Other companions of Thon mi could not survive in the Indian climate. This minister introduced the Tibetan script evolving it from the Brahmi script of Gupta period, which was used in that time in North India. Thon mi sam bhota introduced the Tibetan script which is in use till today and composed eight books, of which unfortunately only two have been handed down to us. He wrote books on Sanskrit Grammar and Language for teaching and learning the language and also books on the grammar of Tibetan Language. He also wrote discourse on Buddhism. From this period the First phase of translation of Indian Buddhist work from Sanskrit into Tibetan started.

The Tibetan dynasty actually existed, flourished and experienced its golden age from the time of *Sroñ btsan Sgam Po* (620-649 A.D.) up to that of Khri *Sroñ de btsan* (755-794 A.D.). During the reign of the latter the Indian scholars Padmasambhava and Santarakshita visited Tibet. In the year 775 A.D. the first Buddhist monastery was founded in Bsam Yas of Tibet. This monastery was built after the model of Odantapuri, near modern Gaya in Bihar. In this monastery during the period between 792 and 794 A.D. Kamalasila defeated the Chinese scholar monk Mahayana is a scholarly debate; and the great expansion the Indian Buddhism in Tibet started marching in a grand scale.

During the reign of the king Ral Pa Can (815-838 A.D.), the second phase of translation of Indian-Buddhist scriptures into Tibetan started, which is marked by the organized composition of a systematised Sanskrit Tibetan Dictionary of all terms and expressions for use by all the translators so that the translation could be kept uniform. The translation work was always done as a joint effort of a Sanskrit Pandita (*Pan Chen*) and a Tibetan translator (*Le tsa ba*). Occasionally there was also a reviser.

After the decline or the great Tibetan dynasty Tibet was scattered in to sectarian groups and small feuds; and over large areas of the land there was lot of anarchy. From the middle of the 9th century up to 13th century this anarchy continued. There were at least ten instances of sectarian clashes among religious sects and feuds as well. During this period the regional kings and sects were active in propagating Buddhism in the land of Tibet.

In 1040 A.D. the ruler of Gu-ge in Western Tibet invited the Indian Scholar Atisa Dipankara to Tibet (i.e. Gu-go). During this period along with innumerable Sanskrit works many of the *dohas* of Saraha, *Nãropa*, *Mãrpa*, Tillopa and many others were translated into Tibetan. Most of these mystic songs ,poems or *dohas* are now lost in original language and are available only in Tibetan translation. This was the so called third phase of translation programme initiated in Tibet.

In the year 1260 A.D. the 'Phogs Pa ruler of the Sakya sect met the Mongolian Emperor Kublai Khan and offered Tibet as a tribute to the Mongolian emperor. This emperor initiated the organized collection of the Tibetan translation of Indian works, which were till then in forms of scattered manuscripts only. The whole range of works under the sections of Sutra *Vinaya* and *Abhidharma* commentaries on them, other literary works of different types were arranged systematically and the complete form of *Kanjur* (*Rka*' '*gyur*) and Tanjur (Bstan 'gyur) took shape. The Mongol emperor sponsored the supply of requisite paper and ink. The Sakyas became very powerful at this time. Bu ston performed the unique job of editing and organizing the whole set of literature and added a detailed index, list of index and appendix. This is actually the original Narthang manuscript of the Tibetan canon.

The Sakya power came to an end during the period 1357-1419 A.D. The *Dge Lugs pa* sect under the leadership of Tsoñ Kha Pa rose to power and political importance. The Ming dynasty was the ruling power in China. In 1403 A.D. Yung Lö was the Ming emperor. Yung Lo sponsored the production of the first Xylograph block prints of the Tibetan canon in the year 1410 A.D., the archetype of which was the Narthang manuscript. The purpose of the Ming ruler was obviously to compete with the Mongol rulers in the matter of improving its political relation with Tibet, which was quite bitter during the previous centuries.

The *Dge lugs Pa* ruler B sod nam rgya mtsho was the first to receive the title *Dalai Lama* in the year 1578 from the Mongolian Emperor Altan Khan. But he was declared the third Dalai Lama. Two of his predecessors Dge 'dun grub pa and Dge 'dun rgya mtsho were awarded the title posthumously. In Mongolian language the word *Talei* means 'Ocean'.

Thereafter Dalai Lama's guru Chos Kyi rgyal mtshan (Sanskrit: Dharmadhvaja) was declared the first Pan Chen Lama. It should be noted that Dalai Lama is Lord Avalokitesvara, who is the most important of the eight *Bodhisattvas* in Tibetan Buddhism. Pan Chen Lama represents Lord *Amitãbha who is* one of the five Tathagatas.

During the period 1641-1642 the Mongolian ruler Gu Šri Khan (of Khoshot) occupied the whole of Tibet and thereafter entrusted the fifth Dalai Lama with the total sovereign power of ruling the country which meant religious as well as political supremacy in power politics. Actually it is from this period that Dalai Lamas are the highest authority both in religious and political life of the country of Tibet and its people.

It can be recalled once again that in spite of the political ups and downs in the country of Tibet, its academic, literary and cultural interrelation with India and Indian Buddhist literature continued through translation activities. Three marked phases of such organized initiative have been identified. There is no other country which preserves the literary heritage of another country so meticulously through such organized and planned work This is a unique feature, for which so many lost works or Indian Buddhist Logic, Grammatical digests, Commentaries and pieces of creative literature lost in the original language (i.e. chiefly Sanskrit) can be re-collected and evaluated. Many original *Sanskrit* texts were also lost and destroyed in India, the manuscripts of which could be collected from Tibet and published for scholars. Pandit Rahul Sankrityayan, Pandit A.L. Thakur and others have contributed immensely in this area. It is well known how Rahul Sankrityayan collected manuscripts or photographs of those from different places of Tibet.

Thus Tibetan canonical literature is actually a part of Indian literature which should be studied and researched upon more vigorously in the present day situation as a mark of social-cultural exchange and integration.

The history of many Buddhist monasteries of ancient and Medieval India can be best gathered from the Biographical (or rather Hagiographical) literature and from the Geographical literature pertaining to the history and geography of the holy places written in Tibetan language. These are the *rnam thar̲* and *lam yiq* works in Tibetan. e.g., the history of:

(a) Somapura *vihãra* (= Ompur, near Paharpur, now in Bangaldesh),

(b) *Tãmralipta Sanghãrãma,*

(c) Odantapuri, (which was the model for Bsam yas monastery), at present Kurkihar near Gaya in Bihar,

(d) *Vikramasîlã*, identified as present day *Patharghãtã*,

(e) Maynamati Lalmati,

(f) *Kãpetya,* (not yet identified) where Bedhivarman and his pupil, the great Prajñãvarman resided.

In all these University monasteries Tibetan monks and scholars lived and studied. There was a regular inflow of students and scholars from Tibet. Indian scholars also visited Tibet and worked together with Tibetan scholars to fulfill the programme of translation.

The Newari artisans and architects played a very significant role in the cultural interrelation between India and Tibet. The Newari artisans of Nepal were regularly engaged in construction work, and work of inner and outer decoration, mural painting etc. of the buildings for monasteries. Till today in Indian Tibetan enterprises Newari artisans are seen to work as trained hands for the job.

Tibetans in Tibet, Tibetan people in India, (i.e. Indian) and Tibetan refugees in India–the language, literature and culture of these three types of Tibetans of today are the same. So is the case of the Tibetans living in Europe or elsewhere. On the other hand, the whole range of Trans-Himalayan areas continue to be the witness and background of several layers of ethnic-religious culture. In brief, it could be said, the temple, mural paintings, theories and rituals prove and show that all the *šaiva, šãkta* and Buddhist Tantras are surviving, sometimes in an amalgamated multiplayered form, but quite often in an integrated yet simultaneously operating feature. The minute details of these aspects could be elements of research from the viewpoints of behaviour, arts, icons, rituals, painting, sculpture, literature, festivities, myths and mysticism and so on. Till these are studied as integrated part of Indian studies, a major area of India and her people remain misunderstood and alienated. Till these people are studied in their own terms of Indo-Tibetan, Tibeto-Chinese, Tibeto-Mongolian and Tibeto-Burman feature in respect of ethnicity, society, religion, culture, literature, art, art forms etc. and all again in their historicity as well as current sensibility the mind of Himalayan people remain obscure. The seed of distance, estrangement and insurgence remains hidden there which flares up in any crucial situation.

On the other hand the controversial and sensitive issues of current times should not be just put under the carpet. Those should rather be studied and analysed without bias or dogma. Sometimes the study of recent past is unpleasant due to many touchy factors. Scholars need to have the feeling of distance but not lack of sincerity in researching up on such aspects. Not only the ancient period, the recent past emerging into the present is to be understood and realized in its proper value and historicity. Personal interest, chauvinism or regionalism should not stand in the way of scholarly endeavour. Scholarly activities again need rather to respond and react in cases of social crisis and contribute in a positive way towards integration and not the contrary.

BIBLIOGRAPHY

Bacot, Jacques, *Introduction à l 'histoire du Tibet.* Paris 1962.

Bell, Sir Charles, *Tibet–Past and Present.* Oxford 1924 (deutsch: *Tibet einst und jetzt*. Leipzig 1925).

Haarh, Erik, *The Yar-lué Dynasty*. Kbenhavn 1969.

Hoffmann, Helmut, *Tibets Eintritt in die Universalgeschichte. In: Saeculum* 1 (1950), S. 258-279.

Hoffmann, Helmut, *Die Religionen Tibets. Bon und Lamaismus in ihrer geschichtlichen* Entwicklung. Freiburg/MÜnchen 1956.

Hoffmann, Helmut, *Tibet–A Hand book.* Bloomington, Indiana 1975 (Kap. V: The History of Tibet, S. 39-82).

Pal, Pratapaditya, *Tibetan Paintings* Vaduz/Basel 1964.

Petech, Luciano, Tinbet. In: *Handbuch der Orientalistik*, 1. Abteilung, 5. Band: Altaistik, 5. Abschnitt: Geschichte Mittelasiens. Leiden/Köln 1966, S. 311-347.

Richardson, H.E., *Tibet and Its History* /Toronto/Melbourne, 1962.

Richardson, H.E., *A Corpus of Tibetan Inscriptions:* London 1985.

Schulemann, Guenther, Geschichtc, der Dalai-Lama. Leipzig 1958.

Shakabpa, Taepon W.D., *Tibet–A Political History*. New Haven/London 1967.

Snellgrove, David, Richardson, Hugh, *A Cultural History of Tibet*. London 1968.

Stein, R.A., Ia civilization tibétaine. 1 Paris 1962; 2 Paris 1981 (English: Tibetan Civilization. Übers. V.J.E. Stapleton Driver. London 1972.

Tucci, Giuseppe, *Tibet–Land of Snows*. London 1967 (Kap. II: History, S. 19-63).

Wang Furen; Suo Wenqing: *Highlights of Tibetan History*, Beijing 1984.

THE STATUS OF TIBETAN LANGUAGE

Thubten Tsering

To know the status and importance of Tibetan language one must first understand its origin and how it has developed over the centuries. Hence, let me discuss the topic under three board headings:

1. Source and origin–historical background
2. Its development over the centuries.
3. The present status and its importance

TIBETAN LANGUAGE–SOURCE/ORIGIN AND HISTORICAL BACKGROUND

Tibetan language refers to both written and spoken language. The latter has its origin as far back as the human languages. This is universal. However the written language or the literary language developed much later with invention of scripts. Tibetan literary language too came into existence much later.

There are two theories as to its origin and source:

(a) The theory advocated by scholars on Bon religion of Tibet &

(b) Generally accepted theory of Buddhist Scholars.

Many Bon Scholars–especially Prof. Namkhai Norbu of University of Naples believe that the source of Tibetan writing system goes as far back as Bon kings of Zhangzhung (name for Western Tibet) prior to the introduction of Buddhism from India. He further examines that it was wrong to conclude that Tibet had no writing system or written language before king Songsten Gampo. According to him there are ample reasons to believe that Tibet which was called Zhangzhung before it came to be called as Bod, had its own religion which was Bon and hence its own culture and writing system–on which the present written language was based.... He refutes that if Tibet had no writing system at all before king Songsteen Gampo, it would not have been possible to record the history of 32 earlier kings (Bon). The Zhangzhung script was called Smar–Yig which was there during king Nyatri Tsenpo–(The first known kin in Tibetian history). During his reign, it is recorded in Bon histories, that many Bon treatises into Tibetan–for which Smar–Yig was used. Otherwise there would be no such records. Prof. Norbu further advocates that since the former writing system was not adequate for an accurate translation and rendering of profound and vast teaching of Lord Buddha into Tibetan language present writing system was devised and developed by Thonmi Sambh in the 7th century–A.D.

(B) The generally accepted theory of Buddhist scholar is that Tibet had no written language prior to king Songsten Gampo. He was the greatest and the most enlighted ruler of Tibet whose influence had reached both her neighbours (India and China). Necessitated by the learning of vast teaching of Lord Buddha which were either in Sanskrit or Pali language, he dispatched Thonmi Sambhotta and many other bright young Tibetans to India to study Sanskrit and other language of that time. Tnonmi Sambhotta on his return created the present Tibetan script based on few Indian like Dev Nagric and Sharda characters of North India. The exponents of this theory refute that the so-called Mar-Yig is not tranceable and hence the written language originated with the creation of Tibetan script by Thonmi Sambhotta in the 7th century.

However while this needs little deeper study and under standing one cannot outrightly deny the fact that the record of 32 kings prior to king Songtsen Gampo can be kept without existent of any writing system. A careful and logical thinking tells us as Buddhism almost disappeared from its place of birth due to in of people with different cultures, so is the case with Bon religion in Tibet after the introduction of Buddhism.

DEVELOPMENT OF TIBETAN LANGUAGE OVER THE CENTURIES

After the creation of Tibetan script by Thonmi Sambhottia many changes took place from time to time necessitated by the world of translation of Lord Buddha's teachings- from Sanskrit into Tibetan. Tibetan Grammar was prepared on the lines of Sanskrit grammars. Tibetan scholars did not spare any effort to probe into the intricacies of Sanskrit Grammars. They studied the large collection of homonyms and synonyms preserved in Sanskrit Lexicons. They knew that for a standard translation it was essential to have a through knowledge of Sanskrit Grammar and vocabulary.

During King Trisong Dhetsen the most powerful ruler, who captured Ch'ang An, the capital of the Tang dynasty, called a Great Conference in which both Indian and Tibetan Pandits participated. It was presided over by Acharya Bodhisattva Jnanendra. The aim was to set definite rules and directions for the translation works. They joined hands in compiling Grammers and Lexicons of Homonym and Synonyms in Tibetan and Sanskrit to enable the younger generation of monk scholars to continue the work of translation. In short, the cultural activity of Tibet reached its peak during his time–(8th century). The art and technique of rendering Sanskrit texts into Tibetan was a unique achievement of the Tibetan scholars. Their contribution in the preservation of Sanskrit texts in literal and accurate Tibetan translation, surpassed the Chinese both in accuracy and volume. The collaboration of Tibetan and Indian monk scholars rendering Buddhist Sanskrit texts into Tibetan resulted in the production of some 4569–texts of Kajur and Tanjur. Thonmi Sambhotta translated Dhodhe Namje and Dodhe Pakong Chaggyapa, Lotsava Chodrup translated Sutra (wise and foolish) of Lord Buddha. Books on medicine, astrology and poetry were eventually translated starting from 8th to 15th century A.D.

Many other books were written in Tibetan–of which few widely acclaimed ones are:

1. Biography of Pandit Dhipankar Atisha by his discipline Dron–tonpa–11th century.

2. Bhiobum Ngonpo–by master Potava 12th century–a treatise of Kadampa School of Buddhism.
3. Biography of Saint Milarepa by Master Heruka Sangyre Gyaltsen–15th century.
4. A drama and a book on Tibetan Colloquial by Master Gungthang Tenpe Dronme of Ando–province of Tibet–19th century.

Some of the authors like Master Heruka Sangye Gyaltsen stressed importance on regional language–as it happened during the Bhakti Movement in the 13th century India. Towards the beginning of 15th century Xylographed Kanjurs reached Tibet from Nenjing King China–as present to Sakyapa, Karmapa and Tsongkhapa Lamas for the first time. Since then many books were xylographed in Tibet and are preserved to this day. Moreover the uniformity in handwriting, spelling and language come to stay eversince. The xylographic works of Dherge of Khan province and Narthang of Utsang are famous for their clarity and spelling works. However, so much have been destroyed by the Chinese during the Cultural Revolution of 1960s. Not only that appealing number of rare manuscripts were either burnt or thrown in the river during that time. This is an irreparable loss lot only to Tibetans but also to the entire Buddhist world.

PRESENT STATUS AND ITS IMPORTANCE IN LEARNING AND UNDERSTANDING OF BUDDHISM AND BUDDHIST CULTURE

The survival of a nation is mainly dependent on the preservation of its culture. The value and importance of the culture is based on the uniqueness of its language and writing system.

Tibetian script is based on phonetic system like those of Sanskrit, Latin and French etc. As a result it is rich in vocabulary unlike the Chinese picture writing system. Moreover Tibetan characters too are limited and not complicated. Tibetan scholars and grammarians of the past have defined (writing) itself as composition of names and words producing different sounds–when these different sounds are sketched on paper it becomes handwriting. Such definitions have deep meaning. When Thonmi Sambhotta devised Tibetian script–he had to base the characters on the spoken language of Tibet and hence vowels and 30 consonants in Tibetan it is wrong and absurd to say that Tibetan written language is based on Sanskrit–as written language has to be based on the spoken language.

Basically Tibetan scrpt is of two types–U–Chen (with head character) and U'-Med (without head character). About 90% of Buddhist text are all in U'Chen which is very similar to Dev Nagric script of India. Most of xylographs are in U'Chen. U'Med is quite different. As discussed earlier the Bon writing system called Mar-Yig is said to have been the origin of U'Med writing which came from Tazig (Tibetan name for Persia). U'Med itself has different ways of writing. Like in English–it has big letters–Tsugchen, small letters–Tsuagchung and flowing letters–as Khyugyig. It too like English has ornamental writing system called Drutsa of different types.

U'Med is generally used in official letter writing, general letter writing and in fact in most of lay literature. Like in Arabian countries Tibet too had special calligraphers called Yigkhen. Some of them were very famous who had done great service to the development of Tibetan handwriting from time to time. The uniformity of present Tibetan U'Med writing brought about during the famous Regent Rabten Kunzang Phakpa in the 15th century after consultation with many renowned calligraphers (Yigkhen) of that time. The line drawing rules called Thigri and Thigshe for both U'Chen and U'Med for different types of writings were set at that time. Detailed information about this can be had from Dhese Sangye Gyatso's (The Regent and famous scholar of Tibet) book titled Bindure Yasel. It was written that such line drawing rules were preserved in the form of xylographs at Kunbum Monastery of Tibet–which are said to have taken to the People's Museum of Beijing–China. They are the best and the most authentic writing system of Tibetan calligraphy of both U'Chen and U'med–according to one of the most renowned 20th century scholar of Tibetan Literature–Late Prof. Rev. Dnungkar Losang Trinley.

As to its importance in the Himalayan regions it is understandable that proper learning and understanding of Buddhism is impossible without certain knowledge of Tibetan language. Today surprisingly, when many ancient Buddhist texts in Sanskrit are not at all available, Tibetan texts of olden days have substituted more than adequately. Bilingual scholars of Tibetan and Sanskrit today are amazed at the accuracy of the translation works done from 8th to 15th century in Tibet. Hence one can proudly say that for serious understanding of Buddhism it is imperative to have knowledge in Tibetan language. Be it trantric or Vinaya Sutras there is no authentic books in any language other than Tibetan.

Tibetan language and its coverage, as a medium of learning Buddhist culture, goes beyond some 60 million people of entire Himalayan Region of which ethnic Tibetan accounts for just 6 ***or 10% of the total population. Though it may not be used as spoken language Tibetan literary language is understood by people inhabiting the regions from Ladakh to Auranachal Pradesh, Bhutan, Sherpa, Tamang, Newar and Neshangpa of Nepal and also in Mongolia. According to late Tibetan historian and former Cabinet Minister of free Tibet Tsepon Sakabpa Wangchuk Dhedhen–during 7th century Tibetan king Srongtsen Gampo occupied northern Burma/Myanmar and hence traces of Tibetan Language such as names for fire, wood and human etc are found in their language. So also from there same influence reached Manipur and there are so many Tibetan words used in Manipuri Language today. Strangely, Shakapa writes, the number names from one to nine in Tibetan and Japanese are one and the same–he suggested that further research is needed in this line as well.

As such this language whether one may agree or not has become indispensable for learning and understanding of Buddhism especially of Mahayana sect. Tibetan language which is as rich as Sanskrit, Latin and French, if not preserved, through understanding of the essence of Buddhism is impossible. Nor the same task can be carried out in any other language in the absence of Tibetan. As to the richness of Tibetan language it is found out that a person with certain knowledge about Tibetan literary language finds little difficulty in picking up any other language with near perfect pronunciation. Prior to the Chinese occupation of Tibet there was age old tradition of Tibet for learning Buddhism. Those monks after completion of their studies went back to their respective countries and became teachers. As such Tibet served as fountain head of Buddhism until recently. However, it is to all ours knowledge that the situation has changed completely today. It is only about 1% of Tibetan in exile are trying to keep up the Buddhist culture and teachers in the west. Sadly speaking, authors on Tibetan language are very few and the number is on the decline.

Let us now have serious introspective thinking on this line and collectively as the most important duty of Buddhist people of Asia see that the flame of Tibetan language is kept burning for our coming generation, if at all the essence of Buddhism and its culture is to be understood properly for the peace of this world. His Holiness the Dalai Lama once remarked that it is shameful that, in future, we have to depend on western countries for the learning of Buddhism.

AN INTRODUCTION TO TIBETAN LANGUAGE AND LITERATURE

Narendra Kumar Dash

Regarding the racial origin of the Tibetan people we find two different traditional views. Some think that Rupati, a military commander of the *Kaurava* army, after having been defeated by the *Pandavas*, fled to Tibet with his followers and those people are the ancestors of the Tibetans. This view is based on the letter written by an Indian *Pandit*, Deje Dak-po, about one hundred years after the death of Buddha. Some of the educated Tibetans prefer to believe this view, which may be called the tradition of Indian ancestry.

A tradition of mythological origin is also current among the Tibetans. The tradition maintains that Tibetans are descended from monkey who was an incarnation of the compassionate Avalokiteswar (*Tib, Chenresi*), who produced six progeny through a mountain ogress. The descendants of these two inherited the qualities of both the father's compassionate and merciful, though often playful traits and the mother's stubborn characteristics. However, the children of the pair lost their various similar characteristics. Tradition accepts that the whole thing happened near Tsethang in the centre of U-Tsang region of Tibet. There is a mountain called Gong-po-ri behind Tsethang where the caves of these monkey ancestors are found till today. The Jokhang pillar inscription at Lhasa provides evidence in support of the second tradition.

Modern anthropologists claim that the Tibetans belong to the Mongoloid race. Shakabpa supports this view of the anthropologists. He says that "such a classification seems plausible since Tibetans have had a close relationship with the Mongols for centuries; but up to now, no comparison of the skulls of the Tibetan and the Mongol have been made". (T.W.D. Shakabpa, 1967, p. 6)[1] The archaeological findings however, suggest that the Tibetans were autochthonous and they did not come from outside the country. (Gupta and Ramachandran, 1999, p. 13)[2] The view of Gupta and Ramachandran in this regard is noteworthy. They think that "the earliest evidence of this comes in the form of Old Stone Age or Palaeolithic tools. These are roughly chipped tools made on river-borne pebbles and are called '*choppers*', *datable* to a period between 1,00,000 and 50,000 years back from now. At a later period, called Neolithic or New Stone Age, people used polished stone tools and earthen pots and pans and live in caves and tents. Some of these important archaeological sites are sure in southern Tibet and Lu Ling in central Tibet. At Karub, near the town Chamdo in eastern Tibet, the remains of a whole Neolithic village, with streets and houses, some 5000 years old, have been found in excavations. Stone ploughs, hoes, axes, millstones as well as earthen pots and pans have been found in individual houses. Neolithic remains, including chipped tools made on stone flames and used in hunting, have also been found at some other sites, such as Nyngchi and Medong on the Tsang-po river in eastern Tibet" (Gupta and Ramachandran, 1999 pp. 13-14)[3]. Thus, we may safely suggest that there were existence of villages in the mountains of Tibet at least 3000 years before the beginning of the Christian era.

Like many other countries, the early history of Tibet is shrouded in mystery and mythical traditions. There is no documentary evidence to enlighten us about the most ancient period of the history of the Tibetans. Buddhistic tradition suggests that the Purgyal dynasty started from a descendent of a king named Nyatri Tsampo who was exiled from *Magadha* of Bihar, India and was elected as the ruler of the Yarlung in 127 B.C. and. The *Rdzogs-Ldan gzhon-nu'i dga'-ston,* composed by the 5th Dalai Lama, refers that the father of Nyatri Tsampo was Mak Gvapa. This view of the 5th Dalai Lama differs from that of Bu-ston. He thinks that the first Tibetan king was a descendent of the royal family of king gSal-rgyal of Kosala[B] in India[4].

It is believed by the Buddhists of Tibet that the boy who was born with long blue eyebrows, a full set of teeth and webbed figures, was hid by his father and when the boy grew up he wandered into Tibet. There he met some farmers who were adherents of the Bon[C] religion. The boy was wandering aimlessly and when the farmers asked him from where he had come the boy without understanding the language, gestured towards sky. The innocent farmers thought that the boy has come from the sky which was considered very holy and decided that the sky has sent him to be their leader. Placing him on a wooden sedan chair, they carried the boy to the village and called him *Nyatri Tsampo* meaning "Neck-enthroned king". The Tibetans believes that the king built first house in Tibet for the purpose of residence known as Yumbulagang. It is needless to mention that before the construction of a house the Tibetans were living in the caves(Nos-kgi-yul-dan No-kyi-mi-man,2000,chapter one)[5].

Before going into a discussion on the history of Tibet I would like to give some information about the origin of Tibet. The Deb-ther Sngon-po of Gos Lo-tsa-ba Gzhon-nu-dpal describes that the name 'Bod' for Tibet had originated from the name "Pugyal" long before the emergence of the religion. Other historians think that the name 'Bod' was derived from 'Bon' itself, which was the name of the religion of the people before the introduction of Buddhism(Dge-dun chos-phel'sDeb-ther tkan po, chapter one)[6]. Another group of scholars think that the name 'Bod', orally meaning 'fled', was given to the country because the king Rupati and his followers fled to Tibetan territory after being defeated by the Pandavas(Tsug-lag(Tsug-lag-treng-wa's Mkhas-pa-I-dga-ston)[7]. The Indo-Tibetan border people refer to Tibetans as Bhotias, a name derived from 'Bhota', the name of Tibet given by the Indian Pandits. The country 'Bhota' seems to be referred to in the *Mahabharata* of Vyasa, which was probably composed during the lifetime of Gautama Buddha.

The country is known as Tibet in modern times. It is similar to the Mongolian word Thubet; Chinese word 'Tufan', the Thai word 'Thibet' and the Arabic 'Tubbat', which are found in the early works. We cannot opine definitely from which one the word Tibet is derived when the word Tibet became popular or when it was used in the literature for the first time. In many poetical compositions the country is referred to as '*Khawachen*' or '*Gangjong*' meaning the 'the abode of snow' and '*sildanjoing*' means 'the cool climate land'.

Buddhist historians are unanimous on the fact that the seven kings of the Purgyal dynasty returned to sky by a sky-rope after their deaths and therefore there was no need to make tombs for them. The tomb of the 8th king of the dynasty still exists in Kongpo in U-Tsang. No record about the political or religious activities of the kings before Drigum Tsenpo, the 8th king, is available to us. It is believed that the first seven kings ruled over the Yarlung area smoothly. The orthodox Bon followers became active and started revolt from the period of Drigum Tsenpo. This king was killed by a minister named Longdarma and the three sons of Drigum Tsenpo fled to the forest and after some years the eldest son Chatri Tsenpo was able to capture the throne. The contribution of Chatri Tsenpo, also known as Podekungyal, to the development of agriculture in Tibet is noteworthy. During his time (the king is believed to be a contemporary of Wu-ti of former Han dynasty who reigned in first century B.C.)[8] both iron ore and copper ore were discovered. He instructed to dig the canals for the purpose of improvement in agricultural sector and he also built bridges over the streams for better transportation.

Tibetan historians are silent about the immediate eighteen successors of the king Podekungyal. The eighteen generations after Podekungyal, Tho-tho-ri Nyantsen was born in 173 A.D. The historians believe that the king received the Nyenpo Sangwa (the secret) at the age of sixty. This is the initial stage of the introduction of Buddhism into Tibet. This period is very important in the history of Tibet, because two important things happened in Tibet when the king was sixty years of age. First, the introduction of Buddhism and the second the introduction of Tibetan currency notes (233 A.D.),

Tho-tho-ri became the twenty eighth king and when he was sixty years, he received a book of Buddhist scripture, while living in the palace of Yumbulagang. Since the book was written in Sanskrit language, neither the king nor any of his subjects or ministers could understand the language. Therefore the king called the book *Nyenpo Sangwa* meaning the 'Secret'. An early historian from Tibet, Nel-pa Pandita by name, opines that the secret book was received through a Indian Pandita named Sosemtso. Others maintain that the book came from the sky and the king Tho-tho-ri Nyantsen was informed in a dream that there would be a king in the dynasty after four generations from him who could be able to read the book and subsequently could be able to understand the subject matter of the book. As per the records the king Tho-tho-ri Nyantsen died at the age of 120 years and after 324 years of Tho-tho-ri, the king Songtsen Gampo was born in 617 A.D. He ascended the throne at the age of thirteen. After his enthronement, the king introduced ten moral principles and sixteen rules of public conduct in Tibet.

The king had five wives viz., Nepali Princess named Bhrkiti Devi (Belsa), Chinese princess named Wen-ch'eng kung-chu (Gyasa) and three Tibetan ladies. The daughter of the Nepalese King Amshu-verman sent his daughter to Tibet with an image of Aksobhya Buddha. This image is considered as most sacred as the Tibetans believe that the image was blessed by Lord Buddha himself. The Chinese prince Gyasa reached in Tibet in 641 A.D. with many articles of personal use and also with an image of Shakyamuni, the Gautama Buddha and it is believed that this image of Shakyamuni was also blessed by Lord Buddha himself. It is needless to mention here that we have no records to support this view of the Tibetans that images were constructed during the life time of Buddha.

The Nepalese Princess Belsa and the Chinese Princess Gyasa requested the king to build temples for the images they had brought with them from their own country and two temples were built near Lhasa. The temple built for the image of Shakyamuni was called *Ramoche Tsukla-khang* and the temple, which was built for the Aksobhya on a small lake, was named as *Rasa Trulnang Tsukla-khang* and latter this temple was popularly known as Jokhang. The doors of these two temples were faced towards China and Nepal respectively. Thus, during the time of the King Srongstsen Gampo Buddhism was introduced in Tibet. The king decided to develop contact with India, the land of Buddha and therefore he sent his minister Thon-mi Sam-bhota and sixteen companions to India to learn Sanskrit language and the Indian scripts. The names of these sixteen companians are not known to us as we do not find any document in this regard. Thon-mi Sam-bhota went to Kashmir in northwest India and learned Sanskrit language from Devavidyasimha and Indian scripts from Lipikara. It is not known exactly when Thon-mi Sam-bhota and his companions had come to India and which route they followed during their visit to Kashmir. The sixteen companions of Thon-mi died in India as they could not bear Indian climatic condition. This simply indicates that Thon-mi and his party went to Kashmir through plain land and his companions could not bear the heat in Indian plain land.

Thon-mi alone returned to Tibet after the completion of his study under the Indian teachers. He devised Tibetan alphabets and translated "The secret", preserved since the time of Tho-tho-ri Nyentsen into Tibetan for the benefit of the people.

When Thon-mi Sam-bhota visited India to learn Indian scripts and Sanskrit language the post-Gupta scripts were in use in North India and he selected those alphabets for his purpose. Now it may be a general query that whether any alphabets were in use in Tibet before the introduction of 30 letters by Thon-mi Sam-bhota? It seems that there was also a set of alphabets, which were developed form Central Asian Brahmi, and the set of alphabets were prevalent mainly in the valley of Tarim. Sankrityayana suggests that the u-med alphabet "letters without head" were developed from the North Indian scripts. Some scholars also opine that the Tibetan alphabets of Thon-mi Sam-bhota were based on the Kutila scripts. Whatever may be the source, Thon-mi did not follow the alphabets in toto. He changed the set of the alphabets as per the needs of the Tibetan people. Tibetan never pronounced some of the Indian letters and therefore, some letters were dropped. The long vowels, the fourth letters of the *vargas* i.e. *gha, jha, dha* and *bha* have been dropped and some more new alphabets were also made to fulfill the needs the pronunciation of Tibetan language. Those letters were developed adding a stroke on some letters and thus *ts, tsh, z.dz, h* and *sh* were formed. Thus the total of letters became 30 including '*a*' as consonant excluding *i, u, e* and *o* signs.

Thon-mi Sam-bhota not only devised the new set of alphabets, he composed eight books on the rules and regulations of the Tibetan grammar. When Thon-mi visited India, the grammatical composition of Panini, the *Astadhyayi*, was very popular in the land of Buddha and it is obvious that he might have gone through the sutras of Panini under Devavidyasimha, his tutor of the Sanskrit language. Unfortunately the eight books are not available in complete form. Only two Chapters (the fifth chapter of the first book and the 6th chapter of the second book) are available in the academic world. The fifth Chapter of the first book entitled *Sumcupa* deals with the letters of the Tibetan language and the sixth chapter of the second book entitled *Tag-kyi-jug-pa* discusses about the gender of the Tibetan letters (K. Angarupa Lahuli, p. xvi)[10].

At the beginning of the fifth chapter the author Thon-mi salutes to Manjusri who is the god of *Vak* in Tibetan tradition. In Indian tradition, *Sarasvati* is the goddesses of the *Vak* or language. Tibetans believe that Manjusri, the god of language, is very young and very beautiful to look at viz;

ངག་གི་དབང་ཕྱུག་འཇམ་པའི་དབྱངས་ལ་ཕྱག་འཚལ་ལོ།།

Tibetans believe that the god of the *Vak* is endowed with three jewels

བདུ་ལ་ལོ་ནུ་ནུ་མཆོག་མངའ་བའི།།
དཀོན་མཆོག་གསུམ་ལ་ཕྱག་འཚལ་ལོ།།

Thon-mi Sam-bhota thinks that Manjusri taught the accent and the structure of words but the letters were devised for the first time by lord *Siva* viz;

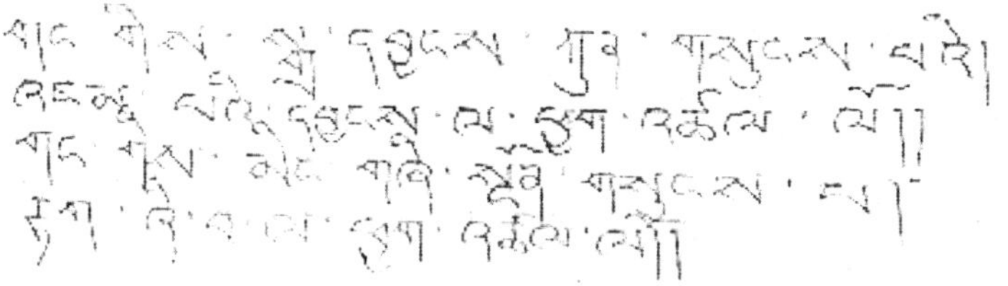

This interpretation of Thon-mi regarding the root of communications is seemed to be influenced by the Indian tradition. Regarding the history of grammatical tradition in India, the Tibetan historians believe that during the reign of thirty three Gods, a god named *Sarvajnana* composed a great grammatical treatise which was used by the Gods and subsequently ceased to exist and therefore, the text was not available in the Jambudvipa, (B.C. Law, 1984 p. 1)[11]. There after *Sakra* composed the Indravyakarana. This Indravyakarana was perfectly apprehended by *Brhaspati* who demonstrated it to the children of Gods and became known as the preceptor of the Gods or the teacher of Grammar. Due to profound knowledge in grammar Brhaspati became proud and therefore, Indra the king of Gods got an urn full of water from the ocean, took a drop of it by means of a helm of *kusa* grass and said to *Brhaspati* that the science of grammar as a whole is like an ocean. That part of it, which I know, is like the water of this urn and that which thou knowest is only like this drop.

Then the science of grammar came to Jambudvipa and was expounded there. When grammar ceased to exist, Panini appeared. The fortuneteller to whom he showed his hand foretold that it will not be possible for him to acquire the knowledge of grammar. Panini then drew the corresponding line of his hand with a sharp knife and set out in search of a teacher but did not find any. Then he propitiated *Mahadeva* and acquired the knowledge of grammar from him. The Buddhist texts *Manjusrimula kalpa*, however, does not agree with the view that Panini acquired the knowledge of grammar from *Mahadeva*. According to the text, Panini came to the knowledge of grammar through having propitiated *Avalokitesvara* (Taranath, pp. 53-54)[12].

As per the Tibetan sources, Panini composed his treatise with 2000 rules, which is known as Paniniya *Vyakarana*. On this treatise of Panini, a King of the Nagas composed a commentary called the Mahabhasya consisting of 100,000 *slokas*.

This tradition regarding the origin and development of Sanskrit grammar differs from its Indian counterpart in many respects. As per the Indian tradition *Brhaspati*, the Devaguru taught grammar to Indra for *divya-sahasra-varsa*, but Indra could not complete his studies of this branch of knowledge (Patanjali, Paspasahannika)[13]. It is interesting to note that both the Indian and the Tibetans traditions believe that *Mahesvara* is the root cause to explore the seed or basic rules of the Sanskrit grammar viz., *Nrtyavasane jatarana raja nanada dhakkam nava panca varam* etc. (Paaniniyasiksha)[14] From the sound of the *damuru* of Lord *Mahesvara*, Panini got the basic fourteen rules of Sanskrit grammar (Paaniniyasiksha, p. 1)[15].

It is a popular belief that Thon-mi devised 30 letters for the Tibetan language beginning from ka (Tib: ཀ) to 'a' (Tib: ཨ) but in his treatise on grammar Thon-mi clearly suggests that like any other language, there are two types of Tibetan alphabets named ali (A-li means vowels which are four in number in Tibetan language)[16] and *kali* (consonants)[17] viz.,

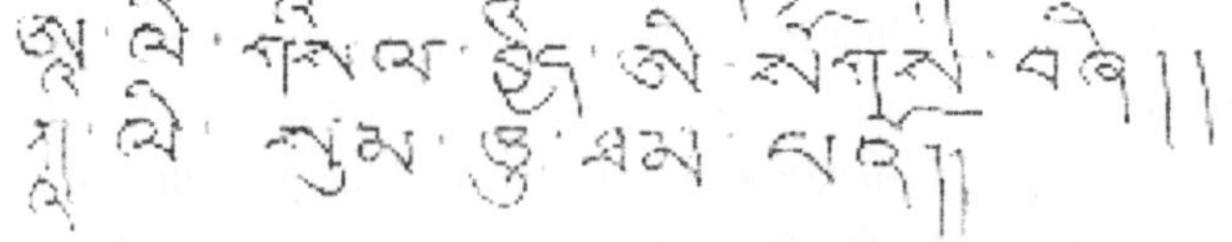

The 30 consonants are divided into seven and half Vargas and in each Vargas there are four letters in Tibetan.

It has been told earlier that the first Buddhist work was translated into Tibetan in the second half of the seventh century by Thon-mi Sam-bhota. Many more Indian works on Buddhism and other branches of human knowledge were translated after the visit of Santaraksita to Tibet for the second time. It is a well-known fact that the Indian Pandita Santaraksita was invited to Tibet by the King Trisong Detsen from Nepal. However, he could not sustain in Tibet due to the opposition from the Bon priests. Realizing the fact that the time is not yet ripe for spread of his teachings in Tibet, Santarakshita advised the king to invite the great Tantric teacher Padmasambhava to counter the magical powers of the Bon priests and returned to Nepal.

Padmasambhava was well versed with the magical arts and therefore, he was able to subdue the Bon priests. Padmasambhava vanquished the Bon Priests and caused them to take an oath to defend Buddhism in Tibet. Gradually Buddhism began to spread and when the king realized that the ground is ready to invite again Santarakshita, he sent invitation for the great Indian scholar. After his arrival, Santarakshita requested the King to build a monastery in the Drakmar region similar to the one at Odantapurī in Bihar. It was based on the conception of the Buddhist Universe. Twelve years later the monastery came to be known as *Migyur Lhungi Dubpai Tsukla Khang* "The temple which is unchangeable, perfect mass". However, popularly the monastery was known as Samye (Tib. Bsam-yas). Recent discoveries suggest that the monastery was constructed in 766 A.D. and it was inaugurated in 767 A.D. (T.W.D. Shakabpa, 1967. pp. 37-38)[18] Seven Tibetans were selected by the king as a trial group to become monks and Santarakshita trained them in the Buddhist lore. Gradually many more became monks and a good number of Sanskrit works were translated into Tibetan. The same king also established a centre for study of Indian language at Samye monastery. It is needless to mention that Tibetans were very careful and practical regarding the translation of Indian works. Atisa the great scholar of 12th century A.D., who visited Tibet from India, has remarked that he had never seen such an extensive and thorough system of translation of Buddhist texts, even in India.

Now I would like to focus some light on the history of the translation activities in Tibet so that we could have a rough idea that how careful the Tibetans were about translation of Indian works and how our cultural properties are being preserved in Tibet.

Though Buddhism entered Tibet during the time of the King Sron-btsan-Sgam-po, the new religion emerged as a significant political power for the first time during the reign of Khri-Ide-sron-btsan sad-na-legs, the immediate predecessor of Ral-pa-canwho was believed to be murdered by two pro Bon ministers Be and Chogro [19]. The king Tride songtsen is popularly referred as Sadnaleg in Tibetan sources. The king invited Indian Pandits to the Samye monastery to help the translations of the Buddhist texts. The king called a meeting of his ministers and various vassals from different parts of the kingdom. An extensive document was prepared pleading support for the propagation of the Buddhist faith. The temple of Karchung Lhakhang was erected near Lhasa by the King (T.W.D. Shakabpa, 1967, p. 48)[20]. The third son of the King, *Tritsug Detsen* or Ral-pa-can, became the King after the death of his father. He made *Bande* Dangka Palgyi Yonden the chief minister of his kingdom. Ral-pa-can invited Silendrabodhi, Danasila and Jinamitra to Tibet. These three famous Indian Pandits translated many Indian texts with the help of the Tibetan *Lotsava*, Kawa Paltsek and Chogro Lui Gyaltsen. With the help of these scholars from India and Tibet, the king strengthened the translation activities of various treatises from Sanskrit to Tibetan languages, which were initiated by his predecessors. The king is well known for his contributions to the process of modernizing and standardizing the Tibetan language. It is known from the Tibetan documents that the king was responsible for the revision of the Buddhist texts, which were translated earlier to give uniformity to all the works that had been translated into Tibetan before the arrival of the three famous and erudite Indian scholars. They not only revised the earlier works but standardized the terms used for translating Buddhist concepts from Sanskrit. This team of Indian and Tibetan scholars prepared the *Mahavyutpati* (Tib. *Bye-brag-tu-rtogs-byed-chen-po*). This hand book for translators or the Sanskrit Tibetan Lexicon played a vital role in the creation of the rich Indo-Tibetan translation literature. In this work no alphabetical or similar ordering has been adopted but the entries (*Mahavyutpati)*[21] are arranged on the basis of the meaning (*Mahavyutpati)* [22] categories, beginning with the names or epithets of Buddha (Tib. *Sangs-rgyas-kyi-mtsnan*) and ending with the names of all sorts of disease or maladies (*skad-go-'thun-la*). Now we are not going to study about the entries of the *Mahavyutpatti*, but a detail study of the text in comparison with other ancient and mediaeval Lexicographical works from India should be done to focus on the Indian cultural influence on Tibet.

The King Ral-pa-can not only made considerable contributions in the field of cultural development but also made reforms in the field of socio-economic sector. He tried to maintain the status-quo in the field of the land reforms done by Muni Tsenpo. He introduced the new system of weights and measures, particularly to weigh silver and gold, based on Indian model. He also ordered that seven households should be responsible for the maintenance of one Buddhist monk or *Bande*. This seems to be the first or earliest case of monastic taxation in Tibet. Thus Ral-pa-can did his best for the country and its religion.

The second phase of the translation of Indian works began only after the arrival of the great scholar Atisa Dipankara in Tibet in mid 11th century A.D. A major portion of the Indian works of the *Bstan-gyur* and *Kan-gyur* were translated during this period. The famous works on Buddhist logic like the *Pramanavarttikalankara*, the *Pramanavarttikalankaratika*, the *Vadanyayaprakarana*, Sri *Paramaditika*, the works on *Prajnaparamita* like the *Astasahasrika Prajnaparamita*, the *Abhisamayalankaratika* and many grammatical and other works were translated by the joint effort of Indian and Tibet scholars during this time.

The third phase of the translations of Indian works may be confined during and after the fifth Dalai Lama. The fifth Dalai Lama was said to be a good Sanskrit scholar. The academic institutions established by the great fifth Dalai Lama included the study of Sanskrit with other subjects. During his time the famous grammatical work of Panini was translated into Tibetan.

It is said that the period of the second phase of the translation activities in Tibet include a major portion of the total translations into Tibetan. Just before the arrival of Atisa in Tibet there was several impurities crept into Buddhism in Tibet. To check further degradation Yesehod selected twenty-one young men and sent them to study the scriptures in Kashmir. Rin-chen-zang-po and Legspahis-shes-rab survived out of those twenty-one. With the help of Pandits like Sraddhakara Varma. Padmakara Gupta, Buddha Srisanta, Buddhapala, Kamala Gupta and many others. Rin-chen-btsan-po translated many Sanskrit works after completion of his studies. Rin-chen-btsan-po also translated the *Hastavala-prakarana* (Aryadeva), the *Abhisamayalankaraloka* (Haribhadra), the *Astangahrdayasamhita* (Nagarjuna), the *Caturviparyayakatha* (Matricetta) and the *Saptagunaparivar-nanakatha* (Vasubandhu) etc. into Tibetan. Since the climatic condition of India was not suitable for the Tibetans, they decided to invite Indian scholars to Tibet for the academic purpose. They noticed that in the Vikramasila Vihara there is a great scholar who educated himself at Nalanda, Rajagriha, Vikramasila, Vajrasana and also in the distant Suvarna Dvipa. The great scholar was invited to Tibet and he spent 13 years there. He reached Yer-pa in 1051 and completed the famous commentary on Kalachakra there.

Now I would like to mention about an Indian Pandit who translated the Indian works into Tibetan single-handedly. The Pandit, who was invited by Lo-tsa-ba Padmaruci, unfortunately lost host Lo-tsa-ba due to cholera on his way to Tibet. The Pandit Smrtijnanakirti was forced to take shelter with a shepherd. He acquired good knowledge of Tibetan language during his travel in the country land along with the shepherds and translated the works single-handedly. It is said that the translator established a college in Wtams of eastern Tibet for the study of *Abhidharma*.

After twenty years of the sad demise of Dipankara in Tibet (1074) the Sakya monastery was established in Tibet in the province of Gtsan by Khon konchou Gyalpo. The role of the monastery for the spread of Buddhism in Tibet, Mongolia and even in China is noteworthy. During the reign of Chingis Khan (in the year 1222) one of the hierarch of the monastery introduced Buddhism in Mongolia for the first time.

Kashmir Pandita Sakya Sri Bhadra, who was the disciple of Ravi Gupta, Chandra Gupta, Vikhyatadeva, Vinayasri Abhayakirti and Rabisrijnana, was an erudite scholar. Due to his scholarship he became the head of the great monastery at Vikramasila. He was shifted to Jagattala monastery established by Rampala (1057-1102), the king of Magadha by the 7th year of his reign.[23] after the destruction of Nalȧnda and Vikramasila by Mahammadbin-Bakhtyar. He however went to Tibet by the request of Khro-phu Lo-tsa-ba who met him in Nepal. During his ten years living in the Sakya monastery he taught Nyaya to his disciples. One of his disciples Vibhutichandra who accompanied him from India lived there even after the return of his teacher in 1213, and he obtained such a command over the local language that he translated many texts into Tibetan without help of any Lo-tsa-ba (R. Sankrityayana, 1984, p. 47)[24].

Any discussion on Tibetan language, history or culture is incomplete without the mention of the contributions of the historian Bu-ston, reformer Tson-kha-pa and the religious leaders Dalai Lamas. Bu-ston Rin-chen-grub was born in 1290 which was a crisis period for the survival of Buddhism both in India and Tibet. During this time there was rivalry among the powerful monasteries and the monasteries were more concerned with name and fame rather than the service to the *Dharma*. Many works were translated into Tibetan language but there was no list of those works for ready reference of the scholars and others who were interested in the subject. Bu-ston realized this when he was working in the library of the Sha-lu monastery as a monk. He translated only two works from Sanskrit, viz., the *Kalapadhatukaya* of Durga Simha and the *Tyadyantaprakriya* of Harsakirti.

Bu-ston employed himself to collect all the translated works up to his time and systematically compiled those in two volumes named *bKa-'gyur* and *Bstan-'gyur*. The Sanskrit equivalent of the term Kangyur may be '*Buddhavacana*'. This very term consists of three words viz. '*bka*' (words of Buddha) '*bstan*' (the 'Sastras') and '*gyur*' ('translations'). The *Bstan-'gyur* includes the works on philosophy, logic, poetry, astrology, *tantra,* in commentaries of the works collected in the *bka-'gyur* and the works of the *acaryas* other than Buddha. Beside the collection of works, he composed more than fifty works[25] including the masterpiece-*The History of Buddhism in India and Tibet.*

Tson-kha-pa the religious social reformer and scholar was born in the year 1351. To achieve the goal he learned all the branches of Buddhism in Tibet, viz., *Sa-kya-pa, bka-rgyud-pa* and *Bkah-dam-pa* and he incorporated the teachings of these schools in his life but he was a follower of the *Bkah-dam-pa* sect. His disciples think that the religious teacher was a *Neo-ka-dam-pa.* At the end of his student carrier in 1395, he realized that superstitions could not be removed so long as the people remained uneducated. Therefore he taught the common people the basic principles of religion and philosophy. His disciples, *Ja-dbyans* constructed the monastery *Hbras-spur* (De-pun or Dhanya-kataka) in 1416 and Sakya-ye-ses established Se-ra in 1419 to fulfill the mission. During the Tson-kha-pa period, Pandit Vanaratna from India visited Tibet who seems to have translated some *siddha* songs into Tibetan.

Before a discussion of the history and tradition of the Dalai Lamas, I would like to focus on the title Dalai Lama which was given to a Tibetan monk by a King of Mongolia. It is known from the history of Tibet that Altan Khan gave the title Talai Lama to Sonam Gyatso of Drepung monastery. Sankrtyayan suggests that the "Tibetans use the word rGyal-ba-rin-po-che for Dalai Lama ... In the language of Mongols Ta-le is the word for 'ocean'. At the end of the names of all the Dalai Lamas except the first ones, the word rGya-mtsho (*Sagara*) is added, and so the Mongols began to use the word *Ta-le-lama,* of which the corrupt form is Dalai Lama."[26]

The title was actually given to Sonam Gyatsho, the 3rd Dalai Lama; but it was also given to Gedun Truppa and Dedun Gyatsho posthumously. Gedun Truppa (1st Dalai Lama) was a true disciple of Tsonkhapa, the founder of Ge-lug-pa sect. The great monastery of Tashilhunpo at Shigatse was founded by Gedun Truppa in 1447. Thus the origin of the Dalai Lamas and their emergence to power started from the mid 15th century A.D. Gedun Gyatsho was born in the year 1475 and he was considered as the incarnation of Gedun Truppa and became known posthumously as the second Dalai Lama. He studied at Tashilhunpo and Drepung and he founded the monastery of Chokhorgyal.

The 4th Dalai Lama was born in Mongolia and he was the great grandson of the Mongol King Altan Khan. He received his basic and religious training in Mongolia and latter he was brought to Tibet. His name was Yonten Gyatsho and he was initiated into the monk-hood by Sangye Rinchen. During his student carrier he got philosophical training from Panchen Lozang Chosgyan of Tashilhunpo monastery, to whom he gave the title of Panchen Lama as a token of recognition to his scholarship. Since then the reincarnations of Lozang Chogyan have been known as the Panchen Lama.

The 5th Dalai Lama (1617-1682) was a great scholar of Sanskrit and Buddhism. He sent Phun-chog-thun-grub to India to study Sanskrit grammar. He learned Sanskrit grammar at Kurushetra with Pandit Balabhadra and Gokulanath Mishra. They translated the Panini *sutras* into Tibetan in the year 1658. The text, however, seems to be the translation of the *sutras* incorporated in the *Prakriya Kaumudi* of Ramachandra. However, the translation is not a ditto of the Prakriya Kaumudi as the translators have included more *Varttikas*, omitted some *Varttikas*, altered the arrangement of the *sutras* omitted some words of a particular *sutra* and in some cases they have changed the word order of a *sutra*.

The same group of scholars has also translated the *Sarasvata* into Tibetan in the year 1665. It seems that the same *Lotsaba* translated a work on Ayurveda with the help of Gautama Bharati, Omkara Bharati and Uttama Giri in the year 1664. Sankrtyayana suggests that Phun-chogs-thun-grub was the last translator of Tibet to translate Indian classical texts.

Thus, this translation activity in Tibet was carried out for a long time of eleven hundred years (from mid 7th century. AD. To 17th century A.D.). During that period around, four thousand and five hundred Sanskrit works were translated into Tibetan. Modern explorers have also discovered the Sanskrit originals of a few hundred books in addition in 19th and 20th centuries. A large number of Sanskrit manuscripts were, however, lost when the monasteries at *Bsam-yas* and Tholing were burnt down. Sankrtyayana thinks that the Tibetans no doubt venerated Sanskrit as the *devavani* or the divine speech but when all-important Sanskrit works were translated into Tibetan, their Sanskrit originals no longer remained indispensable. The Sanskrit originals remained quite undisturbed in the inaccessible racks of the few monastic libraries due to the want of adequate knowledge of the language of the most of the Lamas in Tibet and gradually many of the works were affected by the insects.

From the personal experience of the great scholar Rahuljee it is known that the Tibetans believe that Sanskrit Manuscripts have the miraculous power of healing diseases; if a patient drinks the water sanctified by dipping a leaf of Sanskrit Mss, his ailment is bound to disappear. Tibetan Lamas, therefore, were in the habit of breaking palm leaves of Mss. in order to give their fragments to pressing supplicants. This practice has naturally destroyed a large number of Sanskrit Manuscripts.

The Sanskrit literature that was taken to Tibet contains several works of non-Buddhist also. Grammatical works and works on Lexicography were very important for the Tibetans. They have translated the *Amarakosha* with its commentaries, the *sutras* of Panini and Candra, *Unadi sutras, Dhatu sutras, Kalapa Vyakarana, Sarasvata Vyakarana* and the *Manjusri Sabolalaksana* for their practical purpose. A total number of 47 treatises on Sanskrit grammar were translated into Tibetan. This included six works, which are not affiliated to any particular branch of Sanskrit grammar. The works on poetics like the *Kavyadarsa, Subhashitaratnakaramdaka*, the poetical composition *Meghaduta*, a drama on the Mahiravana legend also attracted the Tibetan Lo-tsa-bas. We find a Tibetan translation of the *Chandasastra* of Pingala; works on Ayurveda like *Astangahrdayasamhita, Rasasiddhi Sastra* and *Ayurveda Sarva Samgraha* are found in the Tibetan translations. The works like the Arya *Nagarjuna Bhasita Bhesajakalpa* and the *Sarvesvara-rasayana-sarvarogahara-sarira-pusthi-Sastra* have been preserved in the *Bstan-gyur* collections. The original Sanskrit of these two works is not found in India. Tibetans were also translated some works on education. The *Adhyayana pusthaka pathana kriya viddhi* and the *Gurukriya Karma* that are available in Tibetan do not seem to be available in India. The *Rahaprasniya*, the *Yuddhajaya*, the *Nitisastra-prajnadanda* and the *Rajapari-Katharatna* are the works on the politics, which are available in the collections of the *Tangyur*. It is very interesting that the Tibetan Lo-tsa-bas have not ignored the works on erotics. They have translated the *Kamasutra*, the *Ratirahasya* and the *Narisiddhi labhavakhya* with great care and labours.

I am not going to discuss about the philosophical works those are available in Tibetan Tripitaka. It will be justice to the subject to discuss about the works separately. At the end I would like to comment that in comparison to Chinese translation of Indian texts, the Tibetan ones are accurate and faithful. The Tibetans never give a corrupt translation of the technical works/terms which were difficult for them to understand correctly, but they have included the transliterate form of these words in their translation which help us to reconstruct their works again in Sanskrit.

NOTES

1. Shakabpa, T.W.D., *Tibet A Political History*, Yale University Press, 1967, p. 6.
2. Gupta and Ramachandran; *History of Tibet*, Delhi, 1999, p. 13.
3. Ibid., pp. 13-14.
4. Refer: Bu-Ston Rin-Chen-Grub; *Bsung-rab rin-po-chei mdzo*n (*A History of Buddhism and its sects in Tibet*) translated by Obermiller into English for short note on Magadh, Koshala and Bon religion.

5. Refer: Dalai Lama XIV; *Ńos-kgi-yul-dań Ńo-kyi-mi-mań;* Tibetan Cultural and Religious Publication Centre, Delhi, 2000, Chapter–One.
6. Refer: *Dge-dun chos-phel's Deb-ther tkan-po* (Tibetan Xyolgraph), Chapter–One.
7. Refer: *Tsug-lag-treng-wa's Mkhas-pa-i dga-ston* (Tibetan Xylograph).
8. It is believed that the King Podekungyal was contemporary of Wu-ti of former Han Dynasty who reigned from 40-85 B.C. Refer–Shakappa, T.W.D *op.cit.*
9. Sankrityayana, Rahula; *Selected Essays*, New Delhi, 1984, p. 2.
10. Refer the Hindi introduction to the *Sambhota Vyâkarana* of K. Angarupa Lahuli, p. XVI.
11. Law, B.C., *Historical Geography of Ancient India*, First Edition, 1984, Delhi, p. 1.
12. Taranath's *History of Buddhism in India*, pp. 53-54.
13. *The Mahābhāsya* of Patanjali–Paspasāhnnika.
14. *The Pāniņīyasīkşhā*, ed. By Manmohan Ghosh, University of Calcutta, 1938.
15. Ibid., p. 1.
16. Ā-li means a set of alphabetic beginning with Ā i.e., vowels. There are four vowels inTibetan language.
17. Kā-li means a set of alphabets beginning with Kā i.e., consonants.
18. Shakappa, T.W.D., *op.cit.* pp. 37-38.
19. It is believed that Ralpachan was murdered by two pro-Bon ministers Be and Chogro.
20. Shakappa, T.W.D. *op.cit*; p. 48.
21. See the *Mahavyutpatti.*
22. Ibid.
23. The Jagadalla Monastery was established by Rampala (1057-1102) the king of Magadha by the 7th year of his reign (Refer the colophon of the *Aşţasahasrika*).
24. Sankrityayana, Rahula; *op.cit.*, p. 47.

REFERENCES

Bu-Ston Rin Chen-Grub-Bsung-rab rin po-chei mdzon,Translated into English by Obermiller (A History of Buddhism and its Sects in Tibet).

Dalai Lama XIV Nos-kgi-yul-dari No kyi –mi-man, Tibetan Cultural and Religious Publication Centre, Delhi, 2000.

Gupta and Ramachandran–*History of Tibet*, 1999.

Ghosh Manmohan-*The Paniniyasiksha*, University of Calcutta, 1938.

Lahuli, K. Angarupa–*Sambhota Vyakarana* (Hindi Translation)

Law, B.C.–*Historical Geography of Ancient India*,, Ist edition, 1984.

Patanjali–*The Mahabhasya*.

Sankrityayana Rahul–*Selected Essays*, New Delhi, 1984.

Shakabpa, T.W.D.–*Tibet, A Political History*, Yale University Press, 1967.

Taranath-*History of Buddhism in India*.

THE RELICS IN THE TIBETAN TRADITION

Rachel Guidoni

Relics have an important place within many societies, However when we consult dictionaries or encyclopedias related to social sciences, there is nothing at the entry "relic". This topic has been especially studied in the domains of History of Religions, Philosophy, or Theology. In the Anthropological field, it is most often studied as being a small part among topics concerning Sainthood, Death, or Funeral practices : the bibliographies and books suggest that this subject has almost never been treated for itself.

On the other side, although all the specialists of the Tibetan culture admit the importance of religion in everyday life of the. Tibetans, whether Buddhists or Bonpos, the studies in this domain have, until recently, approached very few questions of the religious practices. It is the same conclusion for the veneration and cult of relics, which has kindled very small interest in the studies concerning all the Tibetan cultural area (at the moment, I could find out only 4 articles written by 3 researchers and dealing precisely with this topic).

The topic of relics can be analysed in many different ways, but I have chosen an anthropological approach, which will consider relics as *a material object fitted with special values, and associated with particular ritual and devotional practices*.

I also want to be precise about the geographical area concerned. What we call Tibetan cultural area, or sometimes Tibetan world, is made of the four historical regions of Tibet: Amdo, Kham,U-Tsang and Ngari, plus the areas at the boundaries where the influence of Tibetan culture is very strong: Bhutan, valleys bordering Tibet in Northern India and Northern Nepal. Despite the variety of the populations concerned, some common features in the ritual tradition and in the way of life enable to gives relative unity to this territory.

In the first part of this presentation, I will detail the different frames of my subject, and in the second part, I will be more pragmatic by giving some particular examples.

THEORICAL FRAME: THE RELIC: DEFINITIONS FROM TEXTS

Relic: All the corporeal remains and also all the objects, kept and worshipped, which have belonged to a person that the tradition considers as having famous spiritual qualities. In this context, I will only consider the corporeal or contact remains associated to a person which is known and clearly nominated.

The English word "relic" (relik, in Middle English) derives from the Old French word. This French word 'relique' itself derives from the Latin 'reliquiae': it appeared in the 11th century, and indicated the remains of the body, or any object having belonged to or having served the person a saint or a martyr. This uniformity does not exist either in Sanskrit or in Tibetan languages, as two different words at least can define this notion. The Sanskrit tradition makes the distinction between the relics linked to the body (*sharirika*) on one side, and the objects that were used by the venerated people (*paribhogika*) on the other side.

In Tibetan, we have to notice that dictionaries do not really agree on the various definitions. For example, *sku-gdung* can designate the body of the deceased, his bones or his relics; some also use this word to designate the *stupa*[1] (The Sanskrit word Stupa indicates a Buddhist monument originally aimed at enshrining ashes of a spiritual master, but its employment has evolved and it can also preserve a whole body or on contrary nothing at all).

The second word, *ring-bsrel*, signifies "which can be kept for a long time"; More precisely it designates the relics having the shape of small white beads, hard and shining, which emanates from the body usually after the cremation. But in the written tradition, the use of the two words *sku-gdung* and *ring-bsrel* refers to a broader significance, which does not implicate only relics from bodily origins : this category extends on one side to all the objects used or touched by the concerned person, on the other side it extends to the religious texts. The other terms for relics are, amongst the most popular, '*phel-gdung*', or "increasing bone", *sha-ri-ram*, the Tibetan equivalent of the Sanskrit word for corporeal remains of a dead body, and also *byin-rten*, short-cut for *byin-rlabs kyi rten*, "support for a wave, floods of grace", and important as it is related to the central notion of *byin-rlabs* which will be detailed hereafter. From an etymological point of view, it is relevant to notice that the Tibetan words for relics almost always remind of the body, and especially of the bones.

SACRALITY AND SAINTHOOD

1. The analyses of some epigraphical texts from India have shown that the value of a relic is its ability to contain the living presence of the Buddha. So a relic is worshipped in the same way as the Buddha would be worshiped if he was still alive. But Tibetan research does not emphasise this dimension, and seems more interested by the notion common to the veneration of all these objects: this is what Tibetans call *byin-rlabs*. This word, that we can translate approximately as the English "blessing", is equivalent to the Sanskrit *adhisthana*, and it is mentioned in the Buddhist texts from the Dunhuang caves (8th–11th century)[2].

   In a literal translation, *byin-rlabs* means "a wave (or floods) of grace". The relics are venerated and worshipped because they dispense, they emit this *byin-rlabs*, but this conception goes far beyond this simple kind of object, it can also apply to any object or any person possessing these same qualities : a statue, a religious text, a master, a pilgrimage place can also emit *byin-rlabs*.

2. Another important theme is sainthood, because the question of relics is directly linked to the question of sainthood; usually, every Saint and only Saints can let relics. At least in the Christian tradition, relics are always associated with Saints (or to Jesus Christ, and his family). But this concept of sainthood is still subject of discussion in the Buddhist Studies because of the very specific connotation of this word.

According to dictionaries, a saint is somebody perfect, or pure, and who leads a life in accordance with religious principles. But a Tibetan scholar (*Sa-skya Pandita*) from the 13th century has contradicted this idea: he has argued that *ring-bsrel* can also be produced by evil spirits, or by the four natural elements.

My purpose is not to discuss the philosophical implications of the concepts of sacrality and sainthood, but rather to illustrate through examples the Tibetan idea on who can let relics, and try to understand exactly how it is conceived by those who worship them, how it can be explained in the larger context of Tibetan Buddhism, and finally to see if it has the same features in the Bon tradition.

CHARACTERISTICS

Relics present some particular features which should be described in the beginning:

1. Who can let relics: men, women, religious or lay people? For the moment, it seems that most of those who let relics are men, mainly clergy, who live in monasteries and hermits . Women are very less represented. Most of the reincarnate masters (*lamas*) let after their death bones, small beads, and sometimes their heart, eyes and tongue. Though rare, we also find mention of liquids, for example the nose blood from lamas (very important in the Tantric tradition). It can also happen that the body disappears after death as, according to the tradition of *Dzogchen* (a very deep but very efficient method to attain

liberation within this life), the body of these practitioners dissolves in a rainbow light, or the body gets smaller and smaller until it totally vanishes. Another idea seems interesting to investigate: it is said that a master, whatever his spiritual level, will let relics (*ring-bsrel*) (Martin, 1987.31) only if he has disciples. This suggests that the qualities of the spiritual master are not the only conditions to let relics, and it could suggest a spiritual lineage through relics.

2. What are the most common, and the most extraordinary relics? Can all parts of the body become relics? Does a hierarchy exist among relics?

   If bones are the most often mentioned, together with teeth, three other parts are also very much valued: eyes, tongue and heart (Martin 1987 p. 31) these three parts are respectively associated to the Body, Speech and Mind of the Buddha, and it is believed that if they could escape from cremation fire, it is a proof that the master really attained Buddhahood. It is also said that the one who could catch heart when it jumped outside the fire is the designed one to be the successor of the deceased master.

3. What characteristics do they have? It has already been noticed that they can get multiplied: Tibetans often tell that the round little white pearls must be kept in a place both dark and clean, and if the faith is sincere, they will get multiplied. Others have features linked with their colour, or with their size, as they are called "similar to a mustard seed", and some show other specialiies: some *ring-bsrel* can be produced when the person is still alive, from his hair, his skin or his blood. It is indeed said that by scratching his head or his arms, a master can produce spontaneously this kind of relics. Lastly, I will try to constitute a catalogue of relics, where I will consider their nature, the person to whom they are attributed, the period concerned, and the geographical location. In this way I will see if these information prove to be as pertinent as in the Christian tradition, and if it is possible to deduce correlation between a period and a kind of relics.

WESTERN RESEARCH ON THE TIBETAN AREA

The topic about the cult of relics has produced a few works limited mostly to the Indian area, China, or Southeast Asia, and very often these are from an historical perspective. Concerning the Tibetan area, references on this topic are very scarce. Firstly, the accounts of travellers or missionaries[3] often contain some mentions or anecdotes with relics. Actually these Westerns did not miss the opportunity to detail whatever they considered curious, and beyond their preconceptions. Their tales are full of interesting data, often provided by Tibetans who were accompanying them, or interested on this particular tradition.

Das mentions relics of horses, Bacot explains how they are used simply as medical pills, Waddell says that some Tibetans wear around their neck the dried excrements of their lamas..... Secondly, some biographies or autobiographies written by Tibetans sometimes contain interesting information. And thirdly, from a scientific point of view, the few articles having discussions on relics are based only on textual references and concern only their classification or their nature. Y. Bentor has written on the topic of relics because they are used during the consecration of stupas, which is her main concern, but it is not treated as a major theme; her research lies on textual references, and she often follows the theories developed by G. Schopen in the Indian context. Only one of her articles clearly refers to relics, where she details the different classifications in the Buddhist traditions of India and Tibet. From another side, D. Martian also mentions different traditions of classifications, but based on guides of stupas, and he points out many ideas arising from these texts, for example the symbols of fertility and of vitality. Some anthropologists have already explained and illustrated these themes of fertility and rebirth in funeral rituals, and have shown that in this way, death can also be a source of life. (Bloch et Parry, 1982: 3-8).

[4]But the interesting point is that both Bentor and Martin, at the end of their work based on scriptures, agree to admit a deficiency in a sociological approach of this phenomenon. So my work will

mainly lay emphasis on anthropological material, and will be compared to the written tradition existing in texts.

CIRCUMSTANCES OF RESEARCH

Until now, my fieldwork has mostly consisted in meeting people, interviewing them, observing when possible uses of relics, and collecting written references on the subject. The Tibetans constitute an important population within India, around 1,30,000, so it is very interesting for me as it provides the opportunity to meet people from very different backgrounds: religious or lay, rich or poor, in exile for a more or less long time……until today, I have led about 60 interviews, and collected more than 40 texts. Concerning interviews, I talked with Tibetan people from different backgrounds some being religious, others being lay, but both categories having unique testimonies to tell about my research: some have a good knowledge of written traditions, some have incredible accounts of miracles after the death of lamas, some remember special accounts; through this way, I could collect really interesting and sometimes unique data which are not mentioned in the written tradition. Concerning the scriptures, I could localize some very unknown texts dealing exclusively with relics, and the most ancient dates from the 13th century. I could also witness funerals, see many relics, some mummies, and collect other accounts about them. I have visited many places, among which I can mention Dharmasala, which has an extraordinary Library on Tibetan texts, the bonpo settlement of Dolanji (near Shimla), the bid monasteries in Bir (HP), and some important religious places in Sikkim. I have seen almost all the Tibetan mummies of lamas which exist in exile, and could record the account the way they were done.

The main themes of my Research

I have chosen to divide my research into four main branches, of which I will now give a detail:

1. The terminology and characteristics of relics. In a first step, it has to be explained as to how Tibetans conceives a relic, and what they mean when they use the words linked to this idea.

For example, there exists at least 5 different Tibetan words which correspond to what we call "relic", so it has to be detailed, and so it has to be studied in which way the oral and written traditions are same or different. This part will give a new light on the Tibetan concept of relics.

2. The circulation. This discussion will treat relics as material goods which are moved, carried, and brought to new places. My aim is to observe under which circumstances they are displaced and who can join this exchange. I will also study the question of transmission: relics may be given, or sold, or offered, or exchanged, or sometimes stolen, but how is all this really happening? This discussion will enable to show if relics can be assimilated to commercial goods, or if on the opposite, they do not join these exchange and constitute a special group apart. I would like for example to follow a relic from the place where it appeared, usually the cremation ground, until the place where it will be kept, in order to observe all the circumstances of its movements and transmission.

3. The uses. Concerning the uses, very few can be found in literary references, and for this question the fieldwork is very important. Relics seem to enter in many different ways of being used : they can just lie on an altar or inside a reliquary, or they can be used in some medical pills, or served at the time of the consecration (of a stupa, for example), or else they are inserted into statues, eaten by very sick people, mixed with ink to copy some very holy scriptures…in general, they are used in a purpose of protection, or of curing diseases.

   Then, another very interesting point will be discussed here : the relation between relics and politics. It is known for example that relics were used to legitimize the central power in countries like Burma and Sri-Lanka (Bechert and Richard Gombrich, 1984, p. 137)[5], and this tradition has not been studied in the Tibetan context, although it seems to be rather important. For example, it is well known that the foundation of the Bhutan Kingdom is linked with the relic of *Tsangpa Gyare*: it is a part of the backbone on which the image of a deity has naturally appeared. After a controversy and a fighting between two lamas, one of them stole this relic from the monastery where he was living, and escaped from Tibet to Bhutan. Over there, he used it to legitimize his power by explaining that the one who possessed this relic is for sure the winner of the fighting, and by this way, he became the founder and first ruler of Bhutan. Till date, this relic is preserved by the royal family in the Palace, as one emblem of his power, and is one of his most precious treasures. Interestingly, it was stolen last year, but the King ordered a fast and huge search, and it was rediscovered after some days near the border with India. It seems it had been ordered by a man in Nepal dealing with antiquarians. So contrary to the common thought, relics are not only linked with the religious realm!

4. The last part is a comparative section. I would like to offer a perspective to the Tibetan tradition, by confronting it to other traditions, first the Buddhist ones (Japan, Southeast Asia) and then the non-Buddhist ones (India, China, Central Asia). As for the *ring-bsrel*, their Indian origin does not seem to be contested by Tibetan texts, and they are also attested in China, Korea, and Japan. The mention of the tongue jumping outside the pyre is known in China and Japan, but the heart or images on the bones seem to be less popular outside the Tibetan world. (Martin 1992. p. 191).

Evolution of this Phenomenon

The Relics constitute a phenomenon common to many religions: they exist particularly in the Christianity, the Muslim tradition, or even among certain Central Asian populations who keep them in order to preserve the power and the well being of the tribe (Loseries 1992, p.171). On the other hand, however, it seems that the Hindu tradition does not have anything to do with relics; and as for the *tantric* tradition there is mention of using human bones and skulls, but they are not considered as relics as their provenance is not clearly known.

As relics seem to be unknown on the Indian subcontinent, it is important to think on circumstances of their appearing of this cult within the Buddhist tradition. According to written sources, the cult of Relics has been established by the founder of the religious current, the Buddha Siddhartha Gautama (about 6th century BC) himself. The first mention appears when he was alive: two Burmese merchants came once to offer him some food and to receive his blessings, and at the time of leaving, they asked the Buddha to give them somethings so that wherever they went, they might be able to worship. The Buddha then took some of his hair, and cut some of his nails, and offered them to the two merchants for veneration. He also explained them how to keep them by enshrining in a *stupa*, he explained how to build a *stupa*, and he showed which shape it should have. This is the first reference to relics in the Buddhist tradition. Later on, after the Buddha passed away, his body was cremated, and the ashes were divided carefully in eight equal parts, and given to the eight leaders of the Kingdoms newly converted to Buddhism. This also proves that from the beginning the relics were a stake of power. Later on, the King Ashoka again divided the eight parts, by spreading them all over the Asian world, and by the way delimiting the boundaries of his new Buddhist empire. Till date these relics, with others, are very much venerated, and most of them are enshrined within *stupas*.

If we consider the Bon tradition, the Biography of the founder *gShen-rab mi-bo* indicates that almost the same tradition was followed his body was burnt, the relics were carefully enshrined in a *stupa*, and the ashes and other remains were divided into three equal parts, and for each part 100 *stupas* were built and the remains enshrined inside.

In the Tibetan world in general, very little is known about relics, except that with the tradition of the many spiritual masters (*lamas*), the relics are known to have a certain evolution, a diversification, and also an increase of these objects. But if we want to know whether this tradition already existed in Tibet before Buddhism was introduced from the 7th century onwards, we will have to go through the archaeological works, as there are quite a lot of data concerning the remains of dead bodies, and funerals at these early times.

Classification

The written and more or less scientific Tibetan tradition is not unanimous on the subject: there are divisions into 3,4, and even 5 different kinds of relics; but the one with 4 parts seems to be the more well known. The general term used is *ring-bsrel*, and it can be divided in this way:

- corporeal; relics: especially bones,
- relics like mustered seeds (*'phel-gdung* and *ring-bsrel*)
- annex relics: hair, nails, cloths, etc.

Relics from the Dharma body (*dharmakaya*): some particular texts (Bentor, 1994: 17. Her classification is quoted from a text found in a writing of the Vth Dalai-lama (1617-1682)[6].

Whatever may be the classification, the Tibetan tradition seems to always preserve the last part for the texts, more exactly for the *dharani* (*gzungs* in Tibetan), which are short formulas little bit like *mantra*. I do not know for the moment if these different classifications are linked to the different schools, or to local places, or to some particular eras. But I aim to explain these different versions, and by comparing all these sources, I will see if these is or not any underlying link.

Another famous classification gives five different kinds of relics, each being associated with the Guardians of the Five directions : they have a special colour, a specific origin in the body, and some particular characteristics; this classification has been clearly explained in a text from *Padma gling-pa* (16th century).

This section will also deal with the question of recognition, and of the authenticity of relics. For example, I have been told of quite interesting traditions both in Mustang and in Sikkim: after a monk or an hermit passes away and his body is cremated, there is a meeting aimed at checking if some relics have left or not. In a case in Mustang, some Sanskrit letters were seen inscribed on the skull, so the monks agreed to consider this as a relic, then they wrote down these particular signs, before carrying these remains in a near monastery and enshrine them there cautiously. It happens that in other cases there is doubt on the relics being true or fake, and it will be very interesting to see which are the criteria to determine if they are genuine or not.

Some Examples

In a sense, we can say that the relic affords to have a 'second life', because it perpetuates, in a different way, the person whom the relic is produced from. Moreover, the purity of the body of the lama does not seem to disappear after his death, contrary to the common people whose dead body is viewed as very impure. One of the proofs of this statement is the Tibetan language itself, which has a specific term (*sku-gdung*) to indicate the dead body of a master. So arises another question: how can it be that some people can let a corpse which is not impure? How can it be explained that in some cases, the dead body is no more put aside, but on the contrary, transformed, and put again into circulation and use within the community?

Funeral practices

It is surprising to see such a difference in the treatment of dead bodies. For most of the common people, the most popular funeral was what is known as 'sky burial': the body was usually cut into pieces and disposed off to the birds, until no flesh remained, but this practice has disappeared in exile, and is officially forbidden in Tibet. If wood was available, the bodies were burnt; otherwise, there are also mentions of burial, and immersion of dead bodies, but these are particular cases (for children, or people having contagious diseases). Anyhow, for these common people, it is required that nothing is left at the end of the funerals; bones and other remains which were not eaten or destroyed are usually powdered, and mixed with clay in shape of small votive figurines (*tsha-tsha*) looking like *stupa* or deities. These figurines are kept on the family altar, or let in a temple, but it is not considered by Tibetans as a relic.

On the other hand, the high lamas receive some particular funerals, and their body is the focus of a very special attention. If we refer to people having witnessed the preparations of funerals for high lamas[7], the bodies are usually put in the posture of meditation, washed and dressed every day as if alive until the day of the funeral, and sometimes some mercury is put in their mouth to avoid bad smelling. In most of the cases, their body is cremated, but it can also be mummified. In very rare cases, and only if the lama intentionally required it, his body can be offered to birds. Burial and immersion for lamas are almost non-existent.

Case of a Cremation

It is the most common funeral performed for lamas and monks, and was reserved to them as wood was scarce and so, expensive in Tibet. Usually a pyre is built in the shape of a *stupa* with 4 doors, and a *mandala* is drawn on the ground of the pyre; it is little bit like an oven. After long prayers, the body is inserted in the *stupa* through one door, and the cremation can begin. Biographies of lamas and accounts of funerals generally mention some particular signs, as special light or signs in the sky, thunder storms, earthquakes; sometimes there is also mention of rain, rainbows, or blue smoke, which are considered very auspicious signs. In some rare cases, the eyes, tongue, or heart, or all the three together, are described as jumping outside the pyre, which is considered as high spiritual qualities of the departed lama. It has been for example attested in the case of the previous Karmapa, whose funerals were performed in Rumtek, Sikkim, in the late 80's. They were later enshrined in the golden *stupa* (*gser-gdung*) which can be visited near the main temple in Rumtek.

After the cremation, the pyre is kept intact for some days, after which the ashes are carefully collected, washed and checked. Usually they find some relics in the shape of small beads, whitish or colourful they are kept apart, and offered to disciples or lamas to be enshrined or used as described before. The ashes are kept in the same way as relics.

Case of a Mummification

This technique was quite well known in Tibet, where written sources seem to attest that there were quite a high number of mummies. It is particularly well known that it was performed for the two leaders of the *dGe-lugs-pa* school (Reformed school, or 'Yellow Hats'), the Dalai-lamas, whose bodies lay in the Red Palace of the Potala, Lhasa, and the Panchen-lamas, whose bodies can be seen in their residence of Gyantse. By the way, one of the best accounts and descriptions on how to realize a mummy was written by the Regent *Sangs-rgyas rgya-mtsho*, after the death of the 5th Dalai-lama in 1767, which constitutes even today the main worship place in the Potala.

Unfortunately, together with the massive destruction of monasteries and other religious buildings, the Chinese have destroyed almost all the ancient mummies, and the technique has become rare in exile where only few lamas still know how to do it. For example, the testimony concerning *Tshongkapa*, the founder of the *dGe-lug-pa* school in the 11th century is well known. His body was preserved in a *stupa* in the monastery of Ganden near Lhasa, and when the People's Liberation Army of China came to know about it, they decided to destroy it; when they opened the *stupa,* they discovered that the body was in a perfect condition, the flesh was still soft, and the hair was growing. So they got so afraid that they first ran away, then came back and burnt it. Another miracle happened then; the heart, eyes and tongue were not destroyed by fire, and some Tibetans could manage to save them to the Dalai-lama.

I will now give you a short account about the technique of mummification used for Kalu Rinpoche; Kalu Rinpoche was a great master of the *bKa'-rgyud-pa* school, and he passed away in 1989; the mummification was decided by his main disciples. The body is first washed with scented water, dried and wrapped with small pieces of white cotton cloth; in the mouth, they pour a mix of mercury, water and saffron as it stops inside putrefaction and also helps to empty all the entrails. Then it is put in a meditation posture, and put in a wooden box. The box is filled with fried salt (in order to absorb all the grease), and salt is changed every day until the body gets totally dried; in this particular case, no medicine was added to improve the preservation. This process lasted one year and half, then the head and the position of the body in meditation were maintained by some sandal-wood sticks. As the face was also dried, it appeared with many wrinkles and holes, and it had to be corrected to make the face look like alive; this was done by using Tibetan paper, as they can reconstitute the features by making shapes (especially of the nose and the cheeks). Then the body and the face were gilded, except the hair and nails, because it is said they go on growing after death. The body was dressed with nice cloths, a bell and a *vajra* were put in the hands, and then the body was enshrined in a beautiful gold *stupa.* Once a year, they open it and put some treatment on the cloths to avoid insects eating them. The salt is also considered as a relic and is distributed among the disciples; it can be eaten by very sick people, or just before death .Other mummies similar to this one lay in Dharamsala, in the palace of the Dalai-lama, another is in the settlement of Orissa, one is in Arunachal Pradesh, and one is in Nepal.

Many other things are kept from the dead lama: not only the objects he had touched or possessed, but also remains from his body; and far from keeping them apart or hidden, they are shown, located, offered to public worship.

CONCLUSION

As I explained before, as far as I know, until now, no work has yet been undertaken about analysis and synthesis on the tradition of relics in the Tibetan culture: there is no testimony of any field work aimed at providing data about customs and beliefs associated to relics. That is why through the three sections of definitions, movement, and uses of relics, I would like to improve the knowledge concerning relics and their cults, a topic which has especially been studied in both Christian and Muslim worlds.

This subject will keep on following two complementary directions: one based on the anthropological observation, the other founded on the written sources. These two poles are necessary to have a better understanding.

I also feel it is important to lead this research now. As the Tibetan society is at a turn of its history: exile has changed lots of traditions, even those related to funerals; so it is the time when there is still the memory and the knowledge of the ancient traditions, and at the same time things evolve and people are conscious that new tendencies are being introduced. On the other hand, recent researches have focused on Bon tradition as being the true autochthonous Tibetan religion. A cross over study on one specific topic present in both traditions, in the present case relics, will help to see in which proportions they are similar or not. For the moment, I am inclined to think that the tradition of relics does not present any important contrast between Bon and Buddhism.

Lastly, apart of showing a new facet of the rich Tibetan culture, this topic can offer new data for the anthropological reflection related to the representation and the techniques of the body, and also to the death and after-death rituals.

NOTES

1. The Stupa (Sanskrit word) is a Buddhist monument originally aimed at enshrining ashes of a spiritual master, but its employment has evolved and it can also preserve a whole body or on contrary nothing at all.
2. The texts discovered in the caves of Dunhuang can be considered as the most ancient documents written in Tibetan; most of them are chronicles, and religious scriptures. They are interesting not only because of their antiquity, but also because they provide unique data concerning Tibet just after Buddhism was introduced, which occurred around the 7th Century AD.
3. Actually these Westerners did not miss the opportunity to detail whatever they considered curious, and beyond their preconceptions. Their tales are full of interesting data, often provided by Tibetans who were accompanying them, or interested on this particular tradition.
4. Bloch et. Parry, 1982: 3-8.

5. This fundamental feature in often mentioned; see for example Heinz Bechert and Richard Gombrich, Le Monde du Bouddhisme, Bordas, Paris, 1984, p. 137.
6. Bentor, 1994: 17. Her classification is quoted from a text found in a writing of the Vth Dalai-lama (1617-1682) .
7. Amongst the Tibetan religious men he had interviewed, D. Barlocher (1982) could get the testimony of Rakra Tethong concerning the death of Mogchok Rimpoche (p. 493-505).

REFERENCES

Anonymous, *Sangs rgyas dang nyan thos mchog zung gi ring bsrel rin po che bod gzhung nas gdan zhu bskyangs pa. The Visit of the Sacred Relics to Tibet at the Invitation of the Government*, Government of Tibet 1951.

Barlocher Daniel, *Testimonies of Tibetan Tulkus: A Research among Reincarnate Buddhist Masters in Exile*, 2 Vol., Zürich, Tibet Institut 1982.

Bechert Heinz & Gombrich Richard, *Le Monde du bouddhisme*, Paris, Bordas 1984.

Benard Elizabeth, "The Living and the Dead: A Comparison of Buddhist and Christian Relics", in *The Tibet Journal*, Vol. XIII, No. 3, 1988.

Bentor Yael, "Tibetan Relic Classifications", in Per Kvaerne (ed.), *Tibetan Studies. Proceedings of the 6th Seminar of the International Association of Tibetan Studies*, Oslo, Institute of Comparative Research in Human Culture 1994.

Bentor Yael, "The Content of Stûpas and Images and the Indo-Tibetan Concept of Relics", in *The Tibet Journal*, Vol. XXVIII, No. 1-2, 2003.

Blackman Sushila, *Graceful Exits. How Great Beings die*, New-York, Weatherhill 1997.

Bloch Maurice & Parry Jonathan (eds), *Death and the Regeneration of Life*, Cambridge, Cambridge University Press 1982.

CHU Junjie, "A Study of Bon-po Funeral Ritual in Ancient Tibet: Deciphering the Pelliot Tibetan Mss 1042", in Tan Hu (ed.), *Theses on Tibetology in China*, Beijing, China Tibetology Publishing House, 1991.

Cutler Nathan S., "The Early Rulers of Tibet: Their Lineage and Burial Rites" in *The Tibet Journal*, Vol. XVI, No. 3, 1991.

Das Sarat Chandra, "Description of a Tibetan Funeral", in *Journal of the Buddhist Text and Anthropological Society*, Vol. V, No. 2, 1897.

Filippi Gian Giuseppe, *M'tyu. Concept of Death in Indian Traditions*, New Delhi, D.K. Printworld 1996.

Ghimire Beena & Binod, *Hindu Death Rites*, Kathmandu, Nepal Lithographing Co. Pvt. 1998.

Guidoni Rachel, "Les Reliques du Bouddha au Népal", in *Bouddhisme Actualités*, No. 36, September 2002.

Guidoni Rachel, "Entre Relique et Reliquaire. L'exceptionnelle Momie de Gling Rinpoche (1903-1983)", in Philippe Borgeaud & Youri Volokhine (eds.), *Les objets de la mémoire.* Annuaire 2004/05 Studia Religiosa Helvetica, Vol. X-XI, Berne, Peter Lang 2005.

Gupta S.P., *Disposal of the Dead and Physical Types in Ancient India*, Delhi 1972.

Huntington Richard & Metcalf Peter, *Celebration of Death: The Anthropology of Mortuary Ritual*, New-York, Cambridge University Press 1979.

Kvaerne Per, "Tibet Bon Religion. A Death Ritual of the Tibetan Bonpos", in *Iconography of Religions*, Vol. XII, No. 13, 1985.

Loseries Andreas, "Charnel Ground Traditions in Tibet: Some Remarks and Observations", in Charles Ramble & Martin Brauen (eds.), *Anthropology of Tibet and the Himalayas*, Zürich, Ethnographic Museum of the University of Zürich 1993.

Martin Dan, *Pearls from Bones: Relics, Chortens, Tertons and the Signs of Saintly Death in Tibet*, unpublished article 1986.

Martin Dan, "On the Cultural Ecology of Sky Burial on the Himalayan Plateau", in *East and West*, Vol. XLVI, No. 3-4, 1996.

Mullin Glenn H., *Death and Dying. The Tibetan Tradition*, London, Arkana 1986.

Nebesky-wojkowitz René (de), "Ancient Funeral Ceremonies of the Lepchas", in *The Eastern Anthropologist*, Vol. V, No. 1, 1951-52.

QU Qingshan, "On the Funeral Reform in Tibet in 1793", in *Tibet Studies*, Vol. II, No. 2, 1990.

Rinchen Losel, "Burial Costums in Garze", in Tan Hu (ed.), *Theses on Tibetology in China*, Beijing, China Tibetology Publishing House 1991.

Ronge Veronika, "The Corpse Cutters of Sera", in *The Tibet Journal*, Summer, Vol. XXIX, No. 2, 2004.

Schömbucher Elisabeth & Zoller Claus Peter (eds.), *Ways of Dying. Death and its Meaning in South Asia*, New Delhi, Manohar Publishers 1999.

Schopen Gregory, "On the Buddha and his Bones: The Conception of a Relic in the Inscriptions of Nāgārjunikoöa", in *Journal of the American Oriental Society*, Vol. CVIII, No. 4, 1988.

Schopen Gregory, "Ritual Rights and Bones of Contention: More on Monastic Funerals and Relics in the Mūlasarvātivāda-vinaya", in *Journal of Indian Philosophy*, Vol. XXII, No. 1, 1994.

SCHOPEN Gregory, "Relic", in Mark C. Taylor (ed.), *Critical Terms for Religious Studies*, Chicago, University of Chicago Press 1998.

Singh Purushottam, *Burial Practices in Ancient India. A Study in the Eschatological Beliefs of Early Man as Revealed by Archaeological Sources*, Varanasi, Prithivi Prakashan 1970.

Stein Rolf A., "Un Document Ancien Relatif aux Rites Funéraires des Bon-po Tibétains", in *Journal Asiatique*, t. CCLVIII. 1970.

Strong John S., "Relics", in Mircea Eliade (ed.), *The Encyclopedia of Religion*, Vol. XII, New-York, MacMillan 1987.

ṢTRONG John S., *Relics of the Buddha*, Princeton, Princeton University Press 2004.

Subrahmanyam B., *Buddhist Relic Caskets in South India*, Delhi, Bharatiya Kala Prakashan 1998.

Suvajra, *The Wheel and the Diamond. The Life of Dhardo Tulku*, Glasgow, Windhorse Publications 1991.

Thub bstan sangs rgyas, 4, *Bod mi'i 'das mchos. Tibetan Ceremonies of the Dead*, Dharamsala, Library of Tibetan Works and Archives. 197

Uebach Helga, "Eine Kurze Abhangung des Pha-bo°-kha-pa (1878-1941) über Mumifizierung", in *The Journal of the Tibet Society*, Vol. I, 1981.

Wilson Stephen (ed.) *Saints and their Cults. Studies in Religious Sociology, Folklore and History*, Cambridge, Cambridge University Press 1983.

Wylie Turrell, "Mortuary Customs at Sa-skya, Tibet", in *Harvard Journal of Asiatic Studies*, vol. XXV, 1964-65.

MONASTERIES OF SIKKIM WITH SPECIFIC REFERENCE TO THE ECONOMIC STRUCTURE

Ranju R. Dhamala

I

INTRODUCTION OF BUDDHISM IN SIKKIM

Buddism in Sikkim owes its origin to Tibet and Tibetan monks. It was first introduced in Sikkim sometime in the mid-17th century. Some believe that Padmasambhava on his way to Tibet had visited of Sikkim. and sown the seeds of Buddhism. In the history of Sikkim compiled by Maharaja Thutob Namgyal and Maharani Yishey Dolma, they have identified three periods regarding the introduction and spread of Buddhism in Sikkim: (1) Introduction (2) Development (3) Final spread.

These are expressed as "the earliest, the middle and the latter triumphs:"(Namgyal and Dolma, 1908, para 31) The first period coincides with Padmasambhava's visit to Tibet during the reign of Thi-Srong-Det-Tsan in the mid–8th century. It is believed that the Guru on his arrival in Sikkim "exorcised the land of all evil spirits and got rid of every obstacle that would tend to obstruct or disturb that course of devotional practices". He then compiled several works, which were kept hidden under rocks. (Namgyal and Dolma para 31) The middle period of growth was when the 'great incarnate treasure petheri–gter–ston–Tig–dzin–rGod–Kyi–Ldan–phree.

Cherry came miraculously and got the image of Guru Drau Po and Thing – Ka. He spent long periods in devotional and meditation in western and northern passes, and constructed a monastery. (Namgyal and Dolma, para 32) At the final triumph the four monks came from Tibet and took actual possession of the land i.e. Sikkim.

The authors had compiled the above account from the Tibetan sources. The first and second phase of development is much wrapped in mythology, trough it is not improbable that certain monks might have visited Sikkim and preached Buddhism even prior to 1642. According to the available sources of information, the spread of Buddhism to Sikkim started after the arrival of three monks from Tibet and consecration of the first King of Sikkim in 1642. It is said the three monks, Lhatsun–Namkha–Jioned better known Lhatsum Chenpo, Kathok–Kuntu Zangpo of Kathokpa Lama and Ngadak Sinpa Phuntshog Rinzing or Sgadakpa Lama came to Sikkim from three different directions, Lhatsun Chenpo came from north via Dzongri, the Kathokpa Lama from west by way of Singlela and Ngadakpa Lama came from south via Darjeeling and Namchi.(Waddell, reprint pp. 12-13) These three monks met at Yuksom and there they consecrated the first king of' Sikkim Phuntshog Namgyal in 1642. The king was given the title of *Chhogyal*: a fountain-head of both secular and spiritual power. The king proclaimed Buddhism as the state region and built the first stupa Chorten Tashi Wodber in the site of coronation.(Dorjee !989 p.42) During the reign of first Chogyal Phuntshog Namgyal a number of monasteries were either constructed by these monks or the auspicious sites were selected for the future construction of monasteries. Slowly and steadily Buddhism spread throughout Sikkim. It was the State religion till its merger in 1975.

DIFFERENT SECTS OF BUDDHISM IN SIKKIM

The two sects of Tibetan Buddhism prevalent in Sikkim are the Nyingmapa and the Karma–Kargyupa. The Nyingmapa or the old school was introduced by the first three monks visiting Sikkim. As these monks belonged to the three sub sects of Nyingmapa school i.e. Lhatsunpo, Kathokpa and Ngadakpa, the monasteries in Sikkim also belonged to these sub-sects. At present for the majority of people who profess Buddhism, the distinctions among the sub-sects carry little meaning. The common feature of these is the worship of Padmasambhava, known in Sikkim as Guru Rimpoche as the central deity.

Another sect prevalent in Sikkim is the Karma–Kargyupa. The introduction of Karma–Kargyupa sect in Sikkim has a very interesting story. The fourth Chogyal Gyurmed Namgyal (r. 1717-1733) depressed by the events in the state such as frequent raids by the Bhutanese and Nepalese forces and some problems in the family, started forth on a pilgrimage into Tibet, disguising himself as a common man. On arriving at the Tsurphug monastery Karm–Kargyupa, the Hierarch of the sect, the 12th reincarnation of Gyalwa Karmapa could recognize the king and offered him suitable honours. The king, in return promised to construct a monastery of Karma–Kargyupa sect in Sikkim with a suitable estate around it for its maintenance. Accordingly, the Ralang monastery was constructed. (Namgyal and Dolma para 156) During his life-time two other monasteries of this sect, Rumtek and Phodong were constructed.

MONASTERIES OF SIKKIM

The oldest monastery of Sikkm is at Dubdi. It was constructed by Latsun Chenpo, to commemorate the consecration of the first king of Sikkim. He also constructed the monasteries at Sangacholing and Pemayangtse. The Ngadakpa Lama constructed the Lhakhang Marpo, the monastery of Tashi-ga-legs at Tashiding and the Rinchenpong monastery. The Kathokpa Lama constructed the Kathop monastery. Great attention was paid to the construction, renovation and the furnishing of the monasteries by the third Chogyal Chagdor Namgyal (r. 1700-1716). He was greatly assisted in this work by a monk Jigmed Pao who was believed to be the reincarnation of Lhatsun Chenpo. The most important monastery constructed by them was the Guru Lahakhang at Tashiding. With the passage of time the number of monasteries increased. At present there are sixty-seven monasteries. In addition, there are one hundred and thirty-two Manilhakhang (Place for worship for ladies)

Lhakhang or Isankhang (hermitage or place of meditation). (District Census Handbook 1981) Among these/six monasteries i.e. Tashiding, Pemayarigtse, Phensang Ralong, Phodong and Rumtek are considered the most important. Of these first three monasteries belong to the Nyingmapa sect and the latter monasteries belong to the Karma Kargyupa sect. All these monasteries are endowed with vast areas of land.

A BRIEF DESCRIPTION OF IMPORTANT MONASTERIES

1. **Tashiding:** Tashiding Gompa, as is commonly known, is considered the holiest of al the monasteries in Sikkim. It is situated on top of a hill between Ralong and Rangit River in the West district of Sikkim. A number of legends is associated with the site where the present monastery stands. Padmasambhava is believed to have stayed here for meditation. Legend has it that he shot an arrow vowing to meditate at the present monastery is located. It is also believed that the site at Tashiding was accepted as the most sacred in Sikkim by the first three monks following the observance of occurrence of a divine phenomenon. A bright streak of light issuing from the top of Mount Khangchendzonga shone right upon a spot at Tashiding, at the same time a most delicious fragrance of license and sounds of melodious musical instruments filled the air. The monks along with the king Phuntshog Namgyal visited the spot and built the Chorten named Thongwa-Rang-Grol, which means the stupa, the sight of which confers self-emancipation. (Namgyal and Dolma para 83) The Ngadak Lama built the monastery of Tashi-ga-legs and also a Maitreya temple at the site. The Chogyal Lhakhang was build by Pede Wangmo, elder sister of King Chagdor Namgyal, in the first half of the 18th century. In 1715, Jigmed Pao and King Chagdor Namgyal constructed Guru Lhakhang. The internal furnishing of the temple was done by them. An entire set of Kangur written in gold was brought from Lhasa. Jigmed Pao himself performed the consecration ceremony of all Lhakhangs and Chortens at Tashiding.

The main festival of the monastery is *Bumchu*, which falls on the 15th day of the first month of the Tibetan calendar corresponding to February-March. It is the ceremony to open the urn of holy water for the audience of the devotees. The holy water, which is believed to have been consecrated by founder of the monastery, the Ngadakpa Lama, has remained clear till this day and has not dried up. The devotees deeply believe in the miraculous power of the holy water. Thousands of devotees both from Sikkim and outside visit the place during this festival.

2. **Pemayangtse:** This monastery is located near Gyalshing the headquarter of the West district. Pemayangtse means a perfect sublime lotus i.e. the monastery of perfect sublime lotus or Padmasambhava. (Waddell p.21) Regarding the construction and organization of this monastery two phases could be traced:

Lhatsun Chempo selected the site and constructed a shrine there. When Jigmed Pao visited Sikkim in 1709, he instructed the monks of the monastery about the mode of chanting prayers and performing ritual musical instruments as per the practice of the Mindoling monastery in Tibet. Jigmed Pao returned to Tibet after entrusting the management of the monastery to Khanchan Rolpai Dorgee-II. King Chagdor Namgal along with Kanchan Rolpai Dorjee constructed the present building of the monastery. Pure Bhutia blood, good parentage, absence of physical blemishes became the chief qualifications for admission to the monastery for monkshood, and celibacy was strictly maintained, No converts were admitted. The king conferred an importance upon 108 monks and appointed 108 families as chief laymen for supporting these monks.

He also declared that the monks of the Pemayangtse were to be the chief spiritual guides of every succeeding king. They have the customary right of performing all the religious functions of royalty. Its head Lama alone had the right to anoint the Chogyal. The Pemayangtse is considered the premier monastery of Sikkim. All the Nyingmapa monasteries in Sikkim are subordinate to it. Certain monasteries viz., Dubdi, Sangacholling, Linche and Paathing in Sikkim and Ging in Darjeeling are directly under its control and they follow the rites and rituals according to its conventions. The head Lama of these monasteries are sent from the Pemayangtse.

The historical account of the monastery shows that its monks participated actively in secular activities too. They acted as royal advisers, fought in wars against Nepal and Bhutan, represented the State in various negotiations and treaties. They supported the royalty in opposing the British policy of encouraging Nepalese immigrants and fought minor skirmishes at Rhenock, Namchi and other places against the Nepalese immigrants. Thus, from its inception, the monastery and its monks enjoyed privileged position in Sikkim. For the maintenance of the monastery and to meet the expenses of religious performances, a vast tract of land was granted to it by king Chagdor Namgyal and in 1901, king Sidkeong Talku made a grant of certain legal rights in perpetuity.

The chief festival of the monastery is *Chham* (religious dance), which falls on 28th and 29th day of the 12th month of the Tibetan calendar corresponding to February. The monastery has 120 monks.

3. **Phensang:** Another important monastery of Nyingmapa sect is Phensang. It is located in the North district about twenty km. north of Gangtok. The Phensang monastery's religious name is Sang Ngak Choling Gumpa. The site for the construction of monastery was selected by Lhatsun Chenpo and the building was constructed by the third Chogyal Chagdor Namgyal and Jigmed Pao. In 1902, the Princes Chuni Ongmu (later Rani Chuni Ongmu of Bhutan) became a nun and took charge of the monastery including its estate.

   The main festival of the monastery falls on the 28th and 29th days of the 10th month of the Tibetan calendar.

4. **Ralang:** The oldest monastery of Karma–Kagyu sect in Sikkim is located at Ralang in the South district. The full religious name of he monastery is Karma Rabdenling Gompa. The monastery was constructed in 1718 by the fourth Chogyal of Sikkim Chogyal Gyurmed Namgyal (r. 1717-1733), on his return from pilgrimage to Tibet. The monastery was

reconstructed on a larger scale and the number of the novice admitted to the monastery increased considerably during the abbotship of Bermiok Lama Karma Tenzing Rabgay. It is said that when the consecration ceremony of the monastery i.e. *Rabney* was being performed by the Hierarch of the sect viz., Gyalwa Karmapa of Tsurphug in Tibet, the monks and the people of Ralang noticed many auspicious signs.

5. **Phodong:** Another important monastery of Karma–Kargyu sect is Phodong, in the North district. The religious name of the monastery is Karma–Tashi–Cho–Khorling Gumpa. Originally there was a meditation hermitage, *Isamkhang*. In 1723, during the reign of Chogyal Gyurmed Namgyal a monastery was constructed at the spot. The Gyalwa Karmapa sent a monk Karma Tsundu from his monastery to Tsurphug, to take charge of the monastery. During the reign of Chogyal Tsugphud Namgyal (r. 1793-1863) the old monastery was dismantled and a new one constructed in its place. It was reconstructed by the Chogyal Sidkeong Tulku. The present monastery was constructed in 1977.

Like the monks of Pemayangtse, the monks of the Phodong monastery participated actively in the secular affairs of the State as is evident from the account of J.C. White, (10) the first British Political Officer in Sikkim. It is the only monastery in Sikkim, which enjoys the distinction of having two Chogyals viz., Sidkeong Tulku and Palden Thondup Namgyal as its spiritual patron. Sidkeong Tulku was recognized as the reincarnation of a great monk of a Karma–Kargyu sect, whereas the Chogyal Palden Thundup Namgyal was recognized as the reincarnation of Sidkeong Tulku.

The main festival of the monastery falls on the 28th and 29th days of the 10th months of the Tibetan calendar when religious dances are performed.

6. **Rumtek**: The religious name of the Rumtek monastery is Karma Thupten–Choi–Khorling. It is located in the East district, about 15 miles away from Gangtok. The monastery constructed during the reign of Chogyal Gyurmed Namgyal was destroyed

by an earthquake and another one was constructed on the site in 1740. It is believed that the first Chogyal Phuntshog Namgyal on his way to Yuksom had stayed at the place where a monastery was constructed later on. In 1960 when the head of Karma–Kargyu sect, the Gyalwa came to settle in Sikkim, he stayed at this monastery till the construction on the second Rumtek monastery, the Dharma–Chakra Centre was completed.

The main festival of the monastery is the annual dance held on the 20th and 29th day of the 10th month of Tibetan calendar.

At present, the new Rumtek monastery, the Dharma Chakra Centre, which is located about half a Kilometer way up from the old Rumtek monastery has become the chief centre of Kargyu sect. A study centre of Kargyu sect known as Karma Shri Nalanda Institute for Buddhist Higher studies was established in 1981, which attracts a large number of Buddhist scholars not only from Sikkim but also from neighboring countries.

II

The objective of this paper is not only to state the fiscal management pattern of monasteries of Sikkim but also to delineate the change in the economic structure due to the change in the socio-political environment of Sikkim. In order to understand the socio-political environment of Sikkim it is deemed essential to outline, in short, the history of the state.

SOCIO-POLITICAL HISTORY

The history of Sikkim can be authentically traced back to 1642 when Phuntsog Namgyal was consecrated as the first king of the state by the three Tibetan monks of the Nyingmapa sect, from Tibet. Its political history can be broadly divided into four phases of development:

1642-1817, period of Tibetan influence,

1817-1947, period of British Indian influence,

1947-1973, period of Indian influence,

1975 onwards, when Sikkim became the twenty second state of the Indian Union.

I. 1642-1817

In the first phase of its development Sikkim used to look upon Tibet for guidance in the administration of the State and help during the time of crises. The monks acted as advisors to successive kings. During this period, Buddhism was propagated among the non-Buddhist population of the state and numbers of monasteries were constructed. It is also to be noted that during this period the State was engulfed in a series of war. The first attack came from Bhutan in 1706; during the reign of third Chogyal Chagdor Namgyal Tibet helped the king against the Bhutanese menace. The next war was waged by Nepal in 1788 and it conquered the whole of Sikkim, west of river Teesta. Consequently, Sikkim was compelled to pay tribute to Nepal till 1815. The lost territory was restored to Sikkim by the British in 1817 following the signing of Treaty of Titaliya. After this, the political influence of Tibet on Sikkim started waning and the State gradually came under the British influence.

II. 1817-1947

The Treaty of Titaliya (1817) granted Sikkim not only a protection against the Gorkha invasion but it marked the beginning of the end of Sikkim's independence and initiated British penetration. By the Treaty of Tumlong (1801) Sikkim lost all freedom of action became defector protectorate of the British government in India.

Beside the signing of these two treaties, the other landmarks of this period were (i) cession of Darjeeling District to the British by the Sikkim King (ii) large scale migration of the Nepalese thereby changing not only the economy but also the demographic pattern of the State.

Under the British influence the king had little choice to run the administration of the State. Whenever any king showed tendencies of which the British Government of India did not approve, the latter took quick action either to make him refrain from showing such tendencies or replace him with another member of the Royal family.(Basnet 1974) It was only during the reign of Maharaja Tashi Namgyal (1914-1968) that the sphere of autonomous administration was enlarged mainly due to the ability of the Maharaja to work completely under the British influence and maintain good relationship.

III. 1947-1974

The period following the departure of the British from India was marked with a radical change in the political scene of Sikkim. On the one hand, the free Indian Government signed a Standstill Agreement with Sikkim in 1948 in order to remove all confusion regarding their positions and to retain their respective rights and obligations evolved through earlier treaties and conventions, on the other hand, the educated elites of the State, while drawing inspiration from the freedom movement in India, started various political parties. The two political parties, which influenced Sikkim's politics and administration, were the Sikkim State Congress and the National Party. While the former stood for such ideals like abolition of landlordism, starting of a responsible government and accession with India, the latter emerged to counter the demands made by the former. It considered democracy as unfit for Sikkim and merger as a move to abolish the identity of Sikkimese culture and tradition.

The period between 1947 and 1949 was marked by a number of mass demonstration and agitation organized by the Sikkim State Congress. To press its demands for the democratic reforms, it also organized state-wide 'No Rent' campaign resulting in a political impasse. Consequently, the Indian Government took over the administration and appointed J.S. Lall as the Dewan of the state. During his tenure, house tax and forced labour were abolished in order to facilitate the withdrawal of 'No Rent' campaign. The 1950 Treaty signed between India and Sikkim affirmed the protectorate status of Sikkim under India. India undertook the responsibility of Sikkim's defense, territorial integrity and external relations, whether political, economic or financial. This Treaty Spoke and of Sikkim's autonomy with regard to its internal affairs subject to the provisions of the Treaty. The intervening period between 1950 and 1973 was dotted with internal strife between the Durber and the people, which eventually culminated in the revolution of 1973, installation of elected ministry for the first time and the signing of the Tripartite Agreement. Finally the State was merged with the Indian Union in May 1975.

IV. 1975 and onwards

The immediate results of the merger were the abolition of the hereditary rule of the Chogyal and transfer of power to the popularly elected legislative assembly. In the post-merger period the Government of Sikkim has been paying attention to remodel the administration apprentices to suit the process of modernization and an increased investment in different sectors aimed at socio-economic transformation of the society from a traditional and feudal to a progressive and modern one.

Speaking of the social history of Sikkim, the Lepchas are believed to be the original inhabitants of Sikkim. They were animists and politically unorganized. After the establishment of political order in 1642 with the blessings of the Tibetan monks, Sikkim reflected more of Tibetan characteristics in terms of religion, language and customs. The Tibetan form of Buddhism was the State religion. As it was the religion of the royalty, it was quite natural for the subjects to follow the religion of the ruler. Although there were a few instances of conflicts between the Lepchas and Bhutias, (Namgyal and Dolma vol1, para 139, vol. II para 28) on the whole, Sikkimese society presented a uniform character. Another dimension to the otherwise uniform character was added once the British influence started permeating through Sikkim's administration, viz., the steady migration of Nepalese who were predominantly Hindus. However, owing to the fact that the Buddhism was the religion of the Kingdom where the king was the fountain-head of both temporal and spiritual powers (Chogyal), the presence of Hindu subjects did little to alter the social character of the state. Their influence was felt more at the economic level, because the majority of immigrant Nepalese were peasants and land, since long has remained a prime factor in the economic structure of Sikkim.

Theoretically, land belonged to either in lieu of services or as special inducements. Writing in 1872 J.W. Edgar spoke of twelve Kazis and several other officers who exercised jurisdiction over specific traits of lands (*illakas*). The Kazis and other officers exercised limited civil and criminal jurisdiction within the lands the revenue of which they collected. (J.W. Edgar p. 62) Following the British influence in the administration attempt was made to codify the land revenue system and the powers of landlords defined. There were mainly three kinds of estates: (i) Private Estates (ii) Monastery Estates (iii) Lessee-Landlord Estates. The third types of estates were given to various individual landlords on lease. The lessee landlords had again, settled the land with secondary holders. The Lessees acted as the intermediary for the collection of land revenue and exercised some judicial powers as well within the jurisdiction of their estates. The revenue collected from the Monastery Estate was kept with the respective monasteries. (Political Officer's Notification, No. 2328 August 25, 1906).

However, this system of landlordism came under attack in the late 40s. Peasants, majority of whom were Nepalese, were in the forefront of the movement for the abolition of landlordism. The demand of the people was partially fulfilled when the Government issued a notification in August 1949(Sikkim State Rvenue Admiistration Dpartment Notification No. 2753-3252/CF August 1949) *Mandal* (revenue collector) used to be appointed by respective landlord, after 1949 he was in the service of the State revenue administration. With this step revenue collection came to be considered as state function. However, the Private Estates and the Monastery Estates were kept out side the purview of this notification. It has also to be noted that this notification did not usher in any agrarian reform nor did it seek to abolish the system of landlordism though, it certainly curtailed the powers of landlords to some extent. The first attempt towards land reform was made in 1975 when the Land Reform Committee was constituted under the

Chairmanship of N.B. Khatiwada, to study the various aspects of agrarian reforms including the system of land management and cultivation regarding the Monastery and Private Estates. (Government of Skkim: Report of the Committee of Land Reforms 1975, Department of Land Revenue 1975, p. 1).

After 1975, following its merger with the Indian Union the socio-political and economic character of the State has undergone many changes. The society is fast acquiring a cosmopolitan character. Though agriculture still remains the main occupation in rural Sikkim, more industries are coming up in the semi-urban and urban areas. Politically too, democratic processes have replaced the monarchical system of government and the people have adapted to these political process.

After discussing in brief, the changes in the socio-political environment of the state we shall now proceed to discuss the impact of these changes on the economic structure of the monasteries of Sikkim.

III

MONASTERY ESTATES

Among the six important monasteries, all except the Tashiding monastery were granted lands adjoining the monasteries for their maintenance and performance of daily, periodic and annual religious ceremonies. The Tashiding monastery was granted land in 1949 by settling the adjoining areas with the monastery. Before 1949, it was dependent on the Government's subsidy and public contribution. The practice of making grants of lands by the kings or devotees either to the monastery or to the monks of these monasteries increased the size of these estates considerably. Generally, the monastery holds only a small portion of land as the primary holders and the rest are leased out to the secondary holders, known as *bustiwallas*. The different categories of land in the monastery estates are:

(i) Land held by the monastery in its own name or n the name of its monks. They are known as primary holders.

(ii) Land given by the primary holders to the share-croppers on fixed terms and conditions of crop sharing i.e. land given on *Adhia* or *Kut*.

(iii) Land given to *Chakareys*. The *Chakareys* are the servants of the monastery who are given rent-free land in lieu of menial services they render to the monastery or its monks.

(iv) Non-agricultural land, i.e. forest and bazaar area.

AREA OF MONASTERY ESTATES

The Survey Report on Sikkim Settlement 1950-55 (Government of Sikkim, The Survey Report on Sikkim Settlement 1950–1958 [MS] Gangtok, 1958) was the first of its kind to have surveyed the Monastery Estates. According to it, the Monastery Estates constituted 8% of the total number of holdings surveyed. The total area of the estate under different, monasteries were as follows:

Table 1
Area of Monastery Estates (In acres)

Name of the Monastery	*Cultivated land*	*Khas land*	*Total*
Tashiding	916	762.09	1678.66
Pemayangtse	7782.36	1759.49	9541.85
Ralang	4275.32	2153.50	6428.82
Rumtek	1853.87	779.48	2633.35
Phodong	4517.34	5217.69	9535.03
Phensang	2849.97	2377.21	5227.18

Source: The Survey and Settlement Report, 1958.

Besides the cultivated and khasland, Pemayngtse, Ralang and Rumtek monasteries had market areas under it. The markets of Gyalshing and Legship were under Pemayangtse, a part of Ravang market under Ralang monastery and the market area at the Middle Camp near Gangtok was under Rumtek monastery. The reserved forest area under the monasteries was not surveyed during this period (1950-55).

In 1980-82, another survey of settlement in Sikkim was undertaken. The Government is yet to bring out its report but from the records available at the office of Survey and Settlement, Gangtok, the area of cultivated land under each monastery is calculated as follows:

Table 2
Number of Blocks and area of Cultivated Land under Different Monasteries

Name of the Monastery	*No. of Blocks*	*Area*
Tashiding	2	130.6860
Pemayangtse	5	110.7780
Ralang	4	59.6245
Rumtek	4	87.8720
Phodong	7	45.1320
Phengang	4	150.5260

Source: Deptt. of Survey and Settlement, Gangtok.

A comparison of above two tables (I & II) shows that there is a considerable decrease in the area of monasteries estates. There are mainly two reasons for this.

(i) The Govt. of Sikkim had from time to time acquired the monastery land for establishing its offices or residential quarters.

(ii) As mentioned earlier, the monastery had leased lands to the *Bustiwallas* and they were known as the secondary holders of the land. During the Survey and Settlement Operation, 1980-82, these lands were recorded in their individual names as most of these lands were settled with them by the Monastery after taking site salami, whereas under the Monastery, only those lands were recorded which it held as primary holders.

MANAGEMENT OF MONASTERY ESTATES

Before 1973 the monastery estates were either managed by the monastery wing of the private estate or by the *Udor-Tsosum* of the monastery. The estates of Rumtek and Phodong monasteries fall under the former category whereas the estates of Pemayangtse, Tashiding, Phensang, Ralang monasteries under the latter group. (Report of the Committee of Land Reforms, p. 23).

(i) In the estates managed by the monastery wing of the private estates, the correction, transfer and mutation of the records of rights of land were solely in the hands of private estates. The *Udor-Tsosum* was not kept informed of the matter. The land rent, local rates and other taxes such as grazing fees, royalty from forest products, tax on cardamom (*damthay khazana*) were collected by the private estate. Only a share of the revenue used to be given to the monastery for its maintenance and performance of religious ceremonies. The land rents were collected through block *mondals* who instead of getting commission for it received tax exemption known as *minah*, on their holdings.

(ii) The estates of Ralang, Tashiding, Phensang and Pemayangtse monasteries were managed by the *Udor-Tsosum* of the respective monasteries through *Twimi*. They were responsible for the maintenance of records and issue of revenue demands to the *bustiwallas*. Both land rent and local rate (*dhuri khazana*) were collected by the *mondals* on behalf of the monastery. The revenue thus collected was utilized for the maintenance and the performance of religious ceremonies of the monastery.

At present, all the monastery estates are managed by the Government through its respective departments.

INCOME AND EXPENDITURE PATTERN OF DIFFERENT MONASTERIES

SOURCE OF INCOME

The main sources of income of these monasteries are land rent, local rent known as *dhuri khazana*, cardamom *damthey khazana*, and forest royalty share and *bazaar* tax. The *dhuri khazana* or house tax is collected annually at the rate of Re. 1/- per house. Besides these, the monasteries collect a share of agricultural products from its share-cropper.

(a) There are three categories of employees in the monastery who are exempted from land rent payment in lieu of salaries. They are:

(i) Employees who are selected by the committee of a monastery, *Duchi* for permanent period. For them, the exemption is life long.

(ii) Employees employed for a period up to a maximum three years. For them the exemption is for the period of employment.

(iii) The *mondals* are exempted from paying land revenue in lieu of their services of collecting land revenue from monastery estate. They do not get any commission or salary for their service. This practice of exempting the employees from taxation is called *Minah*.

(iv) The last category of employees who enjoy tax exemption is *Chakarey*. *Chakarey* is a servant who renders menial service to the monastery or its monks and in return he is given a rent-free land.

(b) Mode of collection of revenues:

Before 1975, for the purpose of revenue collection block *mondals* were appointed by the *Udor-Tsosum* or the *Duchi* of the monastery. These mondals were responsible for the issue of revenue demands and the collection of revenue from the *bustiwallas*. They deposited the money at the local bank or the monastery.

The responsibility for collecting the cardamom *damthey khazana* was given to a person for two years by the *Duchi* of the monastery on a contract basis. The royalty on forest product was collected by the Forest department, out of which the Department used to give to the monastery 50% share on the sale of timber, and 1/6th share on other forest produce. For the collection of *Kut*, adhia a person was appointed known as grain contractor, by the *Duchi* or for two years.

Since 1975 the land revenue is being collected by the concerned District Officer and deposited in the Government accounts. (Notification No. 138/LR dated Gangtok the 28th August, 1975 and Notification No. 41/LR dated Gangtok the 15th June, 1977).

The bazaar tax is collected by the department of Local Self Government. The Cardamom khazana is included in the land revenue. The grains are collected by the monastery through its grain contractor.

(c) Income of different monasteries up to 1973

Pemayangtse: According to the Survey report, 1958, the land rent was assessed at Rs. 6,765.11. The monastery also collected local rent known as *dhuri khazana* (house tax) @ Re. 1/- per house p.a. The monastery had two markets under it, viz., Gyalshing and Legship. Before 1956, the Durbar used to collect taxes for the sites occupied by shops, houses, stables, godowns and enclosed bazaars through a contractor. In 1956, the monastery took over the administration of these bazaars. Since then the *Duchi* or the committee of senior monks had been looking after the maintenance and upkeep of these with the assistance from the Bazaar department. From the two bazaars it collected the ground rent, bazaar and stable tax. The annual collections from these were Rs. 18,000 approximately. Later, however, the Bazaar department started collecting all the taxes and refunded to the monastery only the ground rent. The cardamom *damthey khazana* was collected through a contactor. The annual collection was Rs. 6000/- approximately. The total income of the monastery from different sources in 1973 were as follows:

Table 3
Statement showing the Income of Pemayangtse Monastery, 1973

Source of Income	*Total Receipt (In. Rs.)*
Land rent and local rate	7,428
Forest royalty share	8,000
Bazaar tax etc.	3,200
Cardamom damthey khazana	8,000
Total	26,628

Source: Department of Ecclesiastical Affairs, Gangtok.

It gets 50-60 *murries*(one *murree* is equal to 80 seers) of paddy, millet and corn as an annual share of agricultural produce from its *kutdars*. Besides these, the Ecclesiastical Affairs department gives Rs. 600/- as annual subsidy for meeting the expenditure on the daily rituals of the monastery.

Tashiding: Tashiding monastery did not have a income of its own till 1949. It used to depend mainly on the annual grant of Rs. 300/- from the Durbar and public contribution. After 1949, the different sources of income consisted of law rent, local rate and the cardamom *damthey khazana*. In 1958, the land rent was Rs. 798.01. In 1973, the monastery collected Rs. 875/- as land rent, Rs. 200/- towards cardamom damthey khazana and the local rate stood at Rs. 72/-.

Phensang: The main income of Phensang monastery was derived from land rent, forest royalty share and cardamom *damthey* khazana. In 1958, the land rent was Rs. 911.37. The total income of the monastery in 1973 were as follows:

Table 4
Statement Showing the total income of Phensang Monastery

Source of Income	*Total Receipt (In. Rs.)*
Land rent and local rate	2073.87
Forest royalty share	1000.00
Cardamom damthey khazana	2728.30
Total	5802.17

Besides these, the monastery has a fixed founds of Rs. 14,360 called *Kang-cha.* The money is provided by the devotees and the monks for regular butter lamps and performance of periodic pujas. The amount is kept with a responsible person who would in turn, as interest on the *Kang-cha* amount, bear the expenditure for the pujas regularly.

Between 1972-1975, it collected 532 mds. of grains as its share of agricultural produce from its *kutdars*.

Phodong: The total land rent of this monastery in 1956 was Rs. 3097.88. Besides the land rent, it also colleted local rent, forest royalty share, bazaar tax and cardamom *damthey khazana.* The total annual receipt in 1973 were as follows:

Table 5

Statement showing the Annual Income of Phodong Monastery

Source of Income	*Total Receipt (In. Rs.)*
Land rent and local rate	5,172.00
Forest royalty share	2,732.00
Bazaar tax etc.	2,402.00
Cardamom damthey khazana	5,784.00
Total	16,090.00

Source: Department of Ecclesiastical Affairs, Gangtok.

The annual *kut* share was 271 kg. of grains (approx). However, according to the *Duchi* of the monastery, normally it does not get the total share of grains from its *kutdars*.

Ralang: According to the survey report, 1958, the total land rent of Ralang monastery was Rs. 3943.39. As the forest royalty share, the Forest department used to give 50% of the proceed on the sale of timber 1/6th share on the sale of dry sticks and grazing fodder. Between 1962-72, its forest royalty share stood at Rs. 37,330/- out of which it received Rs. 32,525/- from the Forest department.

The total income of the monastery from different sources in 1973 were as follows:

Table 6

Statement showing the income of Ralang monastery, 1973

Source of Income	*Total Receipt (In. Rs.)*
Land rent and local rate	5,000
Forest royalty share	7,000
Bazaar tax etc.	6,500
Cardamom damthey khazana	7,000
Total	25,500

The monastery collects its kut share through its contractor. The annual grain share comes to 80 md. approximately.

Rumtek: The land rent fixed for the Rumtek monastery estate in 1958 was 2759.90. The total income of the monastery in 1973 were as follows:

Table 7
Statement Showing the Total Income of Rumtek Monastery, 1972

Source of Income	*Total Receipt (In. Rs.)*
Land rent and local rate	9,700
Forest royalty share	13,700
Total	23,460

The monastery used to collect bazaar toll tax and ground rent from its bazaar at the Middle Camp. The annual collection from it was Rs. 2500/-. The annual collection from cardamom *damthey khazana* was Rs. 5000/-. The annual *kut* share was around 140 murries of grains.

At present, land rent, local rate, forest royalty share and bazaar tax are being collected by the respective departments of the Government. As a temporary measure the Government is giving to each of these six monasteries an annual grant of Rs. 2500/- to meet the expense on performance of daily and periodic religious rites pending the decision on the provisions of the Sikkim Agricultural Land Ceiling and Reforms Act. 1977 (as amended in 1978).

(d) Expenditure:

The expenditure of these monasteries towards the performances of daily, monthly or annual religious rites is met out of the income from their respective estates. The annual expenditure of these monasteries are as follows:

The expenditure includes performance of puja, maintenance of the monastery and its monks, monthly salary of *Kansapa* @ Rs. 30 p.m. and two *Kunners* @ Rs. 14/- each. Ralang monastery pays

Rs. 300/- p.m. to its *Kunner* for looking after the Ralang mani-lhakhang. For the performance of religious rites and burning perpetual lamp at Gumpa, the annual expenditure of different monasteries is given below:

Table 8
Statement Showing the Annual Expenditure of Six Monasteries

Monastery	*Annual Expenditure (in Rs.)*
Pamayantse	26,002 + grains
Ralang	18,830 + grains
Phensang	9,890 + grains
Tashiding	18,762 + grains
Phodong	7,882 + grains
Rumtek	11,469 + grains

Source: Deptt. of Ecclesiastical Affairs, Gangtok.

Table 9
Statement Showing the Annual Expenditure for Performing Different Religious Rites in the Monastery

Monastery	*Annual Expenditure (in Rs.)*
Pamayantse	14,000
Ralang	5,000
Phensang	6,000
Tashiding	6,000
Phodong	6,700
Rumtek	6,700

Source: Deptt. of Ecclesiastical Affairs, Gangtok.

Earlier, each monastery was required to pay 10% of the land revenue collected and all the local tax to the panchayat unit falling within its estate but after 1975 as the government is collecting the land revenue and local tax, the monastery does not pay anything to the panchayat of its area.

MONASTERY ESTATE AND THE QUESTION OF LAND REFORM

In Sikkim, the ideal of land reform was in the air since the late 1940's when various political parties were formed with the avowed objective of abolishing the system of landlordism and ameliorating the poor and oppressed condition of the cultivators. As stated earlier in response to the popular demand the government through a notification dated 20th August, 1949 decided that all the land revenue previously paid to the agents of estates i.e. mondals, would be directly paid to the state treasury. But the Private Estates and the Monastery Estate were kept outside the purview of this notification.

The absolute power of the monastery over the tenants settled in its estate was questioned by the Sikkim National Congress in 1961. In a meeting held on March 1961 the party adopted the resolution, that in the monastery estate, the monastery authority itself made the rules and regulations to the imposed on the *ryots* and the life of the *ryots* of these estates no better than that of a slave. It further demanded that such exploitation by the authority of monastery should be stopped and there should be uniform law governing all the people of Sikkim.

The working committee of Sikkim State Congress at its meeting held on 22.9.60 and on 23.3.61 express surprise at the continuation of monastery and private estates even after the abolition of landlordism in other parts of Sikkim. "Now it is found that there are two administrations functioning parallel in some private and monastery estates. Consequently, the people in these areas are put to great difficulties and disadvantages in various matters of administration and development". It requested the Maharaja to bring every part of Sikkim under a uniform system of administration.

The Land Reform Committee (1975) for the first time expressed explicitly the need for the abolition of monastery estates. It maintained that the existence of private estates and the monastery estates in political and administrative parlance could be seen as a separate organization operating largely outside the control of government. Control over agricultural and forest land, the collection of land revenue, the maintenance of land record were held to be a part of state activities in modern administration.(Report on the Committee on Land Reforms, p. 30) The committee, from its visits to various monastery estates concluded that there was a popular demand for their abolition without paying compensation. Accordingly, it recommended for the abolition of rights of the monasteries on their estates and income. It suggested that on the abolition of these estates entire revenue collection should be brought under the department of Land Revenue and collection agencies would have to be appointed by the government on payment of usual commission or pay and allowance. (Notification No.14/LL 78 dated Gangtok, the 2nd June 1978. the Sikkim Agricultural Land Ceiling and Reform Act 1977 as amended, 1978.) As a first step towards this direction, the Government should acquire the land records hitherto held by the respective monastery for the correct assessment of land revenue and tax. It, however, maintained till the formulation of land reform legislation, the religious institutions (monastery) may be allowed to retain its homestead farm along with the appertaining buildings and structures used for the purpose of accommodating visiting monks and these may be exempted from paying land revenue and other taxes.

IMPACT OF THE COMMITTEE'S RECOMMENDATION ON THE ECONOMY OF THE MONASTERY

The recommendations of the Land Reforms Committee made a significant impact on the status of monastery estates and consequently on the economy of the monastery. As per the recommendations of the committee a new survey operation was undertaken in 1980-82 for the whole of Sikkim. The finding of the survey operation showed that there was a drastic change in the size of the monastery estate as compared to the area as reported in the Survey Report 1958. As stated earlier there are mainly two reasons for this (i) acquisition of some parts of the monastery land by the government (ii) transfer of land title to the Bustiwallas by the monastery after collecting site-salami from them. However, it would be far fetched to conclude that such transfer was a fall out of the recommendations of the Land Reform Committee. One of the reasons cited by the monks was illegal encroachment on its lands.

Earlier, the monastery used to collect all the rent and taxes and deposit the same at the balk under its account. The amount accruing from such source. We have seen earlier how revenue was spent mainly on the maintenance and performance of religious rites of the monastery. As per the recommendations of the Land Reforms Committee the Government issued a notification by which it withdraw the power of the monastery to collect the revenue and other taxes, and authorized the District Officer of respective district to collect the same and deposit with the Government. It maintained that it would give a share of revenue to the monastery concerned after it decided on the status of the monastery estate. The Sikkim Agricultural Land ceiling and Reforms Act was passed in 1977. According to it the six big monasteries were entitled to hold sixty standard acres of land. But the Government has failed to take any steps towards this direction. As a result, the monasteries are still deprived of the income from estates. In order to enable the monastery to meet the expenses the Government decided in 1978 to pay each monastery an annual subsidy of Rs. 2500/- pending the Government's decision on the implementation of the provisions of Agricultural Land Ceiling and Reforms Act 1977. The position has not changed till this date. According to some monks this has affected the monastery's economy adversely and they have to depend more on public contribution for the performance of various rites.

SUMMARY

The process of state formation in Sikkim was influenced more by its neighbouring states rather than by internal situations. In the initial phase of its political growth, the Tibetan system of government influenced the structure and processes of government significantly. Here too, like in Tibet, religion (Buddhism), religious institutions (monasteries) and religious teachers (monks) played important role in the state administration. However, after the British influence in the Himalayan kingdom over shadowed the political influence of Tibet, sacerdotal influence on the secular affair also relegated to the background. After the British left the country, there were significant social and political changes in the State and finally it joined the Indian Union in 1975, thereby changing the monarchical character of the Government.

The monasteries performed multifarious functions which included socio-religious, political economic and judicial. Of these, the last two functions i.e. economic and judicial were limited within the jurisdiction of their respective estates. As we have noted earlier, changes in the character of political structure affected the functions of those institutions, especially the temporal functions.

The political movements of late 1940's, with its focus on the amelioration of poor conditions of peasants brought a political awareness among the peasants of the state and the peasants settled within the monastery estate were not immune to these changes. Although the socio-religious role of the monasteries were never challenged disgruntled voices of the peasants could be heard, for example, in 1948 the *chakareys* of the Pemayangtse monastery refused to render their service to the monastery and monks for which they were given rent free land with the exception of house rent. They demand equal status with other peasants of the estate (secondary holders) and showed willingness to pay the usual rent and taxes on their holdings.

It is to be noted that during this movement or even after it, no decision of the Government adversely affected the position of the monasteries, nor did it interfere in their administration. Consequently, when the notification of August 1949 was issued in order to abolish the intermediary role of landlord, the monastery estates were kept outside its purview.

However, after1973, various decisions of the Government have affected the position of monasteries to a great extent. It is reported that during the 1953 political movement, the monastries of Pemayangtse, Ralang and Tashiding became the target of mob fury. Soon after the turmoil, the Mondals were appointed by the respective district officers on the order of the Chief Executive in December 1973 "to collect the taxes from the Estates and deposit the same at the District Office". The recommendations of the Land Reform Committee have not been favourable to these monastery estates either. Following the Committee's recommendations the notification of 1975 (Notification No.138/LR) authorized the district officers to collect the land revenue and deposit the same in the government account. The idea was to give the monastery a share of the land revenue after the status of its estate was determined, but so far nothing has been done towards this direction.

The bazaar tax and forest royalty were collected by the respective departments during the pre merger period too and the monasteries were given a share of the income. The practice is continuing to this day although there are complaints by various monasteries against these departments for being defaulters.

Equally noteworthy fact regarding these monasteries is that after 1975 successive Governments through the Ecclesiastical Affairs and Cultural departments have been paying more attention to the renovation and maintenance of these monasteries.

The functions undertaken and privileges enjoyed by the monasteries were unquestioned till the 1940's. However, with the changing socio-political scenario the monastery too passed through a transitional phase of confusion and doldrums. Although a degree of uncertainty still prevails regarding the status of its estate and the income there from the fact has come to stay that the state would like to perform the secular functions but leave the socio religious domain of the monastery unaffected and unchallenged.

REFERENCES

Basnet, L.B. *Sikkim: A Short Political History,* Delhi, S. Chand & Co., 1974.

Dorjee N., 'Role of Buddhist Institutions in Sikkim', *Shunyata,* 3: 1, 1989, p. 42.

Govt. of Sikkim, *District Census Handbook,* Gangtok, 1981.

Kuloy, H.K. (ed.), "Report on a visit to Sikkim and Tibetan Frontier in October, November and December, 1873" by J.W. Edgar, Manjushri Publishing House, New Delhi, 1967.

Namgyal Thutob, Maharaja & Dolma Yeshey, Maharani: *History of Sikkim* (1908) (MS).

Waddell, L.A., *Lamaism in Sikkim,* New Delhi, Manjushri Publishing House (Reprint), 1978.

White J.C., Sikkim and Bhutan: *Twenty-one years on the North East Frontier, 1897-1908,* Manas Publications, Delhi (Reprint in India).

MONASTERIES IN SIKKIM: A GEOGRAPHICAL STUDY

D.P. Boot

Establishment of a *Gonpa* or Monastery is one of the characteristic features of Tibetan Buddhism where religious professionals, students, teachers and others, reside together within a framework of social organization. (Trevor Ling, 1991, p. 49)The monastery, which also has its own hierarchy of monastic grades, is virtually a residential college for religious studies and teaching centre for craft, script, art etc.. At present, there are 95 monasteries in Sikkim. As per the information provided by the Ecclesiastical Department of the Government Sikkim (2004) there are also 190 *Mani Lhakhang* or place of worship for ladies and 37 *Lhakhangs* or temples in Sikkim.

RELIGIOUS HISTORY OF SIKKIM

History has it that Lama Lhatsun Chenpo, lama Sempa Chenpo and lama Rigdsim Chenpo all from the Nyingmapa. sect, i.e. the oldest school of Tibetan Buddhism met together at Yaksum to install the first *Chogyal* in the unruly territory of Sikkim. The territory extended between Arun river (in Nepal) on the west to the Ha valley (Bhutan) on the east and Khamba *Dzong* (Tibet) on the north to Phulbari-Kisanganj (West Bengal and Bihar) on the south (Map 1). The territory was settled by three major communities- the Lepchas, the Limbus (*Tsong*), and the Mangars besides the early

Map 1

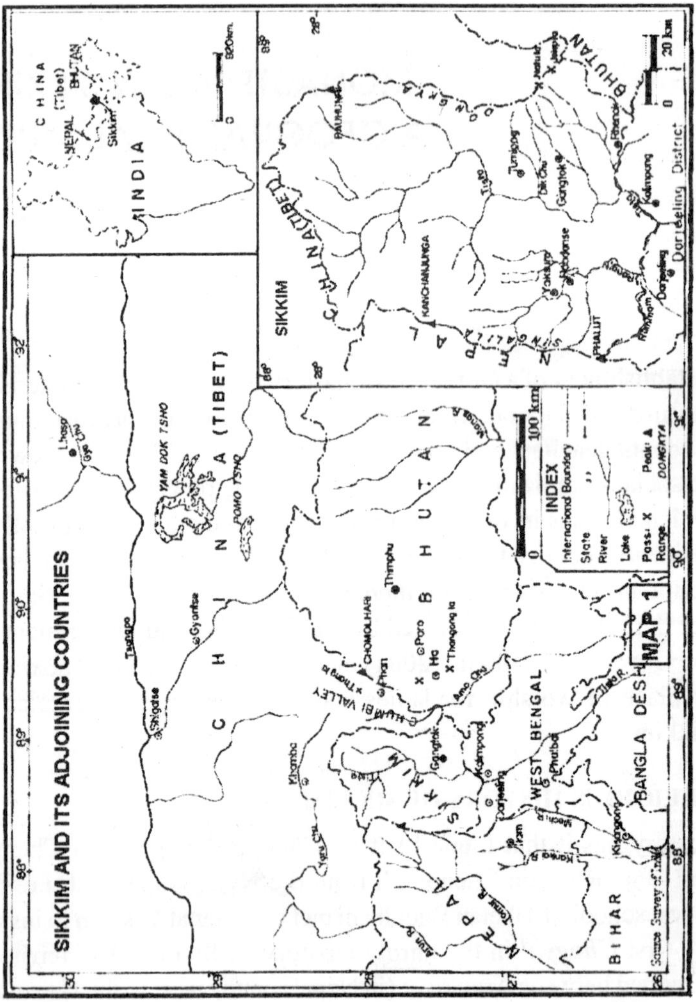
SIKKIM AND ITS ADJOINING COUNTRIES
C H I N A (TIBET)
YAM DOK TSHO
POMO TSHO
Lhasa
Shigatse
Gyantse
Khamba
CHUMBI VALLEY
CHOMOLHARI
Thimphu
B H U T A N
S I K K I M
Gangtok
Kalimpong
Darjeeling
WEST BENGAL
BANGLA DESH
N E P A L
B I H A R
INDEX
International Boundary
State
River
Lake
Pass X
Peak ▲
Range DONGKYA
MAP 1
100 km
Source Survey of India
SIKKIM
C H I N A (TIBET)
KANCHANJUNGA
PAUHUNRI
Gangtok
Kalimpong
Darjeeling
Darjeeling District
BHUTAN
20 km
C H I N A
(Tibet)
NEPAL
BHUTAN
Sikkim
I N D I A

Tibetan colonists. The descendants of the Tibetan immigrants who came to Sikkim in different waves from 13th century onwards and established the kingdom in 17th century call themselves *Lhopo, lho pa* or the people from the south (Anna Balikci Denjongpa, 2002, p. 5). But generally they are referred to as Bhutias in Sikkim. The term Bhutia refers to any Buddhist highlander of Tibetan origin living in the Himalayas. Probably there were some other groups as well but they seem to have been numerically very insignificant and there is no specific record of any other community of this period. The Limbus were mainly settled in the area between Rangit river on the east to the Arun river on the west. They occupied the eastern most part of Nepal, western Sikkim and Darjeeling District (Darjeeling and Kurseong Sub-division of West Bengal) (T.B. Subba, 1990, p. 42). Majority of the Limbus never accepted Buddhism although some cases of conversion did take place in the early phase. During the regime of the fourth *Chogyal* the relation between the Bhutia *Chogyal* and the Limbus sharply deteriorated. Finally they formed a separate territory-Limbuana, covering the area between Singila on the east and Arun river on the west. Thus Sikkim lost the western front permanently. The Mangars were mainly settled in the lower part of the Rangit river system and were loosely consolidated in the unruly territory. Although they took part in the various military expeditions of Sikkim (Thutob Namgyal and Yeshey Dolma,1908), their relation with the ruler was never very good and they never followed Buddhism. The Lepchas formed the most important community both in terms of number and power and they were also consolidated under different chiefs. The first Chogyal divided the country into 12 Dzongs and appointed 12 Dzongpens from influential Lepcha chiefs. They were mainly settled in lower part of the Tista-Rangit river valley system. They were converted to Buddhism in course of time. The Bhutias were mainly settled over the valleys and ridges on the northern and eastern parts of the country that offered similar ecological condition as their homeland-Tibet and was also easily accessible to it. Actually, the entire land east of Tista including upper catchment area (Lachen-Lachung) were known to the Tibetan traders, glaziers, herders and Buddhist missionaries. The ancestors of the first *Chogyal* had settled there long before 1642.

The state recounts its legend/religious history from the 8th century when Guru Padmasambhava named it as *Bay-Yul Demojong*, means the hidden valley of treasures (A.D. Lepcha 1995, p. 29-30). According to a recent text by Jigme Pawo the Demojong (*hBras-mo-Ijong*) covers the area south and surrounding Mount Kangchendzonga in West Sikkim which has the highest concentration of powerful sacred sites and hidden treasures within Sikkim. Thus Demojong is the heart of the historical Sikkim. The centre of Demojong is Drakar Tashiding where Guru Rimpoche is said to have given many teachings (Anna Balikci Denjongpa, 2002, p. 24.) During the first dissemination of Buddhism in Tibet in 8th century, Guru Padmasambhava and 25 disciples (*Je-baṇg nyer-nga*) had blessed the land of *Bey-Yul Demojong*. They also erected a number of places of worship, such as monasteries and stupas and the land was thus transformed into a great sacred and holy place (Dokhampa R.N. 1992. p. 36) After the visit and blessing of Guru Padmasambhava in this Himalayan kingdom primitive religion called Bongthingism continued to be followed by the thin community of Lepcha (A.D. Lepcha, 1995, p. 30). Thus the seed of Buddhism spread in to Sikkim long before the establishment of the kingdom of Sikkim. Rigzin Godem (1337-1409) is thought to be the first high lama visiting Sikkim. The treasure text discovered by him is called "the Prophetic Mirror of Sikkim". He built the first known 14th century monastery at Pawo Humri, hill top between Yuksum and Silnon and the ruins can still be seen today. His visit had no effect in the religion and politics of Sikkim with the exception that the lamas of Tashiding and Silnon monasteries follow the teaching brought to Sikkim by this Lama. On the other hand Lhatsun Namka Jigme (1597-1650), the Tibetan Dzogchen master referred to as Lhatsun Chenpo is regarded as the chief propagator of Buddhism in Sikkim and his followers known as *Zogs-chen-Pa*. (R.N. Dokhampa, 1994, p. 58).

ORIGIN AND DEVELOPMENT OF MONASTERIES

Three neighbouring territories-Tibet, Bhutan and Sikkim-unified as states under the fold of Buddhist religion during the early 17th century. Both in Tibet and Bhutan the monastery and *Dzong* (Tibetan terms for districts and also fortifies monasteries) played a dominating role during the period of unification under particular Buddhist sects: *Gelugpa* in Tibet and *Drugpa* in Bhutan. The state of Sikkim on the other hand, emerged overnight under the guidance of three lamas from Tibet and Buddhism became the state religion after this. Three Nyingmapa lamas from Tibet installed Phuntsong Namgyal, a Tibetan colonist, as the first *Chogyal* (a fountain head of both secular and spiritual power) in 1642. While both in Tibet and Bhutan successive heads of the state were the reincarnations of the previous heads, in Sikkim religion was never given such a top priority in the selection of the head of the state. It maintained a hereditary ruling system. Sometimes, the hereditary head was rather accepted as the reincarnation of some important religious personality. Therefore, even though the head of religion never acted automatically as the head of the state in Sikkim, a "priest-client" (A.C. Sinha, 1975, p. 40) relationship prevailed within the fold of this hereditary ruling system. The system of reincarnation under the fold of hereditary succession was not uncommon in Sikkim e.g. the last king was the reincarnation of the famous Karmapa lama of Kham (Tibet) and also recognized as the spiritual head of the Rumtek and Phudong monasteries (A.C. Sinha, 1975, p. 39).

After the installation of the Bhutia *Chogyal* Phuntsong Namgyal in 1642 Buddhism became the state religion and it was propagated by the lamas with all the zeal and enthusiasm. Immediately after the installation of the *Chogyal* they started either building or at least selecting site for a number of monasteries around Yaksum. A *Stupa Chorten-Tashi Wod-hBor* was built at the site of coronation at Yaksum during the time of consecration. This *stupa* is the first religious structure of any kind in Sikkim. On that occasion of coronation all the Lamas as well as the *Chogyal* requested lama Lhatsum to select a spot for a monastery. The monastery at Dubdi (near Yuksum) was said to have been built (1701 AD) by lama

Lhatsum and it is the first monastery in Sikkim. However, this information given by Thutob Namgyal and Yeshey Dolma has been contradicted by L.A. Waddell who holds that Sangha Choling and Pemayangtse were built first. (L.A. Waddell 1894). Lama Lhatsum also selected site for Pemayangtse monastery and Rabdanse palace and also marked Pemayangtse as a proper site for a monastery for *Tasongs* or pure monks (H.H. Risley, 1894, reprint 1985, p. 110). At this time, lama *mNga-bDag* also built/selected site for two monasteries at Tashiding (R.N. Dokhampa, 1992, p. 36), one at the junction of Barbong and Karma, and the other at Rinchenpong. Kathog lama built/ selected site for Kathog monastery i.e. Kartok in East Sikkim. In course of time monasteries were built in those selected sites.

Lama Jig-med Gyatsho, incarnation of Lama Lhatsum Chenpo, came from Tibet during the regime of second *Chogyal* Tensung Namgyal and was engaged in monastery building activities (R.N. Dokhampa, 1992, p. 36.) During the period of the third *Chogyal* Chakdor Namgyal (1700-17), Bhutan invaded Sikkim.They kept the Rabdantse palace under their control for about eight years and built a number of dzongs and the monastery of Paro-gon near the Pemayantse monastery. The *Chogya*l himself took refuge under the 6th Dalai Lama in Lhasa (Tibet). There he attended monastic school and became a learned scholar. During his tenure Buddhism got strong footing in the soil of Sikkim. Lama Jig-med Poa of Tibet came into Sikkim in1709 under the request of *Chogyal* and under his guidance Buddhism and the monastic establishment further spread and rituals were systematized. The King not only granted land to the Pemayangtse monastery but also introduced the custom that every second son of a three-child Bhutia family should join the monastery. This resulted, not only in the increase of the number of lamas but also generated a demand for more monasteries. During this period, the three monasteries of Silnen, Chogyel Lakhang of Tashiding and Sanga Cholling (were established. Lama Jig-med Poa also organised the Pemayangtse monastery on the model of the Mindoling monastery of Tibet. Thus, though founded later than Dubdi, Pemayangtse became the first monastery in Sikkim to be systematized. In course of time, it became the Royal monastery in Sikkim and served as the head monastery of the Nyingma sect. Lama Jig-med Poa also played active role in the state affairs after the death of the third *Chogyal* (1717) as the fourth *Chogyal* Gurmed Namgyal ascended at the infant age of only 10. After the death of the great lama Jig-med Poa, the *Chogyal* became depressed and went to Tibet on a pilgrimage where he met the famous Karmapa lama Chang Chuti-Dorjee. To him he promised to build a Karmapa monastery in Sikkim. Thus the Ralong monastery was founded in 1730 with landed estate for its support (Thutob Namgyal and Yeshey Dolma 1908). In this way, the Karmapa sect received royal patronage for the first time in Sikkim. The King also founded two important Karmapa monasteries at Phudong and Rumtek. Interestingly, these two monasteries were established for the first time outside the monastery cluster around the capital, Yaksum-Rabdanse. He also granted more land to Pemayangtse monastery. During the period of the successive rulers most of the monasteries were established on the north and eastern part of the country because this area was mainly inhabited by the Buddhist population (Bhutia and Lepcha). The following reasons may also be responsible for the shifts of location—(i) the southern part of the state was almost uninhabited during that period and in the later part of the 19th century the land was occupied by the migrant Nepalese; (ii) the formation of Limbuana restricted the establishment of monasteries on the western part; also, (iii) the old capital region had already become overcrowded by monasteries.

Sikkim faced internal trouble on the issue of succession of the fifth *Chogyal* Namgyal Phuntsong because a group of influential Lepcha opposed his nomination (H.H. Risley, Reprint 1985, p. 15-16). Finally, the Tibetan authority deputed one administrator-Rabden Sharpa-to look after the state affairs on behalf of the infant king (born and succeeding in 1733). During the tenure of this *Chogyal* (1733-80), two monasteries were established-those of Rishihat and Wangdu Dorjiling in Darjeeling (L.A. Waddell, 1894, p. 252). Bhutan and Nepal attacked Sikkim during the later part of his regime in 1770 and 1775 respectively. The King was succeeded by his son Tenzing Namgyal in 1780. Nepal made a fresh attack against Sikkim in 1788. The Raja fled to Tibet with his family and was succeeded nominally by his son Cho-Phoe Namgyal in 1790. After the British-Nepal treaty of Titalia in 1817, Raja returned to the new capital-Tumlong. In this period of political uncertainty monastery building activities were limited and confined to the northern part of Sikkim as the entire southern part was occupied by Nepal (west of Tista) and Bhutan (east of Tista). Only a few monasteries at Lachung, Chungthang, Tolung and Lachen were established during this period (Table 1). In fact, the Hindu Gorkhas even destroyed a number of monasteries during their 26 years (1788-1814) stay in Sikkim. Monastery building activities started again after the 1817 treaty and 13 monasteries were established between 1840 to 1860 (Table 1). Some fundamental changes were initiated in the course of the history of Sikkim after this period. Firstly, this treaty brought an end to Tibet's political control over Sikkim although cultural as well as religious influence remained constant at least till the first part of 20th century.and lamas continued to visit Sikkim of and on. Secondly, Sikkim also faced internal trouble on the question of Nepalese immigration since the 1861 treaty of Tumlong which made Sikkim a British dependency. The number of Nepalese settlers in Sikkim increased very rapidly after this and they received direct encouragement from the British authority. This Nepalese immigration was finally to change the very demographic profile of the state and reduce the Buddhist communities to a minority in course of time. Sikkim also virtually lost its political independence and came under British tutelage.The latter deputed one Political Officer to Gangtok in 1889 and capital shifted from Tumlong to Gangtok. During this period only two monasteries were established in Sikkim (Table 1). Till 1884 there were more than 40 monasteries in Sikkim (C. Acharya, 1995, p. 22). Monastery building activities started once again from the first decade of the 20th century. About 16 monasteries came up between 1912 to 1947. These monasteries are mainly small village monasteries. In the post British period very few monasteries have been established with exception to the Dharma Chakra Centre at

Table 1

EAST DISTRICT

Sl.	*Name of Monastery*	*Map Name*	*Sect**	*Year @*	*1894*	*1993*	*1995*	*2004*
					No. of Monks			
1.	Amba Mamring	Mamring	NA.	NA.	NA.	10	9	9
2.	Bagcham	Bagcham	Ny.	NA.	NA.	NA.	NA.	NA.
3.	Tashi Polding	Pendam	Ka	NA.	NA.	NA.	NA.	NA.
4.	Sang Nayag Rabten-Ling	Enchey	Ny.	1840	15	91	70	96
5.	Dojiden-Kathog	Kartok	Ny.	1840	20	26	26	26
6.	Kagyud-Tse-chog-Ling	Chandmari	Ka.	NA.	NA.	NA.	NA.	NA.
7.	Lingdok Tsenkhar	Lingdok	Ny.	1875	NA.	NA.	NA.	9
8.	Choi-Khor-Yang-Tse	Lingkoed	Ny.	1860	20	79	132	107
9.	Tsenkhar Tashicholing	Martam	Ny.	1947	NA.	28	23	28
10.	Karma Lhundrub Choikhorling	Martam	Ka	NA.	NA.	NA.	NA.	NA.
11.	Sang Ngyor Choi Tsog Centre	Rangnyak	Sa	NA.	NA.	NA.	NA.	NA.
12.	Tashi Choi Ling	Pabyuk	Ka.	NA.	20	35	24	29
13.	Ugen Do Ngyag Choi Khor Ling	Gonjang	Ny.	NA.	NA.	NA.	NA.	NA.
14.	Palzor Phantsog	Rhenock	Ka.	1841	NA.	34	38	28
15.	Karma Choi Khor Thangten Ling	Rumtek	Ka	1740	80	189	137	148
16.	Dharma ChaKra Centre	Rumtek	Ka.	1960s	NA.	NA.	NA.	NA.
17.	Pai Kazmai Sur Mang Shedrub/Choi Khor Ling (Gnar-Wang)	Lingdum	Ka.	1990s	NA.	NA.	NA.	NA.
18.	Ragdong Tensung Tingteg	Rakdong	Ny.	1941	NA.	50	40	33
19.	Sang-Nayag-Dud-Tul-Ling	Simik	Ny.	1850	20	86	NA	68
20.	Kama Drub Gyud Choi Khor Ling	Song	Ka.	1912	NA.	31	46	48
21.	Thub Ten Gatsel Ling	Sumin	Ka.	1924	NA.	26	22	32
22.	Mintog Gang	Samdong	Ny.	1913	NA.	38	21	36
23.	De Chen Choi Ling (Tamang)	Sichey	N.A.	NA.	NA.	NA.	NA.	NA.
24.	Sang Ngyag Phun Tsog Ling (Tsa-Ngney)	Tsaney	NA.	NA.	NA.	NA.	NA.	NA.
25.	Karmacholing	Tumin	Ka.	1915	NA.	43	46	39
26.	Ugen Choi Khor Ling (TagTse Ani Gonpa)	Taktse	Ny.	NA.	NA.	NA.	NA.	NA.

Contd....

Sl.	Name of Monastery	Map Name	Sect*	Year @	1894	1993	1995	2004
27.	Guru Kubum Taglung Sang Chod	Deorali	Ny.	NA.	NA.	NA.	NA.	NA.
28.	Changey	Changey Senti	Ka.	1888	NA.	26	29	23
29.	Palung	Palung	Ka.	1954	NA.	NA.	NA.	NA.
30.	Nagthang	Nagthang	NA.	NA.	NA.	NA.	NA.	NA.
31.	Phatamchen	Phatamchen	NA.	NA.	NA.	NA.	NA.	NA.
NORTH DISTRICT								
1.	Choi Drub Dhar Gay Ling	Barphok	Ny.	1939	NA.	NA.	NA.	NA.
2.	Rinchen Khado	Gor	Ny.	NA.	NA.	47	35	28
3.	Tashi Choi Ling	Hee-Gyathang	Ny.	1935	NA.	20	7	32
4.	Palden Phuntsog Phodrang	Labrong	Ny.	1844	30	39	41	58
5.	Ngyul Drub Choi Ling (Gnedupcholing)	Lachen	Ny.	1806\58	8	90	51	62
6.	Sam ten choling (Nga Dhag)	Lachung	Ny.	1788	8	48	48	61
7.	Choi phel Dar gey ling	Lingtnem	Ny.	1857	20	21	13	19
8.	Samten Choi ling	Thangu	Ny.	NA.	NA.	NA.	NA.	NA.
9.	Malam	Malam	Ny.	NA.	NA.	NA.	NA.	NA.
10.	Ugen Sang Do Ling	Naga	Ny.	NA.	NA.	NA.	NA.	NA.
11.	Karma Tashi Choi Khor Ling	Phodong	Ka.	1740	100	333	314	357
12.	Sang Ngyag Choi Ling	Phensong	Ny.	1840	100	188	225	268
13.	Rin Zin Choling	Ringon	Ny.	1860	30	45	41	39
14.	Kang Sang Choi Ling	Sheep Gyer	Ny.	1944	NA.	65	15	13
15.	Tashi Dhar Gay Ling	Silim Phagyal	Ny.	NA.	NA.	NA.	NA.	NA.
16.	Sontam	Santam	Ny.	NA.	NA.	NA.	NA.	NA.
17.	Kod Ser Choi Ling	Santgtok Shagyon	Ny.	NA.	NA.	NA.	NA.	NA.
18.	Sing Chid (Nga Dar)	Singchid	Ny.	1923	NA.	28	28	17
19.	Santong Tinsing	Sangtong	Ny.	NA.	6	33	39	22
20.	Tsa Wang (Chewang) Ani	Chawang	Ny.	1936	NA.	36	46	65
21.	Rin Zin Thar Ling	Tingbong	Ny.	NA.	NA.	NA.	NA.	NA.
22.	Samten Choi Ling	Tolung	Ny.	1789	90	88	88	59
23.	Tsemo Rinchen Thang (Rig Zon Choi Ling)	Chungthang	Ny.	1768	8	41	31	28
24.	Dhar Gay Choi Ling	Tareng	NA.	NA.	NA.	NA.	NA.	NA.
25.	Kabi	Kabi	NA.	NA.	NA.	NA.	NA.	NA.

Sl.	*Name of Monastery*	*Map Name*	*Sect**	*Year @*	*1894*	*1993*	*1995*	*2004*
SOUTH DISTRICT								
1.	Hod-See-Choi-Ling (Woselcholing)	Barmick	Ny.	1952	NA.	23	36	38
2.	Nam-Drol-Ling	Boomtar	Ny.	1929	NA.	15	21	20
3.	Karma-Choi-Phel-Ling	Ben	Ka.	1905	NA.	NA.	NA.	NA.
4.	Kun-Drag-Yung-Drung	Bhon	Ny.	NA.	NA.	NA.	NA.	NA.
5.	Rig-zin Lono-yang	Dolling	Ny.	1840	8	28	33	29
6.	Kewzing Gonpa	Kewzing	NA.	NA.	NA.	NA.	NA.	NA.
7.	Lig-Ney Pha-gyal	Lingi	Ny.	NA.	NA.	46	15	51
8.	Mangbro	Mangbro	Ny.	1874	NA.	14	15	33
9.	Tashi Chodarling (Tamang)	Melli	Ny.	NA.	NA.	25	9	61
10.	Maniram Gonpa	Maniram	Ny.	NA.	NA.	NA.	NA.	NA.
11.	Namchi Ngadak	Namchi	Ny.	1836	6	14	22	27
12.	Norbucholing	Namthang	Ny.	1933	NA.	16	8	8
13.	Samten-Cholling (Sherpa)	Parbing	Ny.	1934	NA.	107	21	62
14.	Karma-Rabten-Ling	Ralong	Ka.	1730	80	121	101	102
15.	Kun-Phen-Tsechu	Ravangla	NA.	NA.	NA.	NA.	NA.	NA.
16.	Pal-Chen-Choi-Ying	Ralang	Ka.	1980s	NA.	NA.	NA.	NA.
17.	Ser-Drub Choiling	Alley	Ny.	NA.	NA.	NA.	NA.	NA.
18.	Shar-Chog-Bey-Phoog	Sangmo	Ka.	NA.	NA.	NA.	NA.	NA.
19.	Sorock Gonpa (Tamang)	Kitam	Ny.	NA.	NA.	12	8	12
20.	Teg-Ling-Dzog-Chen	Tekling	Ny.	NA.	NA.	NA.	NA.	NA.
21.	Samtencholing	Wok	Ny.	1927	NA.	7	5	5
22.	Tashi Palding	Tashi Palding	Ny.	1841	10	46	59	59
23.	Yangang Gonpa (Gurung)	Yangang	NA.	NA.	NA.	NA.	NA.	NA.
24.	Gyaltshe Rimpoche Centre	Rimpoche Centre	Ka.	1980s	NA.	NA.	NA.	NA.
WEST DISTRICT								
1.	Anden Wolung	Aden	Ny.	NA.	NA.	16	15	73
2.	Chakung	Chakung	Ny.	NA.	NA.	11	12	16
3.	Sang-Nayág	Dubdi	Ny.	1701	30	27	34	62
4.	Pau Hungri	Pau Hunri	Ny.	1860	NA.	7	8	6
5.	Khecshopheri	Khachopari	Ny.	1788	11	41	51	69
6.	Lun-drub-Yang-tse	Luntse	Ny.	1850	15	20	45	36
7.	Sang-Ngyag-Dud-Zom-Ling	Melli Aching	Ny.	1740	15	59	30	56
8.	Ugen-Thong-Mol-Ling	Okharey	Ny.	NA.	NA.	NA.	NA.	NA.
9.	Sang-chen-pema-yangtse	Pemayangtse	Ny.	1705	108	102	125	156

Contd....

Sl.	Name of Monastery	Map Name	Sect*	Year @	1894	1993	1995	2004
10.	Sang-Ngyag-Yang-tse	Rinchenpong	Ny.	1730	8	26	20	25
11.	Ugen-Sam-drub-pema-choi-ling	Rebde	NA.	NA.	NA.	NA.	NA.	NA.
12.	Sangh-Nayag-Choi-Ling	Sangcholing	Ny.	1714	25	49	52	57
13.	Nga-Dag	Silnon	Ny.	1716	8	60	65	61
14.	Sribadam	Sribadam	Ka.	NA.	NA.	NA.	NA.	NA.
15.	Bhod-Chogyal	Tashiding	Ny.	1716	20	59	63	87

* Sect: Ny. Nyingmapa sect., Ka. Karmapa sect., Sa Sakyapa Sect. NA. Not available

@ Year of establishment.

Number of Monk: (1) Waddell.L.A.1894. op cit. p. 257-58. (2) Electoral Roll 1993, 1995 and 2004. Election Commission. Govt. of Sikkim.

Note: Of the 95 monasteries mentioned in Table 1, only 56 are enlisted in the Sangha constituency, consisting of the Buddhist monks, which is a speciality in the case of Sikkim politics; as such, those 56 are only included in Table 2.

Source: Eccelesiastical Dept. Govt.of Sikkim 2004, Waddell, L.A. (1894); and Maharaja Thutob Namgyal and MaharaniYissey Dolma. History of Sikkim, (1908).

Rumtek. During the post merger period a number of monasteries were built like, Gyaltshe Rimpoche Centre at Ralong and Sang-Ngor Choi-Tshog Centre at Rankha (East Sikkim) etc.. These monasteries are not at a with monastery system of Sikkim and they have not received any grant from the Govt. These monasteries with their huge structure and large number of students are functioning properly and the expenditure is borne mainly by devotees from all over the world.

DISTRIBUTION

The literal meaning of the term *Gonpa* is solitary place and thus most *Gonpas* of the area are still found in the lonely places. To escape from the mundane temptations of day-to-day life, the Buddhist monks always desired an isolated place where the spiritual activities could be performed calmly (C. Acharya. 1998, p. 3). The monasteries are usually located on a commanding spot, at a high altitude. The selection of the site follows two essential conditions

"Back to the hill-rock, and front to the tarn "(*rgyab ri brag dang, mdun ri mtsho*). (L.A. Waddell, 1894, p. 254)—(i) monastery be built in the long axis of the hill and (ii) it is desirable to have a lake in front of the premises, even at a long distance. The site in front of a waterfall is considered ideal but it is bad in front of a river. In the regional context, the monasteries are located over the ridge top and higher slope of the ridges.

The distribution of the monasteries in Sikkim is uneven as we find there in every aspect of habitation over the dissected topography. Besides topography, spatial distribution of community and political factors also play vital roles in the distribution pattern. In general, the monasteries are located in the Buddhist dominated areas. Of course the cosmopolitan town like Gangtok is an exception. But Gangtok served as the capital of the Buddhist state for about 86 years (1889-1975). About half of the monasteries in Sikkim are located in some particular localities of religious and political importance (Map 2). The first capital, Yaksum-Rabdanse, for example used to be one such area where seven monasteries are located within a radius of 9 km. in the Rathang Chu basin (Map 2). It has been mentioned earlier that this particular area is the legendary Demojong (*hBras-mo-Ijong*) which has the highest concentration of sacred sites and hidden treasures including the first known 14th century monastery of Pau Humri. This area was known to the Buddhist communities and visited by the great monks long before the formation of Buddhist Kingdom. In this way this areas serve as the seedling ground of Buddhism in Sikkim and still it is very famous among the Buddhist communities. Monastery building activities of this newly emerged Kingdom were confined within this particular area till the regime of the third Choygal. The capital of the state shifted from Rabdanse to Tumlong in 1814 and consequently a number of monasteries were established around this new capital. About six monasteries are located within a radius of 3 km. (Map 2). Finally, the capital shifted to Gangtok in 1889 and a number monasteries were founded around the new capital.

Besides these three capitals there are small clusters or chains of monasteries located in areas dominated by Buddhists, sometimes

Map 2

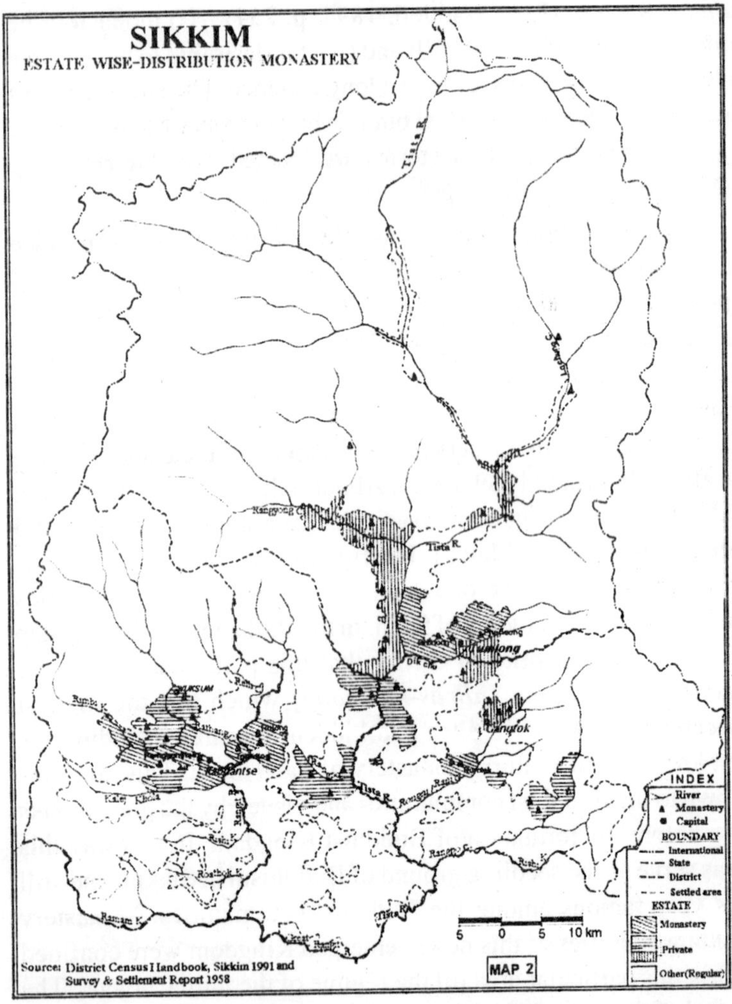

of a certain particular community. For example, there are about six monasteries located within a short distance from each other in the Dzongu area, at present the reserved homeland of the Lepchas. A number of monasteries, about five in number, are located over the ridge between the Rongpo chu and Rongni chu in East Sikkim, which is traditionally inhabited by the Buddhist Bhutias and the

Lepchas. The distribution of village monasteries depends upon the concentration\segregation of Buddhist communities viz the Bhutias, the Sherpas, the Lepchas, and the Tamangs.

The introduction of British administrative system, since the end of the 19th century produced three distinct types of landed estates—Raja's Private Estate, Monastery Estate and Regular Estate. The British land management system continued till the abolition of landlordism in 1949 but the Private and Monastery Estates more or less followed the system till the merger of the state with India in 1975. Thus a parallel government existed in those estates till the end of the hereditary ruling system where Buddhist ethos prevailed under the state patronage even though the Buddhist communities were outnumbered by the Hindu Nepalese at the end of 19th century. The Nepalese were not allowed to settle in the Private estates, (A.C. Sinha, 1975 p. 45) particularly in the North Sikkim (Dzongu area). The area was totally reserved for the Lepcha-Bhutia communities. According to the first Cadastral Survey (1958), there were 389 revenue blocks in Sikkim. Of these 62 revenue blocks were under the Private Estate and 38 under the six monastery Estates (Government of Sikkim, Report of Sikkim Settlement, 1958). The revenue block of the monastery estates were located surrounding the respective monastery (Map 3). In case of Private estate, they were mainly located in some few pockets like around the capitals (Yaksum-Rabdanse, Tumlong and Gangtok) and in Dzongu area. About half of the total monasteries in Sikkim were located in these two categories of landed estate (Map 3). These estates were mainly inhabited by the Lepcha and Bhutia and other Buddhist population and thus offered ideal condition for the establishment of monasteries in those areas. In the Private estate most of the monasteries were very small and most of them are recognized for a particular community like the Lepcha monasteries in the Dzongu area. It may be mentioned here that in Sikkim the distribution of population is sparse on the slopes without any village in the true sense of the term. These revenue blocks are aggregates of *bustees* or hamlets which sometimes consist no more than five or six houses. In many cases such bustees are occupied by members of a particular community.

Map 3

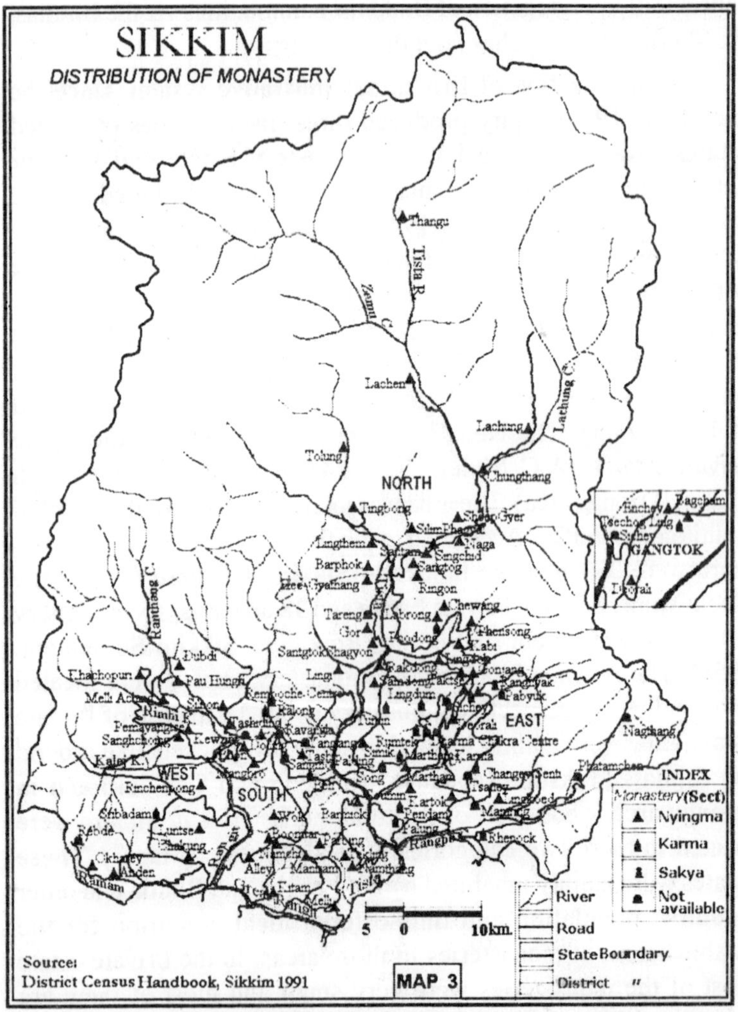

At present, there are 95 monasteries distributed over four districts of Sikkim (Map 2). East district accommodate highest number of monasteries (31) which is followed by North (25), South (24) and west district (15).

CLASSIFICATION OF MONASTERIES

The name of the monasteries in Sikkim are mostly in Tibetan language and are of an ideal or mystic nature but some are physically descriptive of the site. Few are Lepcha names which are also of a descriptive character (C. Acharya, 1995, p. 23). It is very difficult to classify the monasteries on the basis of a single criterion. Hence different classifications are made in terms of their size, number of monks, sect and community.

Type

The monasteries of Sikkim may be grouped into two major categories (i) the so called *Gonpa* founded in or around the village serving mainly as a chapel for the community (ii) proper monastery as defined earlier-a residential college for religious study where religious professionals reside together within a framework of social organization. Most of the *Gonpa* or village monasteries belong to the first category and they consist of merely an *Lhakang* or temple with one or more priests engaged in ministering the rituals to the surrounding villages (L.A. Waddell 1894, p. 253). Most of them are also single storeyed, with a few *stupa or chorten* i.e tombs to preserve the relics of the saints). Some of these monasteries have separate *Mani Lakhang* (places of worship for women). They are mainly maintained from the donation of the local people or grant received from Government. A number of such village monasteries are located at areas dominated by some particular communities where the presiding lamas also belong to the same stock.

To the second group belongs to the important and the premier monasteries of Pemayangtse, Tashiding, Phensong, Rumtek, Ralong and Phudong. All of these have much landed estates for their maintenance. A large number of lamas are attached to these. (Table 1). In addition, the Buddhist community of Sikkim also considers the monasteries of Tolung, Enchy, Kartok, etc.as equally important. These monasteries were either built or the sites were selected by the first three famous lamas or some reputed lamas in the later period. These monasteries also have large number of lamas.

In these major monasteries, the establishment usually consists of a *Lhakhang, Mani-Lhakhang,* school, library, residence for students and monks and a number of *Stupas or Chortens*. The main structure is usually a two storeyed building where the lower storey houses the *Lhakang* and the other buildings cluster around it.

Monk Size

During the regime of the third *Chogyal*, Lama Jeg-med-Pao introduced monastic order in Pemayangtse and also appointed a batch of 108 monks to perform the monastic functions. It has been mentioned earlier that the third *Chogyal* also introduced the custom that one son from every Bhutia family should join a monastery. This resulted in the growth of lama population in course of time. According to Trevor Ling (Trevor Ling 1991, p. 53) there was a rise of 742 lamas during the period between 1720 and 1890 and the changes were noticeable among the districts (Table 2). In this period the lama population was mainly concentrated in the east whereas the number of lama population remained almost static in the west. However, it seems that Trevor Ling miscalculated the number of lama population in the North and the south districts and probably placed some of the monasteries of the North under the East district. This may be correlated with the limited growth of monastery on the western part during the said period (Table 1) In 1894, there were 6 big monasteries in Sikkim in terms of the size of the lama population. The following numbers are given by L.A. Waddell–Pemayangtse 108, Phudong 100, Phensang 100, Tolung 90, Ralong 80, Rumtek 80.

The record is not available about the lama population in the monasteries of Sikkim during the first half of the 20th century. Monastery wise lama population is again available, only the number of voter (21 Year age), since the election of second State Council election (1958) where one Sangha (Monastery) seat was introduced (L.B. Basnet, 19774, p. 109). This seat is reserved exclusively for the monk voter of the different monasteries of Sikkim. This seat still exists in the post merger Legislative Assembly also. At present, out of 95 monasteries there are 3098 voters in 56 monasteries in

Sikkim. During the period of 1894-2004 each monastery increased lama population (Table 2).

Table 2
District-wise Distribution of Lamas in Sikkim: 1720—2004

Year	*West*	*East*	*North*	*South*	*Total*
1720	191	03	—	—	194
1730	206	03	—	80	289
1740	221	183	—	80	484
1790	232	183	103	80	598
1840	232	318	103	80	733
1850	232	378	111	104	825
1860	232	428	147	104	911
1890	237	448	147	104	936
1894*	248	185	405	104	942
1993#	477	792	1168	428	2866
1995#	520	663	1037	338	2558
2004#	704	759	1128	507	3098

Source: Trevor Ling (1991) * Waddell, L.A. 1894. op cit.
Number of Lama in the Electorate List.

In addition, the three large monasteries of *Karma-Kagyudpa* sect at Rumtek, Ralong and Rankha have recently started functioning as mentioned earlier. At present, two of these monasteries are functioning as proper residential college and huge numbers of lamas are attached to these. However, due to their different style of functioning it is difficult to compare them with the major old monasteries of Sikkim.

Sect

The monasteries in Sikkim belong to two major sects of Tibetan Buddhism—*Nyingmapa* and *Karma-Kagyudpa*. It is mentioned earlier that the three lamas belonged to three different sub-sects of Nyingmapa sect from Tibet who installed Phuntsong Namgyal as the first *Chogyal*. These learned Nyingmapa lamas fled the religious war between the Gelugpas on the one hand, and the King of Tsang and the Kargyupas on the other which led to the rise to power of the Gelugpas and the unification of Tibet (Anna Balikci Denjongpa,

2002, p. 22). Buddhism became the state religion of Sikkim after this. During the same period Tibet unified under the fold of *Gelugpa* sect (1642) and Bhutan under the *Drugpa* sect (1624/25). Both Tibet and Bhutan witnessed several inter-sect clashes during their processes of unification. *Gelugpa* Tibet also made several attacks against Bhutan during the process of its unification. Interestingly, there is no such record on Sikkim. One of the possible reasons is that the relation between old Nyingmapa and the reformed *Gelugpa* and *Drugpa* sects etc. remained friendly both in Tibet and Bhutan except in 1717 when the Dzungar troops of the Mongols caused severe damage to the Nyingmas and its monasteries.(Dudjom Rimpoche, 1987, p. 13). The then Dalai Lama of Tibet recognised Sikkim's ruler and even sent gifts to him and "....in the context of Tibet, Sikkim was like a small feudal unit" (A.C. Sinha, 1987, p. 349). The relation between Tibet and Sikkim remained friendly, at least in religious matter till the closure of the border with Sikkim following the Indo-China war. Sikkim was actually under Tibet's protection till the penetration of the British power following the Treaty of Titalia. Actually, a 'patron-supplicant' relationship existed between Tibet and Sikkim before this treaty (A.C. Sinha, 1987, p. 360). On the other hand, Bhutan attacked Sikkim twice in 1700 and 1777 and after the first attack even occupied the then capital of Sikkim for about eight years. However, during their stay they never destroyed any monastery. In fact, throughout the history of Sikkim there is no record of any inter sect dispute among the Buddhists. The *Chogyal* also did not differentiate among the sects. The fourth *Chogyal* established the first *Kagyudpa* monastery at Ralong and allotted landed estate to it and at the same time he also allotted more land to the Pemayangtse monastery belonging to the Nyingma sect. In fact, among the Buddhist communities in Sikkim there is hardly any distinction among the sects and the sub-sects. "The common feature of these is the worship of Padmasambhava, known as the central deity" (R.R. Dhamala, 1992, p. 21-22).

Majority of the monasteries in Sikkim belongs to the Nyingmapa sect. Dupde, Samg-Nga Choling, Pema Yang-Tse, Enchey, Phenzang and others adopted the same terma of Lhatsun

Chenpo and Rigzin Ter-dak Lingpa that were practiced and preached by Mindroling monastery, Nyingmapa Center in Tibet, for their ritual practice and traditional system. The follower of Lhatsun Chenpo known as Lhatsunpa/Zogs-chen-Pa/Dzogchen. The monastery built by Nga-Dag Sempa Chenpo, Tashiding and Zilnon along with Namchi and Lachung Thangmoche and many others followed the same ritual practice and traditional system of Dorje-Dag monastery, Nyingmapa Centre in Tibet. This doctrine known as *Byang-g Ter* or *mNes-bDagpai-Lugs* or simply the tradition of *mNga-bDang*. The monastery established by the followers of Kathog Ringzin Chenpo, like, Kathog at Pakyong and Diling at Sosing/Kewzing follow the ritual system of Kathog monastery, Tibet. The follower of Kathog Rigin Chenpo known as Kathog pa. The monasteries (Dubdi, Pemayangtse, Silnon Tashiding and Sanghcholing) established during the first three successive *Chogyal*s belong to the Nyingmapa sub-sect. Among these monasteries, Pemayangtse received landed estate from the third *Chogyal* and served as the head of the Nyingmapa group of monasteries and was also recognized as the Royal monastery of Sikkim. It also exercised control over the Lepcha monastery of Lingthem,, the monasteries of Simik, Phage, Dubdi, Sanghacholing, Luntse and Pathing. Two other monasteries-Phensong and Tashiding also received landed estate in course of time of these Tashiding received landed estate in 1949.There is no past record about Phensang. Its name appeared for the first time in the administrative Report of 1933-34. Besides these three premier monasteries a few other monasteries of this sect viz. Enchey, Tolung etc. also hold important position. Rest of the monasteries of this sect are very small, They receive either small grants from government for maintenance or depend totally upon the donations from the local inhabitants.

Among the monasteries of the *Kagyudpa* sect, Ralong is the most important. It was founded by the Fourth *Chogyal*-Gyurmed Namgyal, in 1730 with landed estate for its maintenance. The same *Chogyal* also founded the monasteries of Rumtek and Phudong. All of these three monasteries received landed estates in course of time. The names of Phudong and Rumtek appeared for the first time in the Administrative report of 1933–34. Ralong serves as the head of the Kargyupa group of monastery. The other monasteries of this sect are very small. They either receive grant from the Government or totally depend upon donation. Recently, three big monasteries of this sect-Dharma Chakra Centre at Rumtek (1960), Gyaltshe Rimpoche *(Pal-Chen-Choi-Ying)* Centre at Ralong and *Choi Khor Ling (Gnar-Wang)* at Rankha (near Gangtok) have been established with the support of Tibetan refugees and other Buddhist devotees from all over the world. These three monasteries are quite different from the existing old monasteries of Sikkim. They have their own study centres and residential facilities for the students thereby attracting a number of Buddhist scholars not only from Sikkim but from other countries as well.

Community-wise

In addition to the Bhutias, the Lepchas, Sherpas, and a part of Tamangs and Gurungs also follow Buddhism in Sikkim. At present, there is no restriction on entry to any monastery on any community in Sikkim. Initially, however there were some restrictions of entrance in Pemayangtse monastery that used to be open only to those of pure Bhutia blood and few Lepchas of high position. Monk hood also was totally restricted to those of pure Bhutia blood. Such restrictions are done away with at present. Interestingly, a number of monasteries are earmarked for some particular communities like Parbing for the Sherpas, Bumter for the Tamangs, Lingthem for the Lepchas, Yangang for the Gurung etc. Some of them are very old and the monks are enlisted in the voter list of the Sangha Assembly constituency like Kitam, Melli, Parbing etc. These are mainly small monasteries, but such monasteries are well known throughout Sikkim. These monasteries are located in areas settled mainly by certain dominant communities, e.g. the Lepcha monastery in the Dzongu area of North Sikkim. In such cases the lamas come from that particular community.

MONKS

Before going into any details of the fnnctional activities of the monasteries it will be worthwhile to discuss the function and the hierarchy of the monks\lamas. The following hierarchical order is followed in the Pemayangtse monastery, (R.R. Dhamala 1991, p. 58-76) whose model is more or less followed by all the big monasteries of Sikkim.

The monastic discipline starts as soon as the students pass the entrance to the noviciate and are formally admitted to monkhood as Junior Monk. After passing two professional examinations that normally take two to three years the noviciate becomes a junior monk. The promotion of the junior monk to higher ranks depends upon the hierarchy pattern of the monastery and not on any further examination.

Junior Monk—*Thungpo*—*Chapdip*—*Konyer*—*U-Chho*— *Umdza* / *Dorjeelopon*

Thungpo is the conch-shell blower. Two junior monks are appointed for one year for this. *Chapdip* or pourer of the holy water is appointed for one year. *Konyer* or temple caretaker is appointed for three years. With the completion of the duties of *Konyer* the stage of learner or *trapa* is over and he becomes an *U-Chho* or elder monk *Dorje-Lopon* and *Umdza* are the two highest posts of equal rank and privileges. *Dorje-Lopon* is responsible for all the spritual aspects while *Umdza* looks after the secular/temporal matter and supervises the monastic establishment and exercises all discretion. These two posts are fixed for life time.

Adda monk is in charge of the office record and their maintenance while the *Thwimi* monk looks after the economic administration of the monastery. *Adda* and *Thwimi* are selected from among the elder monks. *Chinyer* monk is store keeper and in charge of the menials of the monastery. Two monks are appointed to this post for three years. *Chotinpa* is not only the librarian maintaining discipline among the monks but is also the spokesman of the monks. He is selected from among the senior monks by voting. Previously he was appointed by the king but at present the Ecclesiastical Department issues the appointment for one or more terms. *Uchunpa* is responsible for playing the cymbals and looking after the service of *Umdza* during his absence. *Kangsapa* is responsible for arrangement of rituals in the monastery. These two posts do not fall in hierarchical order although they are selected from among the elder *U-Chhos.*

At present, very few monks reside in the major monasteries and most of them reside in nearby village/ town. Since celibacy is not obligatory for the monks of Sikkim the lamas look after their families and are engaged in various occupations starting from cultivation to other tertiary works. This is because celibacy is not followed among the monks of Sikkim. Despite various changes in the society monk population never decline their size, and each and very monk is attached to a particular monastery.

FUNCTION

In Tibet, monks and monasteries used to take active part in the processes of political unification and administration of the state and this model was followed by Bhutan as well. In contrast, even though Sikkim followed Buddhism and remained under Tibet's tutelage for long period, the monasteries played a different though no less important role in the hereditary ruling system where the monks did exert considerable influence on the politics and administration of the state. As a result there evolved a priest-client relation between the clergy and the Ruler (A.C. Sinha, 1975, p. 40). The heads of the major monasteries were chosen from both Bhutia and Lepcha aristocracy including the *Kazis* or the hereditary landlords representing these two communities and they held high positions in the state council till the penetration of British administration, after the appointment of the Political Officer at Gangtok in 1889.

The functions of these religious institutions may be grouped into two categories (i) Religious and (ii) Secular. This distinction was also noticed in functional activities of the monks. Both these functions have gone through changes with the passage of time. After the initial stage of the spread of Buddhism, imparting monastic education was the key function of these monasteries. In addition, the monks also served as doctors, judges, bankers, traders and crisis managers in their localities in addition to performing ritualistic functions. The monasteries that were basically places of worship and rituals also functioned as monastic schools, trade centres and granaries. Traditionally the monastery lands were leased out in terms of grains because there was no provision of storage in the monasteries. Even though there is no mention about the trading activities of the monasteries in the British Reports it is likely that they took part in trade like their counterparts in Tibet. The political role of the monks gradually diminished with the penetration of British power with the Treaty of Titaliya in 1817. The monk, both from Sikkim and Tibet, used to take active part in the politics of Sikkim. They served as ambassador, negotiator and other international policy makers. In the administrative affairs they lost these privilege after the appointment of Political Officer in 1889. Under the guidance of British administration Sikkim witnessed several administrative changes and in the new setup the secular role of the monks became restricted, and they became confined mainly to their estates, although representatives from important monasteries of Pemayangtse and Phudong continued to be included in the state administrative council for some more time. In the post British period, the Sangha seat in the State Council was introduced in 1958 where lamas from selected monasteries could elect one candidate through secret ballot. Normally, the monks contest the Sangha seat and the elected member looks after the Ecclesiastical Affairs. But during the last three Assembly elections they elected member from outside the monk communities and Ecclesiastical Affairs is no longer under his jurisdiction. At present, as per the voters list of the Election Commission of Sikkim there are 3098 voters in 56 monasteries in Sikkim (Table 1). After the merger of state under secular India the role of monk and monastery in the state affairs totally became insignificant but they are very concerned about their heritage. Recently, monk body strongly protested against the establishment of a Hydel Project in the Rathang (chu) basin in West Sikkim. In fact, Rathang chu basin almost overlap with the areas of legendary Demojong (*hBras-mo-Ijong*) It is the homeland of old capitals (Yaksum and Rabdanse) and old monasteries including Pemayangtse and Tashiding. It will be worthwhile to discuss in more detail about the two most important functions of the monastery -Education and Estate management- which also have evolved through the centuries.

Education

Monastery plays an important role in imparting education. An ideal monastery possesses the facility of imparting higher studies through *Sheda* where monks can acquire higher Buddhist studies. In the monastery *Dupta* enables the scholars to utilize their knowledge to train and enlighten their minds. In addition to this it should have a main shrine for worshiping where the students may practice ritualistic systems and works (C. Acharya, 1998, p. 4). A well established *Sheda* and an equally suitable *Dupda* are the two essential components to lend significance and respectability to monastery. It is not always possible to have these two essential organs in all the *Gonps* for many reasons and it is true in the case of Sikkim also.

Initially Sikkim borrowed this monastic education system from Tibet. The model monastery in Tibet which inspired Sikkimese offshoot was the Samye (Tibet), established in 8th century (C. Acharya, 1998, p. 1). In the beginning, Pemayangtse and Tashiding Gonpas and others were sending batches of young monks to Mindrol-Ling and Dorji-Dak monasteries in Tibet for instruction in strict discipline and religious rites. These lamas came back to their respective monasteries and taught whatever they had learned. Only a few people received this education of basically ritualistic practices due to the lack of well organized monastic school in Sikkim (A.C. Sinha, 1987, p. 3) This was the beginning of the Buddhist studies in Sikkim and till the closure of the Tibet border interaction between the monasteries of Tibet and Sikkim remained close in the academic level.

It has been mentioned earlier that the third *Chogyal* introduced the custom of joining the monastery by one child from every Bhutia family which was followed by the other Buddhist communities (Lepcha, Limbu, Tamang, Sherpa etc.) also. In the past, boys from any Buddhist family could get admission to the monastery from the age of seven or eight and each student was placed under one monk. In Pemayangtse however admission was restricted only to the boys of pure Bhutia family. The young student was first taught Tibetan alphabet and afterwards to read, write and recite by heart some special prayer books and so on which took at least two to three years. After that he could be admitted in noviciate. He is ceremoniously shaved, has to take certain vows and take to the dress of monk. He is given a religious name. He has to learn by heart the books of all kinds of rituals. Before being admitted as a junior monk the boy has to work as an apprentice running errands for and helping out the elder monks besides getting trained in making *Tormas* and playing various musical instruments. Monastic discipline started after the entrance to the noviciate and lasted for another two to three years. The second part of the training included blowing copper trumpets, performing religious dances, playing cymbals and the art of making *torma* (votive offering to the gods in the shape of conical cakes) (R.R. Dhamala 1990, p. 61). The monk perfect in ritualistic practices is now free to learn science of language, medicine, astrology and painting etc. He is also given different responsibilities to serve the Gonpa or its over all development. On completing all these services he becomes an important functionary of the Gonpa. However, this system of education was followed only in a few renowned monasteries like Pemayangtse, Tashiding, Phensang, Enchey and Kathok of Nyingma sect and Ralong, Rumtek and Phodong of Kagyudpa sect (C. Acharya, 1998, p. 3-4).

Maharaja Sidkeong Tulku not only granted legal rights to the monastery estate but also opened school in the monasteries. According to 1913-14 Administrative Report of Sikkim, schools were opened in the monasteries of Phudong, Phensong, Rumtek, Pemayangtse and Ralong. At that time there were 29 monks attending the monastic school at Gangtok (Enchay). According to 1917-18 administrative report of Sikkim, Monastery School started at Temi, Pakyong, Rhenock, Kamlet, Chidam, Wok, Chakung, Soreyong, Chambong, Dentham, Rishim and Song. In course of period these monastery schools became defunct because the record of Ecclesiastical Department shows Pemayangtse and Enchey school opened in 1951 and soon other monasteres started their schools (R.R. Dhamala. 1990. p. 61). The closure of the border with Tibet stopped all shorts of interaction which affected the monastic education system in Sikkim. Under this situation to promote the monastic education and to develop ideal monastic setup, Chogal Tashi Namygal established Sheda in Gangtok in the early 1960s. This Sheda was renamed as 'Sikkim Institute for Higher Nyingma Studies. At Rumtek, another such institute offers higher studies to the Kagyupa sect.

During the post merger period those year old monastic schools were reorganized and in 1986, 15 such schools in Enchey, Rumtek, Phodong, Ralong, Tashiding, Lachen, Hee-Gyangthang, Lingthem, Lachung, Ship Kunzang Cholling, Parbing, Rhenock, Chungthang, Singchit Ngodak and Simik. were put under the administrative control of the Ecclesiastical Department. Starting with 15 monastic schools there are now 50 such schools scattered all over the state, mainly located in the rural areas. (C. Acharya, 1998, p. 6) The establishment of monastic schools changed the old monastic education system. One of the main reasons for such change is the declining number of monks for teaching as in the traditional system each student had to be assigned under one monk (R.R. Dhamala. 1990, p. 61) These schools are financed by the Education Department through the Ecclesiastical Department although there are some monastic schools funded by either monastery's own fund or through public contribution. The concerned monasteries have to provide the classroom and accommodation for students. In such school the course extends to a period of five to six years covering more or less the first two phases of the previous system. After the successful completion one can join the Sikkim Institute for Higher Nyingma Studies, Gangtok, which offers courses from intermediate to post-graduate level. The Institute was affiliated to Sampurnananda Sanskrit University in 1983. The courses it offers are Madhyama-four year, Shastri two year and Acharya-three year. Most of the schools do not have any accommodation facilities. The students from nearby villages attend school as day scholars and the number of dropout is high. On the contrary, Dharma Chakra Centre at Rumtek and Gyaltshe Rimpoche Centre at Ralong still offer, more or less, the old monastic education system along with English. A huge number of students are attached to these centers and they are provided with accommodation on the premises.

Estate

Making of grants of land to the monastery and monks by the devotees or *Chogyal* is an year old practice in Sikkim. Each of the five major monasteries have thus accumulated huge tracts of land around the monastery over which the monks and monasteries enjoyed supreme authority (J.C. White reprint, 1986, p. 28). Sikkim witnessed a sharp change in the land management system with the introduction of lease out system of land by the British Administrator in the beginning of the 20th century. Following the implementation of lease out system of cultivated land, it was felt essential to legalize the huge tracts of land under the monk and monastery. In view of this, *Chogyal* Sidkeong Tulku made a grant of certain legal rights to Pemayangtse monastery in 1901 and also demarcated the estate, comprising of twelve revenue blocks and two bazars (R.R. Dhamala 1991, p. 68). In course of time, this system was also implemented in the other monasteries and as per Administrative Report of 1914-15 King personally demarcated the boundary of each monastery in the presence of Surveyor, who mapped the land of each monastery in the presence of lamas (Administrative report, 1914-15, p. 2). In this new system the monastery or monk became the primary holder of the land who could directly lease out the land to the share cropper (locally known as adhia or kut) or the *bustiwallas* who own the holding which is inheritable and transferable and pays taxes to the

Government or the monasteries. Belonging to the different communities of Nepalis, Lepchas, Bhutias etc these bustiwallas used to be the primary holders as per the survey report of 1958. The bustiwallas again leased their land out, on fixed terms and conditions of crops share, to the share cropper (*Adhia* or *Kut*). Besides these, rent free land was given to the *Chakareys*, the servant of the monastery, in lieu of their menial services. As per the Administrative Report of 1915–16 there were 45 monasteries in Sikkim in 1916 of which Pemayangtse, Phudong, Ralong, Rumtek and Kartok were maintained from the land granted against them, 33 received annual grant from the state and 7 were maintained by the people.

The monastery estates held not only cultivable land but a large tract of non-cultivable land including forest and barren land. Though landlordism was abolished in Sikkim in 1949, exemption was granted to the five monasteries and the Raja's private estate. Interestingly, Tashiding received landed estate (Tashiding revenue block) for the first time in the same year. The recommendation of the Land Reform Committee (1975), expressed the need for abolition of monastic estate and thus made significant impact on the age old status of the monastery estates and the economy of the monastery. The detailed picture of the landed estates and their management appeared in the first survey report,1950-58 (Table 3). The income of these estates varies from monastery to monastery and it depends on their area of cultivable and cardamom land, number of bazaars and forest resources (Table 4). In the post merger period the monasteries have gradually lost their control on these lands. The Sikkim Agricultural Land Ceiling and Reform Act of 1977 has limited the holding size of the monastery land to sixty standard acres of land.* Land was classified into three circles based on the locality, productivity of the soil and access to the market. Each was divided into three classes according to altitude (Notification No. 615/LR 1957). Before1973, there were two categories of monastery estates in terms of their management. The monastery estates were either managed by the monastery wing of the Raja's Private Estate (Rumtek and Phudong) or by the *Udor-*

Table 3
Area of the Monastery Estate in Sikkim:1958
(Area in acre)

Monastery Estate	*Cultivated Area*	*Khasland*	*Total Area*	*No. of Revenue Block*
Pemayangtse	7782.36	1759.49	9541.85	12
Phensong	2849.97	2377.21	5227.18	5
Tashiding	917.57	762.09	1678.66	1
Phudong	4317.43	5217.69	9535.03	9
Rumtek	1853.87	779.48	2633.35	5
Ralong	4275.32	2153.50	6428.82	6

Source: Survey and Settlement Report 1958.

Table 4
Income of the Monastery Estate: 1973
(in Rs.)

Source of Income	*Pema-yangtse*	*Phen-song*	*Tashid-ing*	*Phu-dong*	*Rumtek*	*Ralong*
Land rent and Local Rate	7428	2074	947	5172	9700	5000
Forest Royality	8000	1000	—	2732	13700	7000
Cardamom Damthey Khazana	8000	2728	200	5748	—	7000
Bazar	3200	—	—	2402	—	6500

Source: Dhamala, R.R. Monasteries of Sikkim with specific reference to the Economic Structure.Occasional Paper-8. Centre for Himalayan Studies. 1993. op cit p. 25-29.

Tsosum, managing body of the monastery (Pemayangtse, Tashiding, Phensong and Ralong) (R.R. Dhamala 1992, p. 21-22). In both cases, block *mandal* collected the land and other taxes viz. House tax, bazaar tax, forest royalty etc. The Second Survey and Settlement Report of the 1986 shows a drastic reduction in the size of the monastery estates as compared to the 1958 report (First Survey). There are mainly two reasons for such reduction of the monastery land (R.R. Dhamala. 1992, p. 21) (i) The Government acquired the monastery land for different developmental works (including afforestation programme). (ii) During the survey and settlement of 1986, the lease out lands were recorded in the names of bustiwallas as primary holders. In the survey report of 1986, the land recorded under the monastery covers, only those land which the monasteries held as primary holders (major part of this land are under forest, monastery building and negative land like steep slope, bare rock etc.). At present, all the monastery estates are managed by the respective Government departments and handed over 50% revenue to the respective estate. Despite several Government Acts a number of lesser known monasteries of Sikkim still possesses land including cardamom land though their size is very small.

On the recommendation of Sikkim Agricultural Land Ceiling and Reform Act, 1977 each monastery estate receives Rs. 2500/- to meet the expenses of daily and periodic religious rites. At present, about 69 monasteries receive maintenance grant from Ecclesiastical Department (Rs. 12000/- for 17 and Rs. 6000/- for 52 monasteries per year) and rest of the monasteries are not receiving any such grant regularly (Government of Sikkim, Notification of the Ecclesiastical Department No.79/AQSG/EA dt2003/24/4).This amount is not sufficient for any of these monasteries and each monastery depends on the donation from the devotees.

Standard Acres
(Area equivalent to one standard acre)

Land Use	*Paddy & cardamom*			*Dry*			*Banjo#*		
*Class**	*I*	*II*	*III*	*I*	*II*	*III*	*I*	*II*	*III*
CIRCLE									
A	1.00	1.25	1.50	2.00	2.50	3.00	3.00	3.00	3.00
B	1.10	1.37	1.65	2.20	2.75	3.30	3.30	3.30	3.30
C	1.30	1.50	2.00	2.60	3.00	4.00	4.00	4.00	4.00

* I (below 3500′), II (3500-4500′), III (above 4500).
# Uncultivated land
Source: Agricultural Land Ceiling and Land Reform Act, 1977.

In conclusion, it may be said that the monastery is the first and foremost among any kind of institutions in Sikkim. They performed as the pivot of many functions, both religious and temporal, for a long period. But interestingly enough, there has been not a single monastery-based big settlement in Sikkim. It requires further study as to why these monasteries never acted as a growth centre for the neighbourhood. Although recently, the State Govt. is trying hard to preserve these heritage institutes and their localities for tourism purposes.

NOTE

* Land was classified into three circles based on locality, productivity of the soil and access to the market. Each circle was divided into three classes according to altitude (Notification No.615/LR 1957).The following table shows the standard acre in different classes and circles.

REFERENCES

Acharya, C., 'Guru Padmasambhava's Contribution: The Genesis of Buddhism in Sikkim', *Bulletin of Tibetology* ,Vol. 31, (1), 1995.

——— (1998), 'Aspects of Monastic Education in Sikkim', *Bulletin of Tibetology*, Vol. 34 (2).

Basnet, L.B., *Sikkim: A Short Political History*, S. Chand & Co., New Delhi, 1974.

Carraseo, P., *Land and Polity in Tibet*, Seattle University of Washington Press, 1959.

Denjongpa Anna Balikci, 'Kanchendzonga: Secular and Buddhist Perceptions of the Mountain Deity of Sikkim among the Lhopos', *Bulletin of Tibetology* Vol. 38 (2), 2002.

Dhamala, R.R., 'The Monastic Education System in Sikkim'. *The Himalayan Miscellany* Vol. 4, March, 1990.

———, 'A Socio Economic Study of the Pemayangtse Monastery of Sikkim' T.B. Subba and Karubaki Datta (ed) *Religion and Society in the Himalayas*, Gian Publishers, New Delhi, 1991.

——— *Monasteries of Sikkim with Specific Reference to the Economic Structure*, Occasional paper No. 8, Centre for Himalayan Studies, North Bengal University.

Dokhampa, R.N., 'Origin of Bumchu of Dakkar Tashiding', *Bulletin of Tibetology*, Vol. 28 (3), 1992.

———, Notes on the Biography of Lha-Btsun Nam-mkha Jigs-Med (1597-1650) Bulletin of Tibetology, Vol. 30 (3), 1994.

Lepcha, A.D., 'Guru Padmasambhava's contribution to Sikkim', *Bulletin of Tibetology* Vol. 31 (1), 1965.

Ling Trevor, 'Sikkimese Buddhism in the 19th Century' T.B. Subba and Karubaki Datta (ed.) *Religion and Society in the Himalayas,* Gian Publishers, New Delhi, 1991.

Macdonald, A.W., 'Remarks on the Manipulation of Power and Authority in the High Himalaya' *The Tibet Journal* Vol. 12 (1) Spring, 1987.

Namgyal Thutob and Dolma Yeshey, *History of Sikkim.* (MSS), 1908.

Pradhan, K., *Gorkha Conquest: The Process and Consequences of the Unification of Nepal with Special Reference to Eastern Nepal,* Oxford, Calcutta, 1991.

Risley, H.H., 'History of Sikkim and its ruler' in *Gazetteer of Sikkim,* 1894, reprint 1985 B.R. Publisher, New Delhi.

Sinha, A.C., *Politics of Sikkim A Sociological Study*, Thomson, Faridabad, 1975.

———, 'Frontier Feudalism and State Formation in Sikkim' in S. Sinha (ed) T*ribal Politics and State Systems in Pre Colonial Eastern and North-eastern India,* K.P. Bagchi Calcutta, 1987.

Subba, T.B., 'Limbu Ethnicity at Crossroads' Himalayan Miscellany Vol. 5, March, 1990.

Waddell, L.A., 'Lamaism in Sikkim' in *Gazetteer of Sikkim*, 1894, reprint 1985, B.R. Publisher, New Delhi.

White, J.C., *Sikkim and Bhutan: Twenty one Years in North east Frontier 1887-1908*, reprint Manas, New Delhi, 1986.

THE BUDDHIST MONASTERIES OF DARJEELING HILLS

Karubaki Datta

INTRODUCTION

One of the socio cultural characteristics of three hill subdivisions of Darjeeling district, viz. Darjeeling, Kalimpong and Kurseong is the abundance of Buddhist monasteries. This monasteries have been constructed over a long period of time from the 18th century to as late as 1997 when His Highness the Dalai Lama inaugurated the one at Mirik. Big and small, old and new, these monasteries are to be found in almost all the towns and even the villages in the far flung corners of the hills and the tea gardens of Darjeeling.

The lamas residing in and attached to these monasteries are numerous and are regularly visited upon by the Buddhist people of the region for performing the regular religious rites–either in the house of the person who invites them or in the monastery itself.

Very little is known about these monasteries from secondary sources. The District Gazetteers are almost silent about these and so are the common books on Darjeeling. Some Government documents provide the names and locations of these monasteries but these are contradictory at times and cannot be relied upon. To give an example, there are 14 monasteries around Darjeeling town as per the list prepared by the Tourist Department of West Bengal Government. A list of the same also prepared by the District

Administration for the Rajya Sabha in 1995. This second list varies from the first one regarding names and locations of the monasteries. None of the lists is exhaustive and the actual number of monasteries is much more than what has been enumerated. Moreover, the names in the two lists are not identical and there are variations regarding their locations.

The only exceptions are *A Concise History of the Darjeeling District* by Dozey (1922, pp. 76-81) and some travel accounts like *The Way of the White Clouds* by Lama Anagarika Govinda with detailed description of the famous Yiga Choling monastery of Ghoom. (1960) Indira Awasty's book on Pedong *Between Sikkim and Bhutan* (1978) also contains some detailed information about the monasteries situated there. There are a couple of handbook of Tibetan culture giving the names and locations of certain big Tibetan monasteries set up in the recent years. Names and biographical sketches of some eminet and contemporary Tibetan monks can also be found from these (P. Loris and Julie Foakes, 1996, Graham Coleman 1993).

The objective of this paper is to give an overall descriptive account of these monasteries-their location, history and community or sect wise affiliation. Attempt has been made as much as possible to find out an approximate number of the inmates and novices along with some information about their economic resources.

The following account is based on personal visit at the monasteries and discussion with the inmates or knowledgeable persons from the neighbourhood in 1997-98. However, the lamas were often found to be ignorant or secretive about the history or resources of the monasteries and in some cases language also posed a problem. As a result, the information thus collected sometimes tended to be incomplete or superficial. In absence of secondary sources, they could not be substantiated. Some information, particularly those of the new Tibetan monasteries were collected from brochures published by the particular monasteries or sects containing the biographies of their eminent lamas and activities and achievements of the sect. These books are generally not available outside. The information gathered from these could, to some extent be verified from the above mentioned handbooks.

Yet, in spite of these limitation it is expected to give an overall idea about the history, resources and functions of these monasteries which are otherwise not easily available. The present study, however, does not claim to be exhaustive. Even though personal visit was paid to almost all the monasteries mentioned here, in the absence of any comprehensive list of these numerous monasteries it is possible that some have been left out of the discussion.

THE BUDDHIST CONNECTION OF DARJEELING DISTRICT

Historically, the district of Darjeeling used to be a part of the Kingdom of Sikkim whose boundary-extending from Thangla near Phari in Tibet in the North to Tagongla near Paro in Bhutan in the East and from Titaliya or Kishenganj in Bihar in the South to Tamur river in Nepal was much bigger than what it is today. Much of the area what comprises the present day Darjeeling district was handed over by the Chogyal (the king of Sikkim) to the British East India company in 1835. This included "......... all the land south of the great Rangit river East of the Balasur, Kahail and little Runjeet river and most of the Rungno and Mahanaddi rivers......." (L.S.S. O'Malley, reprint 1985, p. 21) The area was basically an uninhabited region at that time.

The present day subdivision of Kalimpong came to be attached to Darjeeling in 1865. This place too was originally a part of Sikkim which had been occupied by Bhutan during the war with Sikkim in 1770 to be converted to its Dalimkot Suba. Bhutan returned it to the East India Company after its defeat in the Anglo Bhutan War of 1865. The British joined Darjeeling to give the final shape to the district.

Although both these regions were basically uninhabited at the time of annexation, the people, however few they might have been in terms of number, shared the same Buddist culture that prevailed in the two states of Sikkim and Bhutan.

In addition to historic ties, the economic relations between Darjeeling and Tibet further enhanced this influence and strengthened the religious bonds between these regions. Kalimpong, particularly the area of Pedong was important to the economy of this region. This is because the traditional route of trade with Lhasa in Tibet passed through this region. Tibetan traders used to bring wool, borax, salt, musk and medicinal herbs to carry back cotton and woolen goods, matches, soap, needle, tobacco, dried fruit, sugar, hardware and precious stones from Kalimpong. The route from Tibet to Kalimpong passed through Jelep-la pass and Nathang. Even though this was basically controlled by Rajputana and Haryana traders it is possible that besides Tibetans a number of Bhutias from Sikkim were their intermediate trading partners conveying goods from Nathula and Jelepla passes from Kalimpong and back to Tibetan border.

Hence, from an early time, small settlements of Tibetans and Bhutias had sprung up along the trade routes as staging houses, strorage points and transit trading centres. There is a small Tibetan community in Pedong whose ancestry can be traced to the Tibet trading times.

Later, in order to further British aims to secure tradind facilities, the British completed an unpaved road to Jelepla in 1879. This road passed through Pedong. Later, the British expendition against the Tibetans also passed though Pedong in 1888 (Indira Awasty, 1978, pp. 14-17).

THE PEOPLE WHO PRACTICE BUDDHISM IN DARJEELING

The two major groups of people to practice Tibetan Buddhism are the Lepchas and the Bhutias who were the original inhabitants of the region. Initially, the Lepchas used to be animists. They were converted to Buddhism by the Bhutias who had brought this religion with them from Tibet, Bhutan or Sikkim. The Lepchas, concentrated mainly in Kalimpong, have now again converted to Christianity and only a few have retained their faith in Buddhism and even a fewer in animism. The Bhutias on the contrary are Buddhists almost without exception. Now, both the communities are given the status of S.T., but it is well nigh impossible to find out their exact number.

The percentage of S.T. population is quite high in Darjeeling. According to the census report of 1981 the percentage of population was 14.75 as against the all West Bengal percentage of 5.63. The individual percentage in hill towns of Darjeeling, Kalimpong and Kurseong were 13.84, 7.55, and 14.21 respectively. To this population belong the Bhutias, the Lepchas and some tea garden labourers of tribal origin as well. Thus, the total number of S.T. population does not indicate the number of only Bhutias and Lepchas.

These Bhutias, who are people of Tibetan origin are not homogeneous. L.S.S. O' Malley, in his Darjeeling District Gazeteer used the term to denote four groups of people. The Sikkimese Bhutias- A mixed race of Tibetans and Lepchas, they are the descendants of Tibetans who had settled in Sikkim a few centurues ago.

2. Sherpa Bhutias- who had come from East of Nepal. 3. Drukpa or Dharma Bhutias whose home was originally in Bhutan and 4. The Tibetan Bhutias from Tibet. (L.S.S.O. Malley, reprint 1985, p. 21).

The large number of Tibetan refugees who have settled down in Kalimpong and Darjeeling are also Buddhists. The political uncertainty in Tibet had initiated the process of migration of Tibetans to this area much earlier even though the actual flight of the nation began with the Chinese invasion around 1950 and culminated into large scale influx in 1959. Almost 80,000 people fled and arrived in India with the Dalai Lama as 'refugees'. Those who had arrived before that do not enjoy status even though their number is considerable. We do not have the actual number of this refugee population in Darjeeling district. The total population of the Tibetan refugees in Kalimpong, Darjeeling and Sikkim together was 8854 in 1976 while in 1978 a special report on them estimated their population to be more than 10.000. In Kalimpong alone the number reported in 1976 and 1978 are 1973 and 2300 respectively. (T.B.Subba 1990.p.39)

There are some Buddhists among the Nepalis as well. The Tamangs, the Sherpas and the Yolmos are Buddhists but they do not enjoy the status of S.T.s The Tamangs claim to be the largest single group to practice Buddhism. However, their religion is not a pure from of Buddhism and some Hindu elements have been mixed with it.

As per the census data the percentage of population by religion in Darjeeling district is like this:

Table 1
Population by Religion

Religion	*Population (81)*	*Population (91)*	*% of total (81)*	*% of total (81)*
Buddhist	120846	155295	11.8	11.9
Total	1024269	1299929	100.0	100.0

The Buddhist monasteries of Darjeeling hills have been set up by these variours groups of Buddhist people of this region.

CLASSIFICATION OF MONASTERIES

Numerous as they are, these monasteries can be classified variously on the basis of their date of foundation, their affiliation to a particular community or adherence to a particular sect. This classification, however, is not very exhaustive because not all the monasteries, particularly the old ones have maintained authentic and reliable information about their origin and date of foundation. We can at best make a tentative assumption about the period when they were founded. Nor is the community wise classification a convenient one. Even though these monasteries are generally set up and managed by the Associations of particular communities, no monastery can be said to be serving any single community as such. The rituals and the liturgies are more or less the same and it is not rare for Buddhists from other communities also to visit these to offer their prayers and invite the lamas to perform the routine rituals either in their house or in the monastery. The ethnic composition of the inmates are varied and there is very little apparent difference between a Tibetan monastery and a monastery belonging to some other community. The same can be said about their classification on the basis of their sects. All the monasteries preach Tibetan Buddhism and all of them are structured on the model of the big monasteries of Tibet. There are of course some minor variations in the practices of the particular sects but they are not generally discernible to the eyes of the lay outsiders.

However, we think it will be convenient to make a broad division between 1. The monasteries that had been founded by various communities at various points of time and 2. Those founded by the Tibetans after 1959 with or without the blessing and active patronage of some eminent Tibetan monks who had fled from their own monasteries in Tibet. These monasteries of the second category are different from the previous ones both in terms of their resources as well as their objectives.

In the first section we will discuss about the older monasteries about their community and sect affiliation as well as their resource and activities and then give an account of new monasteries set up by the refugee lamas and finally point out the overall qualitative difference between the two.

MONASTERIES FOUNDED BY THE LOCAL COMMUNITIES AT VARIOUS POINTS OF TIME

Community affiliation

Buddhism was introduced in the region initially from Tibet. Accordingly, there are certain monasteries that are known as Tibetan while most other monasteries are known by the name of the communities whose need they serve. The Yiga Choling monastery of Ghoom as well as the four old monasteries in Tirpai, Ghoom, Kurseong and Pedong are known as Tibetan. One of the reasons of this is that they had accepted Tomo Geshe Rimpoche a well known lama from the Dunkhar monastery of Tibet as their patron and they maintained regular contact with Tibet. *Sometimes, monasteries founded by certain groups of people of certain communities were handed over to Tibetan Rimpoches. This is the case with some

Tamang monasteries like Peshak but they are not called Tibetan monasteries and very much remained as monasteries of the Tamangs.

There are two old monasteries in Darjeeling town- viz. those of Bhutia Basti and Ging that had been founded under the patronage of some premier monasteries of Sikkim. These two are commonly described as Bhutia monasteries.

Lepchas are a community to practice Buddhism since the 17th century and accordingly, they have some gombas (monastery) in and around the town of Kalimpong. The bigger among these and run by the Lepcha Buddhist Association is the in lower Bong Basti while the Mani Lepcha gomba-a private one, is housed in the residential premises of a Lepcha family in the outskirts of the town. There used to be another Lepha gomba at Kashiog but this is almost defunct now, we have not come across any Lepcha gomba in the town of Darjeeling. Perhaps the reason is that the Lepchas of Darjeeling have converted to Christianity en masse.

In Pedong, Kalimpomg, there are two small communities of Sikkimese and Drukpas. The Sikkimese are said to be an offshoot of Bhutia people who had initially migrated from Sikkim.

The Drukpas have their Gomba in Sakyong, Pedong. In fact, as a result of the course of history of this region, there used to be several Drukpa monasteries here. Originally the place was a Lepcha settlement where the Bhutanese Drukpas migrated to settle in after the place was won over by the Bhutanese. In order to implant their authority and to serve the Drukpas the Bhutanese Shabdung set up this monastery in the mid 18th century. Two more monasteries were set up – known as the Chowsang and the Kagai gombas. In addition to these, some more Drukpa monasteries which have now been destroyed are the Hecheka monastery in the 13th mile and the Chumachen monastery in the 20th mile. Monasteries are also said to have been set up near the two Lepcha forts Tamsang and Dalim which were taken over by the Bhutanese from them.

Previously there used to be a Drukpa monastery in Kurseong also near the graveyard. It was not a full fledged monastery but rather a chapel for prayer with one lama who is dead now. Previously, there used to be some Drukpa ladies but most were married to Nepalis and probably there is no one in the chapel now to look after their interest.

The Sikkimese of Pedong too maintain their gomba which is actually a chapel for prayer rather than a full fledged monastery.

There is a second Bhutanese monastery in Rishi Road Kalimpong. This one is called Bhutanese because of its connections with the Royal Family of Bhutan. The managing committee is still headed by the Queen Mother and also many of the inmates are from Bhutan.

The Sherpas have several monasteries. Of these, one is privately owned by a family in Darjeeling while a much bigger one is at Sonada. Since the Sherpas are in majority in Sonada there is a Sherpa Association and like any other Association it too maintains the monastery for the interest of its community. The name of the monastery is Samdup Targeling Sherpa Buddhist monastery.

The Durpin monastery in Kalimpong too is commonly known as the Sherpa monastery. The term is misleading as the monastery is neither founded nor maintained solely by the Sherpa community. The monastery was actually founded in the 1950s when there was a Tsechu Association comprising all the Buddhists of this region–the Lepchas, Sikkimese, Bhutanese etc. The chogyals (kings) of Sikkim also had connections with them and there were other patrons from Sikkim. In coures of time, however, most of the communities lost interest in the activities of the Association and with drew from it. Only the Sherpas remained and Mr. T.N. Sherpa, a businessman, the Secretary of the Association took renewed interest in it and built the monastery anew. The Yolmos too have their monastery in Darjeeling.

Sects

Almost all the major sects of Tibetan Buddhism are represented in Darjeeling district. These sects are Nyingma, Kagyu (with sub sects of Drukpa and Karma), Gelugpa and Sakya.

In Sikkim, the two sects that used to enjoy premier position are Nyingma and Kagyu while the sect that enjoyed patronage in Bhutan was Drukpa. As a result of Darjeeling's long connections with these places, many of the monasteries adhere to these two sects. Since the monasteries of Bhutia Basti and Ging were established as branches of Phodong and Pemayangtse, these belong to Karma and Nyingma sects respectively.

The Nyingmas have some more monasteries in and around Darjeeling. The Phuntsog Nyabchorling in Jorebunglow is one of these. Originally a Drukpa monastery, it was later handed over to Zate Rimpoche, the famous lama of the Nyingma sect and expanded under his advice. This monastery has a kind of branch in Lopchu. The Bhutanese monastery of Rishi Road, Kalimpong also belong to this sect and so do the Sherpa monasteries.

The Sikkimese monastery of Pedong and the Yolmo monastery of Darjeeling belong to the Karma Kagyu sect. Subordination to Bhutan had introduce the predominance of the Drukpas in the region of Kalimpong. Of the two Lepcha gombas, the one in lower Bong Basti belongs to the Sahebrung ngonam branch of the Drukpa sect while the Mani Lepcha gomba as well as the Sanchen Dorje gomba of the Drukpas of belong to the Kagyu sect of whose sub-sect the Drukpas are. There were probably some more monasteries in Kalimpong when it was incorporated into the British jurisdiction but these can no more be identified now. Dozey, for example, has mentioned a Buddhist monastery as one of the buildings in the town. He says that this was named the Trongsa gompa which was under the jurisdiction of the Kagyu section. (Dozey 1977, p. 174).

A Tentative Chronology

According to the available historical information the first monastery of Sikkim was built in 1701 at Dubdi and since then monasteries have been constructed almost regularly for a period of 3000 years. Since Darjeeling used to be a part of Sikkim, it is likely that the Darjeeling monasteries were built after 1701.

Some monasteries in Kalimpong, however, claim to be older than this. To give an example, of the two Lepcha monasteries in

Kalimpong, the one of the Bong Basti claims 1690 to be its date of foundation. Tradition has it that the first Lepcha monastery of the region was founded in 1690 in Durpin in Kalimpong town. At that time it was known as Gong Lho. It had an area of about 40 acres. It also had its branches at Sindaybung, Menchu. The monastery used to be quite active till 1865, when after the Bhutan War the British authority was extended to the region. First they asked the monastery to vacate this place and later, forcibly dismantled it without even paying any compensation. It was established for the second time in 1920 in its present site on land donated by Lepchas. The landslide of 1968 destroyed part of it-its kitchen and the Dharamsala which had to be rebuilt. The Mani Lepcha gomba is said to be 300 years old.

All this is based on tradition and cannot be verified. Buddhism was formally ushered into Sikkim after 1642 and Lepchas were gradually converted to this religion. In the absence of any historical document all we can guess is that these had initially started as small chapels around these times and were elevated to the rank of monasteries only in course of time.

The Bhutanese monastery in Kalimpong town gives 1680 as the year in which it was founded. In the absence of any historical proof in support of such claims, it is difficult either to accept or to reject such claims.

The Drukpa and the Sikkimese monasteries of Pedong, Kalimpong also claim to be very old. The former claims 1705 as the date of its foundation while the latter is said to have been establised in 1832 or 35. The date 1705 is based on tradition. Indira Awasti holds that it was built in 1836. Its named Sangchen Dorji is given after a sort of Governor or agent of Bhutan Government who had built a number of social services including a school at Sakyoung. (Indira Awasty, 1978, p. 69)

In the Darjeeling town itself, the monastery in the Bhutia Basti is regarded as the oldest one. According to Dozey this was originally built in 1765 and stood on the Observatory Hill. It was loted and sacked by the Nepalese in 1815 leaving only a small shrine called Mahakaal on the site which once marked its location. What remained of it was transferred in 1860-61 to the North East of St. Andrew's Church and it was finally removed to the Bhutia Basti in 1878-79. (E.C. Dozey. 1977, p. 79).

The Ging monastery, the formal name of which is Sanchhenthong Delling Gomba was founded in 1818. Dozey has given some information about its initial location. "Three miles to the North of the town is reached by the Rangit Road to the East of the Mall. It was originally situated below the village of Ging but was demolished under certain political differences after 1860-61. When these differences were settled in 1879 after the Sikkim trouble by Late Sir Ashley Eden, a thatched structure was erected on the present site which in 1896-98 was rebuilt in stone through the exertions of the present High priest, Lodio Lama, to which, let it be added no contributions were received from the Pemionchi body". (E.C. Dozey, 1977, p. 80).

Many monasteries were established in course of the early 20th century. Among them are the famous Tibetan monasteries of the region.

The Yiga Choling monastery was founded by a famous Mongolian monk Lama Sherap Gyaltsho in 1850 who had initially come to India in 1820s. It is not very clear whether it was he who laid the foundation stone of the monastery or it was already there when he came and it was handed over to him. Dozey also mentions this monastery in his work even though he gives 1875 as the date of its foundation. Interestingly, he adds that it was 'intended primarily as a place for political meetings more than as monastery'. He further adds that it used to receive a grant of Rs.60 per menses from the Government, was managed by a Secretary and a Committee and had some 50 monks in residence. 'On 27th March, 1918, this monastery was the center of much interest for some 5000 people visited it on the day to witness the unveiling and consecration of an image of Champa or Maitreya, the coming 5th Buddha. This huge image, which is over 15 ft. in height was constructed under the personal supervision of 'Trome Gishay Rimpoche' an eminent lama of Chumbi. The construction proceeded almost day and night until the image was completed in the course of a single month and cost some 25,000 Rs.' Lama Govinda has given a majestic description of the interior of the monastery, the statue of Maitreya, the frescoes on the wall along with all other details of the actual temple or the chapel (Lama Anagarika Govinda p. 12-16).

The Samten Choling Gelugpa monastery at Ghoom started as an offshoot of Yiga Choling in 1952. According to the inmates of the same, it was founded by one Minjur Babu. Since some corruption had set in among the monks of Yiga Choling who were accused or flouting the Gelugpa norms, some monks, who felt unhappy there shifted to this monastery and then it was offered to Dumo Geshe who was also the Rimpoche of three other Gelugpa monasteries of Kurseong, Kalimpong and Pedong.

Majority of the other monasteries are said to have been founded later. Of the other Tibetan monasteries, the one in Kurseong is said to be the oldest. Tashi Choling by name, it was founded in 1919 by a Tibetan- Jambay Chobayla, who received the title Sardar Bara Injungla by British. He was a railway contractor by profession but a devout Gelupa by religion. When Dumo Geshe Rimpoche visited the place, he accepted him as his mentor and handed him over the monastery.

Thurpa Choling Gelugpa Monastery at Tirpai, Kalimpong was founded in 1925 though we do not know by whom and under what circumstances. It too accepted Dumo Geshe as its Rimpoche. The same Lama is the mentor of the Gelugpa monastery of Pedong, Kalimpong.

The Tamang monasteries have been constructed almost throughout the century under the initiative and supervision of the local Tamang Buddhist Associations. The monastery of Darjeeling is one of the oldest in the region being founded in 1926 while the one in Kalimpong is built only recently in 1987.

The Sherpa monasteries too were built early in the 20th century. The one in Darjeeling was set up as early as 1924 while the one in Sonada ascribes 1952 as the date of its foundation. The Tschesu monastery of Durpin, Kalimpong commonly called the Sherpa mpnastery was founded sometime in 1950s. The Yolmos claim to have founded their monastery early in the 20th century, in 1914.

Some General Observations

In spite of the differences in their sects and community affiliations, there are many similarities among these monasteries. Some of these are registered bodies while other are not but almost all have their own managing committees. All the communities have their particular associations and the maintenance and general administration of the monasteries are looked after by these associations. Since all the religious ceremonies of the Buddhists are performed by the lamas, the lamas are in great need in the society. Almost all the monasteries have several lamas attached to them though not all of them live in the monastery premises. The sects, other than the Gelugpas, do not insist on the practice of celibacy by their monks and most of the lamas, as a result of this, are family men living in their own houses in the nearby villages. Performing the functions of the monasteries can at best be described as their part time job. They usually pursue their own professions–generally that of agriculturists–and gather at the monastery only at the time of the big annual festivals or any other grand occasion. Usually, one or two live in the monastery premise to perform the daily rituals twice or thrice in the chapel. They usually train up some young boys to perform the rituals but almost all monastery authorities complain about the dwindling number of such young boys interested in the task. The reason behind this is said to be the lack of resources in the monasteries and the incentives for becoming a lama. As trainee they learn to perform the various rituals and pick up the Tibetan language in order to read and recite the scriptures but have neither the necessity nor the inclination to go for higher studies in the philosophy of Buddhism.

As to the question of income of the monasteries it was found that even though some monasteries have some properties of their own almost all complain about dwindling income and lack of funds for maintenance. The expenses in general are met from the fees and the donations that the lamas receive by performing the routine rituals for the common people-either in their houses or in the monastery chapel itself. Some expenses like those of maintenance and repair works arc either borne by the associations or subscription is raised from the neighborhood. In some cases, they have received some occasional aids from the Central Government as well.

Here we have tried to collect some information regarding the activities and the resources of some of these monasteries. Needless to say, that since much of it is based on the oral account of the monks themselves it is not always very clear and leaves much to be desired.

Rent Free Holdings of the Monasteries

Going back to the beginning of the 20th century we come across some documents that show that prior to their incorporation into the British territory some of these monasteries held vast tracts of rent free land. At the time of settlement, the British officers too allowed them to hold these plots. Some of monasteries mentioned in the reports do not exist any more even those that still do, complain of having lost their holdings to the families of the lamas or the leaseholders in whose names the plots were recorded.

In the report of C.A. Bell, the Settlement Officer of Kalimpong, dated 21.7.1903 there is some information about the extent of rent land held by some local monasteries and hermitages in or around Pedong. (From C.A. Bell, I.C.S. Settlement Officer, Kalimpong, to the Deputy Commissioner of Darjeeling, dated Kalimpong, 21st July 1903 [camp Pedong], Boards Mis Form No. 162. General Department).

The total area of rent free grants was 617 acres. The rationale behind these grants was that the lamas already held their land without paying capitation tax and that "great weight should be allowed to the customs of the Bhutan Government and the feelings of the people in considering the claims of these lamas to remain on with paying rent."

The report of the previous Settlement Officer Mr. Merendin is also referred to and extensively quoted. He too had advocated that each monastery should have assigned to it a grant of land proportionate to its size, rent free and in no way subordinate to the

Mandal within whose local limit it might fall. The names of the monasteries and the rent free area held by them are given and is being reproduced here.

Table 2
Rent Free Holdings as per Merendin's Report

Monasteries	*Rent Free area (acres)*
Khangoir	46.15
Pheydong	107.52
Chumichain	72.29
Mani	6.38
Pagong	41.15
Khagay	23.54
Rissom	20.45
Phara	Outside surveyed area

While Pheydong seems to indicate the Sanchen Dorji Drukpa monastery at Pendong Chumachain too belonged to the same sect and the community but has become defunct now. The others can no longer be specifically identified.

C.A. Bell suggested that a few monasteries and hermitages be give rent free grant of their then holdings subject to a maximum of 30 acres in each case. This maximum was to apply only to the monasteries in Dabling and Git whose actual holdings were excessive in comparison with the works performed by them. The total area thus granted was estimated to be 183 acres.

Table 3
Rent Free Holding as per C.A. Bell's Report

Name of Block	*Area of Holding*	*Area proposed to begranted*
Gammabum	24.98	24.98
Dabling	69.02	30.00
Git	9.02	9.02

RESOURCES AND OTHER ACTIVITIES OF THE MONASTERIES

The old Tibetan monasteries of Kurseong and Kalimpong used to be big and busy establishments earlier. As a result of their direct connection with Tibet through Dumo Geshe, the places were regularly visited upon by Tibetan monks–usually from Dumo Geshe's own monastery in Yatung. As a matter of practice, at least 5 lamas used to visit Kurseong every year. The practice gradually died down following the Chinese invasion of Tibet.

The present reincarnation of the great Dumo Geshe now resides in America where he is attached to several Buddhist centres. He can easily raise funda for his monasteries in India.

The Tashi Choeling–Gelugpa Monastery of Kurseong however, does not request for any such favour and try to raise resources on its own. The building of the monastery has been expanded and an additional story added. The annexure is rented out and it yields revenue. Money is also raised from performing monthly pujas. Though the number of Tibetans have now dwindled in Kurseong as a result of intermarriages and there are only about 40 Houses of Tibetans or Bhutias in Kurseong every household arranges at least one Puja once a month. It had received grant from Delhi only once about a decade ago.

Previously, the monastery used to run a school to teach Tibetan to the laymen's children. This was closed down there being no more the need to do so after the opening of Government run Tibetan schools in Sonada, Darjeeling and Kalimpong.

Thurpa Choling Gelugpa Monastery at Tirpai is much bigger than this one in Kurseong both in terms of area and the number of its inmates. There are about 35 lamas attached to it and living there though they often go out for various duties elswewhere. Some of them are very old and speak only Tibetan. Some of the lamas are from Sikkim. (This is because in spite of the large number of monasteries in Sikkim none of them belong to the Gelug sect. According to one, recently one has been founded in North Sikkim.) The monastery building is under the process of renovation and extension. The regular rituals are therefore performed elsewhere in a nearby place. The work is going on since 1993.

This monastery however, admitted of receiving funds for renovation from Dumo Geshe in America. In addition to this and the donations received by the lamas from the routine rituals the monastery had also received a grant from the Government in 1989. Finally, it has some landed property of its own.

In the village of Kagoi it owns 22 acres of land that it had received as donation as early as 1937. At present it is given on Adhia to one Jung Bahadur Gurung who actually cultivates it. The owner of the land was one Tashi Yungjum Bhutiani, who was a resident of the Bong Basti, a Buddhist by religion and a 'landholder' by occupation.

It possesses the second plot of land in Kalimpong itself. The lamas showed the sale deed of the land–of the size of 4.57 acres in Bhalukhopa Basti in Government Estate of Kalimpong for Rs. 5500. According to the document, the land was purchased by Nwagang Kesang Bhutia who was the son of late Sangey Bhutia of Kalimpong who was a cultivator by profession. The lamas of the monastery have no idea about how the land came into their possession and merely said that it was the Rimpoche who purchased the land. The Rimpoche's actual name was Nwagang no doubt but it is not clear whether it was he who purchased the land or it was purchased by someone else-by the same name and donated to the monastery.

Among the other Gelugpa monasteries the Samten Choling Monastery at Ghoom too has its own sources of income and does not seem to be suffering from any lack of funds. It owns a plot of land at Pedong that yields about 30 quintals of rice. They have a centre for weaving carpets that are sold in Bhutan and own about 15 cows. They also receive occasional aid from Seva Kendra in Pradhan Nagar, Siliguri. They have received Government aid of about Rs. 60/70,000.

The Gelugpas insist on pursuit of Knowledge and this ideal is followed by this monastery. There are about 41 monks all of whom reside in the monastery itself. The monastery runs a school for them. In the primary classes they study languages like Tibetan and English. They however do not have any separate teacher for English.

The task is being performed by the Tibetan boys who know the language and live in the monastery. Their actual study of Buddhist Philosophy and literature continues for about 11 years. This is done in the monastery itself under the guidance of senior monk teachers. After completion, those who have aptitude, go for even higher studies in the newly setup universities at Sera, Drepung, Ganden etc. in the South.

Government aid of about Rs. 40,000 was also received by Yiga Chjoling monastery. Now the monastery has about 15 resident lamas and houses one library. Previously they used to run aschool but that has been closed down now.

As already mentioned, the Sanchen Dorjee Gomba of Pedong is one of the oldest and the most important monasteries of the region. (Indira Awasty, 1978, pp. 69–77) There are about 15/16 lamas. Since celibacy is a prerequisite only for the head lama and not for the other all of these lamas are ordinary family men living in their own houses and gathering at the monastery only occasionally to perform the rituals at the time of the festivals or the pujas. As is common with most of the other monasteries of the region-these lamas lived in the surrounding villages cultivating their small plots of land.

Their Rimpoche was originally from Bhutan. Jigme Tensing by name, he developed some problem with Bhutanese government in 1930 as a result of which he had to leave Bhutan. He stayed in this Gomba till his reconciliation with the Bhutan Government took place, He went back and died in Bhutan in 1945 at an young age. No incarnation has appeared as yet and the monastery is with any Rimpoche now.

Though an old and important institution of the region, the monastery suffers from acute shortage of funds and in absence of any resource of its own runs basically on donations. It earns a little bit of money by selling bamboo's. Previously it used to own more than 100 acres of land that it has failed to retain. The land used to be cultivated by the lamas. In course of time, these plots of land have remained in the possession of the families even if no one has bothered to take up the profession of lama. On the other hand, the acute economic crunch is also dissuading the young generation from joining the profession.

The monastery used to run school which has shifted to the town now. The primary school, Sanchen Dorjee by name is also known as the club school.

Khaggyocholing-the Sikkimese monastery of the same place is much more modest in terms of resources. It caters to the small Sikkimese population on whose subscription it survives. They donate Makai and some money for its maintenance. The land of the monastery was originally donated by a Sikkimese and it was also with their donation that the last renovation of the building was implemented in 1986. The monastery is actually a small chapel, amidst a small plot of land where the senior resident lama grows some vegetable for his personal consumption. He has been living there for three generations now accompanied by a young boy whom he is training in the work of performing the routine rituals. However, the lamas here used to be some sort of specialists at the death ceremony. A number of death scrolls used to hang in the main temple. (Indira Awasty, 1978, p. 77).

The Bong Lepcha Gomba is placed under the management of the Lepcha Buddhist Association which is a registered body. The association has taken initiative to generate funds through Government sources and utilize it for the upkeep of the monastery premises. They first made application to the Ministry of Human Resources of the Central Government in 1991. They received money of about Rs. 30,000 for two or three times though not very regularly. The Government aid was used for repairing the ground floor, rewiring etc. Now it is in need of far total renovation, extension etc. They made appeals to the West Bengal Governments, M.L.A.s, the Minister of Tribal Welfare etc. but to no avail. So they made another direct appeal to the Ministry of Human Resource Development, Department of Cultural Affairs through the Himalayan Buddhist Cultural Association. In 1996, they received Rs. 35,000. The Gomba has no water connection. The present

Secretary has taken the initiative. She has tried all the possible sources and finally approached the M.L.A.s. They are expecting to get a grant of 25,000 to set up the line of drinking water from the P.H.E. of the D.G.H.C.

It also has a small plot of rent free land adjacent to the monastery-little less than an acre where he grows some maize and millet. The lama has some land of his own in some distant village area which too he cultivates. Whatever he earns he uses for his family and from that he also meets the expenses of the daily rituals of the monastery, like lighting the lamp and offering some fruits etc. In addition to him, there are some 7 or 8 more lamas who are attached to this monastery. They all live in their own houses in the surrounding villages.

The jurisdiction of the monastery covers the areas of Bong Basti, Dungra, Bhalukhola, Porvang, Nassey.

The second Lepcha gomba, the Mani Gomba by name in the upper Sindaybong area in Kalimpong town is located in the household premises of a particular family. The old monastery building is said to have been destroyed by fire. The present head of the family is Nim Dorjee whose ancestores had founded the monastery. There are about 18 Lepcha families and the Gomba is attended by them. There are about 8 lamas all of whom live in their own houses only to assemble at the monastery at the time of the festivals. The family owns about 7 acres of land and the expenses of the rituals and the festivals are met with from this income. So far, it has not received any aid from the government.

It maintains a cordial relation with the Bhutanese monastery in the town of Kalimpong. It also receives occasional aid from the Queen Mother of Bhutan and some of their novice lamas also receive their training in the Bhutanese monastery.

The Durpin Monastery of Kalimpong, as already mentioned has passed through various phases of expansion. A stupa in the monastery still exists which comes from the previous structure. Construction of this present structure was completed only in 1975. The head lama, Dunzom Rimpoche laid the foundation stone of the present monastery. He has passed away now but has two incarnations. One is a Tibetan living at Tibet now and the other is from Bhutan living at present in Nepal. Otherwise also, the monastery used to maintain connections with Tibet. At the time of the foundation of its original building it had received two sets of Kangyur and Tangyur from the Dalai and the Panchen Lamas of Tibet. Dunzon Rimpoche, the Lama, who laid the foundation stone of this present monastery has been dead for some years now. He has two tulkus one of whom is from Bhutan living in Nepal at present, while the other one is a Tibetan and lives in Tibet.

The Tsechu Association gets aid from the Government for repair works. The money is used for maintenance and renovation of the gomba. Construction of the present monastery was over only in 1975.

There are around 60 monks including the very young ones. The lamas also earn from donations by performing the regular rituals.

The monastery has now started its own sheda. It is attended by monks who have come for higher studies from different parts of the country as far as from Himachal Pradesh and Ladakh. It offers a 9 years course of study. The teachers are the senior lamas from the south particularly from Namdorling which is the biggest monastery of the Nyingamas in India. After completion of the course the monks either join the different monasteries as teachers or go to the south for futher specialisation in medicine, meditation etc. The shedas is financially helped by the Queen mother of Bhutan–the present king's grandmother. She had given a lump sum amount of money that had been deposited in a Bhutanede bank and the interest is withdrawn for meeting the expenses of the sheda. The monks however complained of shortage of funds mainly due to rising costs.

The Sheda consists of the permanent members of the gomba. They can either be laymen or monks i.e. the lamas who can marry and those who cannot. The monks who are the permanent residents are either students of the sheda or are ordinary monks performing the rituals.

The name of the monastery in the Rishi Road, Kalimpong, which is commonly known as the Bhutanese monastery is Dechhen Choling. It is known as the Bhutanense monastery because it is still under the patronage of the Queen Mother of Bhutan and she bears all the expenses of the monastery. It is said to have owned about 50 acres of land most of which it has lost now.

The Head lama of the monastery is comparatively young and after completing his studies under the tutelage of a senior monk at Deorali, Sikkim he is now studying and practicing meditation in Kathumandu.

There are about 60 students most of them being form Bhutan and only a few are from Sikkim or surrounding areas. There are two lama teachers at present for giving them training in the rituals as well as the Tibetan language. Though there is no such facility at present, they are going to make arrangement for a teacher to come and teach them English.

As already mentioned, the two important monasteries of the town and surroundings of Darjeeling are those of Bhutia Basti and Ging.

The actual name of the Bhutia Busti monastery in Darjeeling is Kasma Dorje Monastery. It still maintains its connection with the Phodong monastery of Sikkim. In fact, out of 20 lamas attached to this, 10 are from Sikkim itself. About 10 of them live in the monastery while 10 others, known as Gelongs are married householders and live elsewhere only to gather at the monastery on special occasions.

It also receives a sum of Rs. 2,000 per annum from the Governmnt of Sikkim as aid. The resident lamas however, lamented about the shortage of both funds and lamas. The chham (a festival with religious masked dance performed by the lamas), that they used to organise every year has stopped now. The donations they raise from the neighborhood is not enough and the last chham was organized some eight years ago.

One of the important festivals of the monastery is the chhecho or the monthly Puja of the Padmasambhava. The celebration of the

Buddha Purnima is the biggest ceremony when processions are taken out by all the inmates of the monastery. The monks of this monastery also visit the Mahakaltemple regularly to perform the rituals and whatever they receive in return is spent for the monastery. In fact, a part of the food expenses of the resident lamas are met from the fund of the Mahaka temple. This is because the temple was previously a gomba which was later taken over by he Hindus. Even now, there are said to be two Kagyu lamas attached to the temple.

The Ging monastery, the formal name of which is Sanchhenthong Delling Gompa is said to have been established in 1818 as a branch of Pemayantse–the premier monastery of Sikkim. The head lama, who is in charge of the monastery and lives in the premises to perform the daily rituals was trained in Pemayangtse monastery itself for about 10 years. He maintains regular contact with that place till now and visits that monastery twice or thrice every year. He is living here for last 15 years. About 4 young boys who are being trained as lamas by this head lama lives with him. They perform the household works, looks after the cows and learn the rituals as well as the Tibetan language from him. The total number of lamas attached to this monastery is about 20. The main ceremony of the monastery is held for 2 days 15 days after Losar. All the lamas assemble in the premises on that occasion. Even some senior lamas from Pemayantse visit the place on that occasion.

As for the income of the monastery, it is like the other monastery in the sense that the lamas are paid donations for performing the rituals. Initially the monastery used to own about 14 acres of land but the plots which used to be cultivated by the lamas themselves have now been recorded in the names of their family members thereby depriving the monastery of its income excepting some fuel wood. However, since the monastery is under the Pemayangtse monastery of Sikkim, it still gets a grant of Rs. 2000 per annum from the Government of Sikkim. This grant from the Government is a major source of income of this monastery and even the building was renovated and extended with the one lakh 58 thousand rupees that minister of Sikkim, who was also the Rimpoche of

Pemayangtse sanctioned when he visited the place a few years ago. On that occasion the minister had sanctioned an amount of Rs. 20,000 for the Bhutia Basti monastery as well.

Samdup Targeling Sherpa Buddhist Monastery of Sonada, belongs to the Nyingma sect and was established in 1952. Since the Sherpas are in majority in Sonada, there is a Sherpa Association there and they set up this monastery for their community. The secretary of the Association lives in Sonada itself. After his first arrival in Sonada, Kalu Rimpoche, the great Karma teacher had spent some time in this monastery. The land where he founded his own monastery was also donated by the Sherpas. However, it does not have any connection with this one any more. There is only one lama now who performs the daily rituals. A family man, he is paid a salary of Rs. 600 by the Association for this task. there are other lamas, who live elsewhere in the surrounding bastics.

There is another Sherpa Buddhist Association in Darjeeling which had set up another monastery as early as 1924. It is a small institution and even though the monastery is a Nyingma one the lama, who himself is a Tibetan, belongs to the Kagyu sect. They are not very particular about the sect to which a lama belongs and invite eminent and senior lamas from other monasteries of Darjeeling viz. Dali, Tshecho or Jorebunglow on special and elaborate pujas.

The small monastery in Lopchu is actually a branch of the much bigger Phuntsog Nyab Chorling monastery of Jorebunglow of Darjeeling. It belongs to the same sect and has accepted the same Zate Rimpoche as their patron. A very old monastery and looked after by a single lama it used to have no resources at all. The people around it decided to hand it over to the Rimpoche so that it could be better maintained. The Rimpoche has connections with various places in Nepal, Bhutan, Sikkim etc. and sends money for its maintenance and other expenses. There are two Drukpa lamas who are married with families. There is no committee for its general administration. The local Drukpa ladies collect subscriptions from among themselves and observes the regular monthly rituals.

The Aloobari monastery of the Yolmos is said to have been founded by a Yolmo gentleman at the time of the World War I who had given it the name Mak Dhog meaning war. Later his wife also donated some statues and other things to it. Now it is looked after by the local community of the Yolmos.

Coming to the Tamang monasteries they have their Tamang Buddhist Associations in all the three towns of Darjeeling, Kalimpong and Kurseong. All the associations maintain one monastery at least as a part of its regular activity. Monasteries are maintained in several places where Tamangs have settled as also in the tea gardens with Tamang population. Some of these monasteries are old like that of Darjeeling (1926) and Kurseong (1925) while some are comparatively recent and are still under construction like those of Kalimpong, Mungpoo and Mirik (1952). These dates are generally those of the construction of the buildings and not necessarily the date of the foundation of the prayer house which must have existed long before when the Tamangs settled in the place.

Membership of the Association is compulsory for all the families at least for the head of the family. The parent body is the All India Tamang Buddhist Association while they also consult the Himalayan Buddhist Cultural Association on some special issues. These also function as meeting places of the members of the community. Almost all the Tamang monasteries belong to the Nyingma sect. The functions of these monasteries are basically religious even though they also perform some social and charitable functions like running of primary schools as in Kurseong. (the school is now taken over by the Government but still runs on the monastery premises). The newly founded monastery of Kalimpong has many objectives like setting up of an orphanage, herbal medicine center, museum, library and school. At present they are running only one primary school. The number of lamas attached to these monasteries are high and as all the tea gardens do not have monasteries they all assemble on the particular occasions even from the nearby tea gardens.

In addition to these monasteries there are some other Buddhist organizations which are not full fledged monasteries. Among them are the Himalayan Buddhist Society and Japanese temple at Jorebunghlow. The former was founded in 1967 by some Buddhist Nepalese just as an association of some like minded Nepalis who observe the Buddhist festivals by inviting lamas from any big nearby monastery of any sect. They maintain a prayer chapel that was inaugurated by the Dalai Lama in 1993.

The society undertakes some charity works and maintains connections with some other Buddhist countries like Thailand, Taiwan etc. from where they occasionally receive funds as well as monks.

In Kalimpong too there is an organisation of the Newari Buddhistsn who run a school for children and maintain a temple but that too is not a gomba as such.

MONASTERIES FOUNDED BY REFUGEE TIBETAN MONKS AFTER 1959

Monastery building activities were accelerated after 1950s and this is directly related to the course of events in Tibet. Tibetans started arriving in India in thousands after the Chinese takeover in 1959. Since religion and religious institution used to be an integral part of the life of the Tibetans and among the refugees were also members of the monastic community the India Government provided financial and administrative assistance for their resettlements also. Initially the Government had agreed to provide for a scholastic community of 300 monks to be established at the camp at Buxa Duar but later the Tibetans persuaded them to increase the commitment to funding for 1500 monks of all the traditions. These monks had to go through particularly hard times mainly due to the hot and humid climate and outbreak of diseases. Many developed tuberculosis. Nevertheless they studied hard with the determination to keep their culture alive and later spread it to different parts of the country.

Among the monks, who thus took refuge in India either in 1959 or in the successive years were heads of certain sects and some lamas of eminence. Monks of same sects but of lower hierarchy and belonging to the same monasteries of their Rimpoches or some other monasteries of the same sect gathered around them and new monastic centres were gradually founded.

This was the period when a general awareness was being created in the West about Tibet's culture and religion. This interest provided an opportunity to the monks to revive their religion by diffusing its principles and practices all over the world. This they achieved in three different ways – 1. Through establishment of monasteries and refugee communities 2. Through an increase in the number of Tibetan school serving in the faculties of western universities and 3. Through establishment of meditation centres. Of these three, the third produced the greatest impact and in course of time such centres were set up all over Europe, America, New Zealand, Australia, Malaysia, Singapre and other Pacific regions and even in South Africa. The response of the westerners to these have been overwhelming and they donated generously for the survival and diffusion of Tibetan Buddhism in West. The headquarters of all these sects, however, remained in India.

Darjeeling was selected by some of these monks as a suitable place and some new monasteries were set up here as they had been in Sikkim, U.P. Himachal Pradesh, Karnataka and other parts of the country.

In the following section we have given an account of some these new monasteries. We have also identified the monks under whose patronage these have been set up and given some basic information about their life and connections. This, we hope will give an idea about the objectives with which these monasteries were founded and how well connected they are with the rest of the country and even the world.

Among these monasteries of Darjeeling are represented almost all the major traditions or sects of Tibetan Buddhism. Among them are the Nyingma, the Sakya, the Drukpa Kagyu and the Gelug. The date of foundation of these monasteries are 1. Sakya Guru monastery–1959, 2. Sonada Monastery of Kalu Rimpoche–1966, 3. Dali monastery–1974, 4. Bokar monastery of Mirik–1983, 5. Lava Monastery–1988, 6. Zekhor Choede–1975 7. Ponda godown–1994. (Peter Lorie and Julie Foakes, Graham Coleman, Enthronement Ceremony–1993 (about Kalu Rimpoche), 2. The Twelfth Gyalwang Drukpa—The Drukpa Karagyu School of Tibetan Buddhism, 3. The Drukpa Kargyud School of Tibetan Choedhe Monastery at Kalimpong India : Rebuilding Programme etc.)

AN OVERVIEW OF SOME NEW MONASTERIES

The Sakya Guru monastery of Ghoom belongs to the Sakys sect–the only one to belong to this region. The actual head of this monastery is Trizin Rimpoche–the head of the Sakya sect. He was born in Tibet in 1945 and left the country in 1959 at the age of 14. He received intensive training in the study and practice of Sakya tradition and holds the three main Sakya lineages of Sakya, Tsar, and Ngor. He also holds the complete teachings of both the iron bridge and great perfection lineages of Nyingma. He is regarded as the incarnation of both Manjusri and Padmasambhava. He founded many monasteries throughout India and East Asia. His actual seat in exile is at Rajapur in U.P, India some other important centers being at Mussorie and Puruwala. Since 1974 he has made several world tours teaching in Europe, U.S.A. and South East Asia.

Though the monastery has grown under his patronage its actual origin goes back to 1932 when it was founded by some local people who handed it over to Trizin Rimpoche when he visited the place in 1959. He accepted the monastery as his own but since it was not possible for him to spend much time here he appointed one more Rimpoche–Khenpo Sangyen Tenzing to look after the monastery in his absence. The latter is dead now but his reincarnation has been identified who is undertaking his training and visits the place from time to time.

The monastery has a good library and the lamas are encouraged to pursue a course of higher studies either here or in Rajapur or in Varanasi Central Institute of Higher Tibetan Studies. It receives good amount of donation from the foreigners who visit the place from time to in pursuit of religious enlightenment and of course the Rimpoche is there to arrange funds for its upkeep and extension.

One lama of eminence who is not only regarded as a great scholar and expert of meditation but was also a great organizer and succeeded in setting up a worldwide network was Kalu Rimpoche (1904-1989) of Karma Kagyu sect. Born and recognized in Tibet, he began his formal education at a comparatively later age of 13. He studied Sutra and Tantra and received empowerments from many great lamas and came to be regarded as the incarnation of Milarepa. He went into retreat for many years and also traveled extensively in Tibet and other parts of the Himalayas.

After leaving Tibet, he established two centers in Bhutan and ordained 300 monks. In 1965 he established his headquarters in Jamdruo Tarjay Ling at Sonada, He was invited to the West in 1971 where he founded the Karma ling in 1980 along with several centers for Chenrezig Sadhana in France and U.S.A. His principal center in the west is at Vancouver, North America. He began 3 years retreats for westerners in France at his two centers and authored many books.

The Sonada monastery of Kalu Rimpoche had started in a small building which still stands there. The new building was founded in 1978 and the construction work went on till 1988. Another big monastery belonging to this sect is Salugara in outskirt of Siliguri. The Karmapas are very well organized and well connected. They have one more monastery at Dehradun and more than 100 centers all over Europe ion Spain, France, Belgium, Germany, and also in U.S.A., Taiwan and Brazil. The headquarters however is in Rumtek. Kalu Rimpoche's reincarnation has been identified the in son of his own secretary who is residing at present at Thimpu.

There are about 110 monks in Sonada and about 50 in Salugara. They are from different countries like Nepal, Bhutan, Assam, Ladakh, Sikkim and even some Tibetans from Tibet. In Sonada there is a school for the monks but in spite of their connections with the whole world they do not have an English teacher right now. After completion of their studies they are allowed to undertake higher courses in Varanasi or elsewhere.

Bokar Rimpoche, the famous meditation master was one of the direct disciples of Kalu Rimpoche. Incarnated at Baar monastery in North West of Tibet he was recognised as tulku at the age of 4 by the 16th Karmapa. Initially he studied at the Bokar monastery and then at the Karmapa's main school. Later he went to Sikkim. He stayed in Sonada from 1962 and trained in retreat and meditation under Kalu Rimpoche. Later he became retreat master and founded the retreat center at Mirik.

His monastery was founded in Mirik in 1983. Initially a very modest one it was expanded in course of time. His disciple lamas have centers all over the world and almost all have taken retreat sessions under his guidance. At present there are about 65 monks in the monastery. There are also three nuns who belong to the monastery but stay outside the premise. The monastery has its own management committee all the members of which are insiders. The expenses are met with from the donations coming from all over India and abroad. They run a medical clinic supervised by a lady doctor.

The patron of the Dali monastery of Darjeeling is Jigme Pema Wangchen the Gyalwang Drukpa. He is the 12th incarnate head of the Drukpa Kagyu lineage. He is considered an emanation of both Chenrezig Great Compassion and the King of Sambhala. He is also regarded as the reincarnation of Naropa and Gampopa the latter being the founded of the Kagyu order in the 12th century.

Thukse Rimpoche the actual founder of the monastery fled from Tibet in c. 1959. He stayed at Alipurduar and from there he came to Darjeeling. Soon he was entrusted with the responsibility of a couple of old temples of the area.

These included the old monastery at Chitri in upper Manebhanjan in Nepal. The owners handed it over to Rimpoche along with some land. Another temple at Minkamang near Sukhiapokri was also handed over to him. Finally he purchased the original kothi–Forest View Villa by name where the Dali monastery is now situated and started constructing this monastery. The work started in 1974. The monastery was initially very small, it has been gradually expanded. Now it houses the 1. Druk Gar Library that is big and well organised with books in various languages related to religion 2. The Gomba clinic for Western medicine. It is not free but it provides treatment to the needy at a cheaper rate. 3. Meditation center. The Monastery houses around 200 monks including those who came from elsewhere for meditation. The monks are from various places Ladakh, Sikkim, Bhutan and Himachal Pradesh. Recently they have started a higher study center.

It also runs a school that has classes up to VIII which is not exclusively for monks. There are about 80 children. The subjects taught are history, Tibetan language and grammar, a little bit of religion, English, Arithmetic and Hindi. Some teachers come from outside. Few laymen's children are also there. They study along with the monks but their kitchen is separate. After completing the course in school the lay boys go out and the monks who are interested in higher studies are given the scope to join the Tibetan Institute at Benaras.

The Rimpoche resides mainly here and he is well connected with countries like Taiwan, France, Monaco etc. Donations pour in from all the directions and finance is no problem at all. In addition to this, the monastery gets aid from the central Government also through the State Welfare Department. This is specially meant for about 50 poor and destitute children coming from the various Buddhist communities of the Tamangs, Bhutias, Sherpas and the Tibetans.

There is a carpet weaving center owned by the Gomba at 6th Mile, Kalimpong where about 8 weavers work for them. The income adds to the monastery's resources.

Kagyu Thekchenling at Lava was founded by Jamgon Kongtrul Rimpoche. In 1988 a group known as the Lava Mani Gomba Committee approached Rimpoche and offered a small hillock measuring 3.5 acres at Lava Bazar near Kalimpong requesting him to build a monastery there for the benefit of the local populace. The people there are predominantly Buddhist but had no monastery or resident monks or lamas to fulfill their religious needs. On their request the Rimpoche built a small monastery inaugurating it in June 1990. Initially there were 50 young boys from the area who became monks and later the strength grew to 155 representing all the ethnic Buddhist groups of the Himalayan region. They study Tibetan language, literature and religion, maths, and English and take training in rituals and philosophy. It is also a higher study center that offers 15 year study course to those who are interested in higher studies in religion and philosophy. Near the monastery at Lava the Rimpoche also built a retreat center where the monks practice retreat under the guidance of the famous retreat master Bokar Rimpoche.

In Lava, the Rimpoche also has the plan to build a small hospital cum dispensary including outpatient clinic and quarters for a permanent medical staff. The major funding for the projects comes from the individual donors in Switzerland and Rigme Dorje Foundation of Los Angeles. They have their own Paramita Charity Trust in Delhi and Foundations in different parts of the country and abroad. They have a primary school and an old age home at Kalimpong. They also run eye operations camp in Nepal, Sikkim etc.

Like the Karmapas, the Nyingmapas too have some monasteries in and around Darjeeling.

The Ugyen Kunsang Chokhorling monastery belongs to this sect. It was founded approximately 30 years ago by Kangyu Rimpoche who had come from Tibet in 1959. In Tibet his seat was the Taklung monastery. After his arrival in Darjeeling he had spent some time in Ging. Like all the other monks of his stature he too is well connected with various countries of Europe and particularly France, where he often goes and spends long periods teaching meditation. In his absence, the monastery remains in charge of Ven. Nyima Sangpo of Sikkim where he has his own Lhakang in Deorali.

Though the caretaker of the monastery complex complained about paucity of funds and absence of a famous lama the well-maintained premises and the big buildings point to the contrary.

The place is inhabited by approximately 35 lamas many of them being young students. There is a school for them to teach them the rituals by senior lamas while they are also imparted English and math lessons by a teacher from outside. Very recently they have also started a Sheda – a higher study center where 14 lamas are being instructed in the nuances of philosophy by one senior monk teacher.

Zhekhar Choede Monastery, Kalimpong is a Gelugpa monastery founded under direct patronage of the high Gelugpa lamas of Dharamsala. The monastery was originally in the Dhargye district of Western Tibet. It used to have about 70 monks and was famed for its preservation of great teachings and practice of sutras and tartars. The founder was great scholar Jetsun Jampa Tenphel a famous disciple of Ven. Panchen Sangpo Tashi of Tashilhunpo.

After 1959 around 30 monks from this monastery escaped from Tibet and settled in Kalimpong as refugees. Some senior monks passed away being unable to bear the change of climate and the accompanying hardship while several younger ones left the place. Those who remained were disoriented.

They received a new lease of life when Ven. Kyabje Trijang Rimpoche, the tutor of the H.H. Dalai lama visited Kalimpong in 1979. He advised these disheartened monks to reestablish their monastery's former teaching tradition. Thus they began to admit new young monks, give them all the traditional important teaching and provide both English and Tibetan classes for them. However, they had no qualified head lama to give them spiritual guidance. This vacuum was filled up when Ven. S. Chusang Rimpoche–the spiritual head of Chusang monastery at Boudhnath in Nepal agreed to visit the monastery and consented to become its head. He was the most appropriate choice because the previous Chusang Rimpoche had a close guru disciple relationship with the monks of Zekhar Cheode.

The monastery began its rebuilding program in January 1992 with plans to build proper Assembly halls, monk's quarters and a medical clinic for modern western medicinc. Thc land on which it presently stands was donated by a Tibetan who now lives in America. The expenses are met with donations from all over India. Nepal and Europe particularly France through Chusang Rimpoche who maintains an extensive connection with the outside world.

It has about 21 resident monks who perform the traditional religious practices and services for the Tibetan people. Quite a few among them are young about 7-14 years of age whom they are training up in the tradition. Many of them are from Sikkim.

Another Gelugpa monastery that was being revived in this way was near the Ponda godown of Kalimpong at 10-1/2 mile. This monastery whose name was yet finalized at the time when the field trip was undertaken also belongs to the Gelugpa sect. Some very old Tibetan speaking lamas who are not much aware of the world outside have organized themselves under the name of Sed Gyued Datsang Tantric College Association and seem to be old inmates of the above mentioned college in Tibet who fled to India and assembled here after 1959. Their Rimpoche was in Italy and is well connected in Europe. In fact, the monastery was being built with donations from Germany.

CONCLUDING OBSERVATIONS

Before highlighting the contrast between the two types of monasteries it would be better to clarify the term monastery itself and to examine what the term indicates in Tibetan context. A monastery is actually an institution of the monks which were ideally collectivities of individuals who had renounced attachments to materialism and family and had made a commitment to devote their lives to pursuit of Buddhist teachings, including a vow to celibacy. The number of monks in the monasteries was staggering. In 1951 there were approximately 2,500 monasteries and 1,15,000 monks in Tibet proper comprising roughly 10-15% of Tibet's male population. Even though ideally a Buddhist monastery is supposed to be a center of higher education and philosophy by the monks, not all the monasteries of Tibet were centers of such excellence.

Drepung, the biggest monastery not only of Tibet also of the world was virtually a town housing about 100,000 monks and organized in a manner resembling the segmentary structure of classic British universities like Oxford with semi autonomous units conveniently called colleges. It consisted of 4 functioning colleges each a mini monastery with thousands of monks, an administrative structure headed by an abbot and its own sets of rules and traditions. Large monastic colleges were again subdivided into smaller residential colleges. In contrast, there were also monasteries with 5 or 10 village monks. This was because emphasis was placed on mass monasticism in Tibet. In order to induce more and more boys and males to remain in the monasteries all sorts of personalities were allowed to coexist. There were no severe restriction on compartments or insistence on rigorous educational or spiritual achievements. New monks had no exams to pass in order to remain in the monastery and even those who had no interest in studies or meditation were as welcome as the dedicated scholar monks. Even illiterate monks were accommodated. No one was expelled unless he committed murder or major theft or indulged in heterosexual activities. (Melvyn Goldstein, 1999, p. 15-20).

The old local monasteries of the Darjeeling hills are in no way comparable to the ideal monasteries of Tibet where monks remain engaged in higher studies for years. Nor are the monks so numerous and placed in such hierarchical order. These are basically local prayer houses with village monks performing the rituals. With exception of some Tibetan monasteries, the lamas too are basically family persons, small agriculturists by profession and live outside the premises. Performing the functions of a priest can be described as their part time occupation. Nor do they indulge in higher studies. Still these are designated monasteries as different from the lakhangs or mere chapels. They are more akin to the small monasteries of Tibet.

Despite their limitations, these monasteries can be considered as important social and economic institutions of the region. Each monastery can be considered unique with its particular community or sect affiliation as well as impact of and connection with the neighbouring countries/states of Tibet, Bhutan and Sikkim. They stand as institutions that still bear the testimonies of the particular course of history of this region and point to the cultural interaction that this region maintained with its neighbourhood which in its turn shaped the social and religious profile of the land and the people.

The new monasteries set up by the Tibetan refugee monk community are qualitatively different from the old monasteries in all the respects-of their objectives, resources, organisational networks and global connections. Almost all the patron lamas of these monasteries are attached to several national and international centers that are set up all over the world in recent years under their guidance. Not only are they great scholars and teachers but they are also experts in financial assistance and sponsorship for their charitable and educational projects. To give an example–Jamgon Kongtrul Rimpoche-founder of the Lava monastery had first arranged sponsorship for his projects in India with an organisaton in Montreal in Canada in early 1980s. Later, he himself founded the Rigpe Dorje foundation there in 1987 which has now extended its branches in Germany and Switzerland. In addition, he receives donations from corntries like France. (His Eminence the IIIrd Jamgon Rinpoche, Karma Lodro Chokyi Senge-Grand Inaugeration Of the Kudung Lhakhang, 26th April 1994).

In some cases however, the monasteries were not founded completely anew e.g. in the case of the Sakya Guru monastery in Ghoom, it is said to have been already there since 1932. After Trizin Rimpoche's visit in 1959,the local people handed it over to him and made him the patron of the same.

Kalu Rimpoche of Karma sect also has connections with more than 70 centers all over the world. Almost all the monasteries of this period have similar connections.

Since the basic objectives of these monks is to implant Tibetan Buddhism all over India and abroad and not merely earning of livelihood for themselves, most of these monasteries also encourage pursuit of higher studies by their monks. Either they have started their own centers for higher education called Sheda in their monasteries as in Mirik, Dali, Durpin ect. or they send their students to Varanasi. The Gelugpas however, have started their own Universities in the South in Karnataka on the model of Sera, Ganden, Drepung–three premier monasteries in Tibet.

The nature of these new Tibetan monasteries is shaped by the political upheavals in Tibet. Unable to practice their religion in their own country these Tibetan lamas now have the urge to preserve their heritage in these newly founded centers as well as to pass on the tradition to the next generation. In this they are being helped by the Tibetan Diaspora and the world's recent interest in Buddhism and Tibetan way of life.

Darjeeling has proved to be a good location for them because it had an age old historical tie with Tibet through its geographical location. The people were already exposed to the religion of Tibetan Buddhism and have willingly accepted these new institution. Thus Darjeeling, which had originally received its initiation to Buddhism from Tibet through Sikkim and Bhutan is now providing Tibet with a space where Tibetan cultural heritage can survive and prosper.

- Tomo Geshe came from the Dukhar Gompa (monastery of the White Conch) situated on a steep hill with a rocky crest in the middle of a fertile wheat growing valley called Tomo (To-wheat). The meaning of the word Gshe is Doctor of Divinity. The hermit who stayed there in the Dunkhar Gompa came to be known as Tomo Geshe Rimpoche which means "The learned Jewel of the wheat valley", (Lama Govinda op. cit. P. 9), Actually Lama Govinda had accepted Tomo Geshe as his mentor or guru and his book is replete with description of his relation with him as well with information of his guru's life and achievements. Otherwise also, Yiga Choling maintained direct contact with Tibet. 'There was Kachenla who was originally from Shigatse and had been one of the personal attendants of the Panchen Lama, from whom he still received a small pension which he spent for improvement and beautification of the temple while he himself lived like the poorest and humblest of monks the temple door with no other personal possessions than his sitting mats and his monastic robes'... (Lama Govinda, p. 17).

REFERENCES

Awasti, Indira, *Between Sikkim and Bhutan (The Lepchas and Bhutias of Pedong),* B.R. Publishing Corporation, Delhi, 1978.

Coleman, Graham (ed.), *A Handbook of Tibetan Culture: A Guide to Tibetan Centres and Resources throughout the World*, Rider, 1993, First Paperback, Rupa, 1995.

Dozey, E.C., *A Concise History of the Darjeeling District since 1835 with a Complete Itinerary of Tours in Sikkim and the District*, Published under the Distinguished patronage of His Excellency the Right Honourable Baron Carmichael of Skirling G.C.I.E.K.C., First Governor of Bengal, 1922.

Govinda, Lama Anagarika, *The Way of the White Clouds: A Buddhist in Tibet*, B.I. Publication, First Published 1960, First Indian Edition, 1977.

Goldstein, Melvyn C., 'The Revival of Monastic life in Drepung Monastery'in Melvyn C. Goldstein and T. Kapstein (ed.) *Buddhism in Contemporary Tibet Religious Revival and Cultural Identity* Motilal Banarasidas Publishers Ltd. Delhi, 1999.

Lorics, Peter and Foaks Julie, *The Buddhist Directory (A Unique Reference to Europe nad the rest of the World's Buddhist Centres*), New Leaf, 1996.

O'Malley, L.S.S., *Darjeeling District Gazetteer*, Logos Press, Darjeeling, Reprint, New Delhi, 1985.

Subba T.B., *Flight and Adaptation: Tibetan Refugees in the Darjeeling Sikkim Himalaya*. Library of the Tibetan Works and Archives, Dharamsala, 1990.

THE BUDDHIST TRIBES OF ARUNACHAL PRADESH

Hasibul Rahaman

INTRODUCTION

Arunachal Pradesh is one of the seven states of North East India. It is rich in ethnic diversity and rich tribal heritage. It stretches along the southern slopes of the Eastern Himalayas to the western slope of the Patkoi Hills around the Brahmaputra valley. Politically, Arunachal Pradesh came into limelight in 1838 when the British obtained direct control of Assam and converted it into 'non regulation province' of British India. During the two World War periods, there were several administrative reorganisations. Initially it was divided into three frontier tracts–(i) The central and eastern section covering the areas inhabited by the Abors, Miris and Mishmis (ii) The western section covering the areas inhabited by the Monpas, Akas and Dafflas. This section was renamed Balipara Frontier Tract in 1919. and (iii) the Lakhimpur Frontier Tract Following some more administrative reorganizations the entire tribal belt was named North Eastern Frontier Agency or NEFA in 1954 In 1972 it was renamed Arunachal Pradesh and elevated into Union Territory. It became a separate state in 1987.

Arunachal Pradesh is physiographically included in the eastern Himalayan region. The Arunachal Himalayas are broadly divided into three longitudinal physiographic zones from North to South viz. (i) the Great Himalayas (above 3,000 mts) which actually forms the majestic frontier of the whole region, (ii) the Lesser Himalayas (1,200–3,000 mts) and (iii) the Outer Himalayas (upto 1,200 mts). Except in the extreme South east the whole state is topographically very rugged and a considerable portion is under perpetual snow cover with several glaciers and glacial lakes.

According to 2001 census the total population of the state is 1,091,117 of which 573,951 are males and 517,166 are females. The sex ratio is 893 females of per 1000 males. The population is divided over 16 towns and 3257 villages. The total population of rural and urban areas are 8,70,087 and 2,27,881. The literacy rate of the state is 54.3% with male literacy rate is 63.8% and female literacy 43.5%.

Administratively, the state is divided into 16 districts. As per census of 2001 the districts, district headquarters and district populations are as follows:

Tawang (Tawang) 34,705; West Kameng (Bomdila) 74,595, East Kameng (Seppa) 57,065; Lower Subansiri (Ziro) 97,614; Upper Subansiri (Daporijo) 54,995; West Siang (Along) 103,575; East Siang (Pasighat) 87,430; Upper Siang 33,146; Lohit (Tezo) 143,478; Dibang Valley (Anni) 57,543; Tirap (Khamsa) 100,227, Changlong 124,994 (Chaylong) 62211 Papumpare (Itanagar) 121,750; Lower Dibarg (Roing), Kurung Kumey (Yangte).

The population is basically tribal and of the Mongoloid stock. There are 26 Scheduled Tribes and numerous sub-tribes living in this state . They all have their own religion, language, culture and custom. Each tribe has certain distinct characteristic in language, religion, dress and costume and have a rich cultural heritage. The people are simple, friendly and hospitable. The major ethnic tribes of Arunachal Pradesh are–Adi, Nishi, Apatani, Bugun Galo, Hrusso, Koro, Meyor, Monpa, Tagin, Mishmi, Sajolang, Sartang, Tai, Khampti, Tanghang yobin, Singpho, Sherdukpen, Khamba, Memba etc.

ETHNIC TRIBES OF ARUNACHAL PRADESH

The population of the state can be divided into distinct cultural groups on the basis of their socio-politico-religious affinities. There

Table 1
District wise Distribution of Population

District	Headquarter	Tribes	Population
1. Tawang	Tawang	Monpa	21,472
2. West Kameng	Bomdila	Monpa, Mijis, Akas, Khowas	41,474
3. East Kameng	Seppa	Bangnis	42,722
4. Upper Subansirir	Doponiz	Tagon	39,406
5. Lower Sub-ansiri	Ziro	Nishis, Apa Tanis, Solugs, Hill Miris	1,13,300
6. East Siang	Pashighat	Adi, Membas, Khambas, Mishings	7,0274
7. West Siang	Along	Adis, 14 sub seebs, Padam, Minung	7,4152
8. Dilang Valley	Anini	Mishmis, Adis, Mishing	27,716
9. Lohit	Tezu	Khamptis, Mishmis, Singhphos, Deories etc.	69,400
10. Tirap	Khonsa	Nocte, Wangchoo, Tangshas, Singhphos	1,28,135
11. Kurung Kemey	Kurung Kemey	-	-
12. Upper Dibang	Anni RoIMG	-	31,118
13. Lower Dibang	Anni RoIMG	-	30,928
14. Changlang	Changlang	-	62,211
15. Pupum Pare	Itanagar	-	1,12,650

Source: Kamal Mukherjee, Seminar on Problem and Strategies of Development N.E. Himalayan State of Arunachal Pradesh, 1983, 15 & 16 March. (H4 A353) Centre for Himalayan Studies.

are two broad groups of Bodic and non Bodic. Among the Bodic group we find the use of stone and wood for their house and furniture. Their dress is tailored and woolen felt cap is used as head dress. Their religion is sophisticated with their temples, images, sacred literatures and well organized priesthood.

The non-bodic group on the other hand use cane and bamboo for their houses and furniture and do not use tailored cotton dress. Non-bodic religion is faith in spirits and deities with oral sacred literature but without an organized priesthood or centralized place of worship (Durah; 1990: xi-xii).

Religion wise there are animists, Buddhists, few Hindus and some Christians among them. Each religious group is concentrated in some geographically distinct area. The Northern belt of the higher Himalayan region is the area where the Buddhists live, the central belt or the central stretch of hills is the area where animism is still predominant and the southern belt or the foothills where Hindus are in majority. Our focus in this paper is on the Buddhist tribes of Arunachal. The major tribal groups are as under following table.

Table 2
Distribution of Major Tribal Population over Census 1961-1991

Sl. No.	*Name of the Tribes*	*1961 77,187*	*1971*	*1981 120829*	*1991*
1.	Adi	2239	93959	2947	1580
2.	Aka	10793	2345	16580	3531
3.	Apatani	-	12388	3608	22526
4.	Deori	2442	2683	6936	5200
5.	Hill Miri	1110	8174	342	11017
6.	Khamba	2644	348	7010	1333
7.	Khamti	654	4115	625	8339
8.	Khwla (Bugun)	2431	703	2679	1046
9.	Memba	2079	2486	4074	1169
10.	Miji	543	3549	598	5779
11.	Mikir	2817	1298	5201	-
12.	Mishing	197222	3359	24596	5899
13.	Mishimi	20799	22561	32902	3122
14.	Monpa	-	28209	-	38862
15.	Nah	51023	-	87075	
16.	Nishing	19287	82178	26257	116258
17.	Nocte	1144	23416	2096	33720
18.	Sherdukpen	1781	1639	4233	2547
19.	Sulung	957	4288	2353	5443
20.	Singhpho	24055	1567	27124	2978
21.	Tagin	6741	22107	13921	28860
22.	Tangsa	23382	13447	32441	26016
23.	Wancho	78	28650	5	38528
24.	Yobin/Lisu	-	926	14	-
25.	Zekhering	-	23	-	-

Source: Census of Arunachal Pradesh.

BUDDHIST TRIBES OF ARUNACHAL PRADESH

The Buddhists of Arunachal Pradesh belong to the two major schools of Buddhism-Mahayana of Tibet and Theravada basically of South East Asia. Chugpa, Khamba, Loshipa (Idu, Yidu, Midu, Keraah), Hostipa, Memba, Monpa, Nga-Fagin, Sherdukpen, Singhpho and Khamti etc. are basically the followers of the former and on the other side Aiton, Khampti, Phake, Nara, Shyam, Turung, Zekhring and Singpho follow the principle of Theravada Buddhism. Among the six major Buddhist tribes of Mahayan school are Monpa, Sherdukpens of Tawang and west Kameng districts Membas and Khambas of Siang and Dibang districts and Khamptis, Shingphos of the districts of Lohit and Tirap.

HISTORY OF THE INTRODUCTION OF TIBETAN BUDDHISM

The history of Arunachal Pradesh is shrouded in myths and legends. The same is applicable in case of the Buddhists. Legend has it that Buddhism was introduced into Arunachal Pradesh by Guru Padmasambhava more or less the same time as in Tibet. It is believed that Padmasambhava, the great Indian Buddhist teacher who visited Tibet in 747 AD, had spent some time in Arunachal Pradesh while on his way to Tibet. There are a number of places-as many as sixteen, in Arunachal Pradesh which are said to have been visited by Padmasambhava.

It is believed that the Guru himself had spent some time in meditation and preaching the Dhamma in the Tawang area even before entering Tibet. Hence somc tribes had been converted to Buddhism as early as 8th century.

The story of the introduction of Mahayana Buddhism can be constructed to some extent from the existing myths and legends of the region.

The region maintained close contact with Tibet from a very early period. And the religious history of the region is very much a part of thc history of Tibet. In fact the VIth Dalai Lama was born in this place. The Monastery of Tawang has become almost the symbol of Buddhism in Arunachal Pradesh. Before going into a descriptive account of the Buddhist communities a short account of history of this monastery is given here.

The monastery of Tawang is the fountainhead of the spiritual life of the Gelugpa followers of Monpas and Sherdukpens.

The foundation of the monastery indicates a chapter in the history of Buddhism in Arunachal and the rivalry that existed among the different sects of Buddhism in the region. The Dukpas of Bhutan made several attempts to capture Tawang. This explains the strategic location and the purely defensive nature of the layout of the monastery. The monastery was not only a strong base for the propagation of the religion but used to be a military post as well against the Dukpa attacks. Founder of the monastery was Mera Lama.

Gelugpa sect was introduced in the region by Thasngston Gyalpo: a Gelugpa lama from Tibet (1385–1462) and a fellow disciple and associate of the first Dalai Lama. He came to a place called Chankhargor and meditated in a nearby cave in a village of Kraling about seven miles to the Southeast from Tawang. He constructed an iron chain suspension bridge called Chaksam of Tawangchu river connecting the Mukto area with the Kitpi area of Tawang. The bridge survives till today. With his blessing seven sons were born to one Berkhar Terge of Berkhar hamlet near Kraling. The second and the seventh sons had their trainings under one of the disciples of the First Dalai Lama. They built many Gelugpa temples viz. Brakher, Ariakdun, Lhangaten, Sanglamphe, Tadung, Taidung, Surchung, all in the Tawang area and the Talung Gompa at the Monpa village of Sanglem in the Southwest part of Kameng district. Two temples were also built in Eastern Bhutan in the villages of Sakten and Mera respectively.

The Gelugpa sect, thus introduced was consolidated and extended in the areas inhabited by the Monpas and Sherdukpens by a series of his reincarnations. The fourth incarnation was Lodro Gyalpo who got his education at Tashilhunpo and Sera monasteries. He was popularly known as Mera Lama. This was the period of Gelugpa rivalry with the Buddhists of Bhutan The Dukpa subsect was introduced there in the 13th century by the Tibetan monk Lama Phajo. Faced with animosity from his rivals he planned to establish one Gelugpa monastery in Tsosum–a name by which Tawang was known in those days. The Karmapa sects also exerted some influence in the region. There was a Karmapa temple called Gangardung gompa under the jurisdiction of the Karmapa centre of Drosangacholing monastery in Tibet. There was also the Nyingma Thechpa temple at Tsosum established by Mindoling monastery in Tibet.

With the blessing of the 5th Dalai Lama he was able to construct a monastery with the help of the local villagers. Full name of the monastery was Tawang Galden Namgye Lhatse and it is referred to in short as the Tawang monastery. The Dalai himself gave a printing as memento to be preserved at the monastery and also laid down the rules to be followed by the resident monks. He also deputed a learned and pious monk as the abbot and two monastic officials. The monastery became affiliated to the Drepung monastery of Tibet.

The exact year of the construction of the monastery is not known for certain. History has it that the Mongol troops led by one Sokpo Jemkhar came in this area to help the Gelugpa Monpas in their struggle against the Dhukpas of Bhutan. In addition to their local frictions with the Nyingmaps and the Karmapas. From the history of Tibet it is known that the struggle for supremacy among the Dhukpas and the Monpas had started in 1643. Considering all the facts it is inferred that the Tawang monastery was constructed sometime between 1643 and 1647.

In course of time the Gelugpa sect gained supremacy and the Karmapas totally disappeared from the area. Some Nyingmapas exist among the village priests.

The temples at Sakti, Momang, Manjing and Kharung in Lumla area, Urgyeling, Changbu, Shermang, Khromteng, Ariakdum, Kimnash etc in Tawang area and Namchu in Dirang area are affiliated to Tawang monastery.

There were also two nunneries at Tawang established more or less at the same time as the monastery itself. They too exist till today. (N. Sarkar, 1996).

HISTORY OF IMMIGRATION

Monpa

The Monpas live in the northern part of Arunachal Pradesh, now named as Tawang district. Their area, Tawang is so named after the famous Tawang monastery. It is also called Monyul or the land of the Mon (The lower land), because it is bounded by the towering Himalayan ranges of Tibet in the north, Bhutan in the west, Bomdila range in the south, and Zela range in the east. The Monpas are said to have come from Bhutan. Following the persecution by the Chinese soldiery a section of the people from Eastern Bhutan and Monyal in the neighborhood of Tawang immigrated about 200 years ago, to Pemako, the Land of promise which their ancient prophecies had declared to exist somewhere on the frontiers of India. The descendants of this first batch of immigrants are indiscriminately called Monpas or Drukpas. The name Monpa means an inhabitant of Monyul near the Buddhist monastery at Tawang. The people of Eastern Bhutan are called Drukpas by the Tibetans. Hence the Bhutanese immigrants came to be known as Drukpas or as Daktas. Some of the Monpas who accompanied the first batch of colonists in search of the land of promise halted in the upper valley of Siyom to the south of Nepa La, and formed a small colony there and are as *Pachakshiribas* or *Pachakshri* Monpas (P.T. Nair; 1985; 70-71).

On the basis of geographical location, the Monpas are divided into three groups, *a. Tawang or Northern Monpas, b. Dirang or Central Monpas, and c. Kalkatong or Southern Monpas* (K.S. Singh; 1995).

These names given according to the geographical location of their habitat.

(a) The Tawang Monpas

Once Shan-Pradhan with all his nine sons went to a dense forest for collection of firewood. There in the jungle, the father instructed the son to cut down the trees, but due to their tender age, the sons were unable to do so and hence they sought the help of their father. The father found the job very tough, yet with great efforts, he could do it. They then collected the fire wood and moved to a place Dakpa-Chhlengdung where Shan-Pradhan happened to gaze with bewilderment at two sparrows flying away from his vision. One of the sparrows went to the side of Phogmaneng in Bhutan and the other in the direction of Domkho-Movshing village.

Shan-Pradhan looked around and saw the sight of Kalaktang village. He proceeded towards the village but on reacting it found to his utter surprise that there was no other person except an old lady and a young girl. He went near them and asked as to why there was no other person in the village. The old lady replied with stammering that all the villagers had been killed by the great demons. She also cautioned him that there was danger to the life and he should leave the place immediately before the sun set. It is believed that Shan-Pradhan was the representative of Tawang Monastry who had settled down there and had been given the right to receive share of their revenue on behalf of Tawang Monastry and in return he promised to get performed various pujas at Tawang Monastry to counteract the natural calamities. It may be due to that the Tawang Monastry has the right to receive the "*Posa Payment*" which in local term is called "Ṣi-bad." (P.Dutta, 1990; 164-65).

Basically Buddhists, the Tawang Monpas perform several types of religious rituals and ceremonies in different seasons. *Dongyur* is the most important one. This festival is celebrated for three days in a large scale. The rehearsal for the festival dance is done by the participants from the 8th to 9th of the eleventh month of the Tibetan Calendar. The festival takes place outside the monastery. During this festival the following dances are performed. All the dances have their meaning and significance.

(i) Pha-Chham or Abor Dance: introduced by Merak Lama Dore Gyaltso, the founder of the Moanstery.

(ii) Jam-Cham: Grei-Chham: They are twelve in number who are religiously addressed as "Kheta Palapkosi". This dance is performed to receive the blessings of the deity for prosperity.

(iii) Ja Pho Mo:

(iv) Ngan-Chham or Kya-Chham:

(v) Torya or Torgya is an another festival performed every year. Thereafter, the Torgya is taken out in procession by the monks in full warrior dress termed Arpo to five candled at the south western gate outside the monastery to drive away the rest of the demons. The people also throng to witness the Torgya Ceremony and with their inner heart pray to the merciful god to protect them from causing any harm, disease, calamities and anticipate for the best to have a prosperous and happy life in the times to come.

(vi) Tawang Monastry: Tawang is famous for its 400 yrs. old Buddhist monastery locally called Gumpha. Set amidst beautiful wooded mountains, at an altitude of 30484 m. Tawang is the largest Buddhist monastery in India. It is the birth place of 6th Dalai Lama. The monastery houses a 55m high statue of Buddha, numerous sculptures and rare manuscripts.

(b) Kalaktang Monpa

The Monpas of Kalaktang circle are also known as Rongnampa Monpa. They are a small group of people occupying the south-west corner of west Kameng District having many things similar to that of the Monpas of Dirang area.

Like majority of the Monpas they too are Buddhists by religion. However, simultaneously with Buddhism they retain some traits of animism in the form of beliefs in a host of spirits, deities and gods etc. who are both malevolent and benevolent in nature and are capable of causing miseries to human beings. There are number of such deities who are worshipped on a number of occasions to get relief from the miseries.

The priest employed for worship is known as Bonpa. Bonpa, by dint of his super-natural power can contact the appropriate deities and learn how to cure a person from his disease and miseries. Bonpa also determines the good and bad sign by examining eggs and chicken's liver or heart to cure the small disease.

There are some rituals which are performed daily. In addition, on the 10th day of every Monpa month a puja is performed to save the village from all sorts of disasters and for the well-being of its inhabitants. This ceremony is known as '*Chankang Chakar*'.

(c) Dirang or Central Monpa

The Dirang Monpas are the third group of the greater Monpa tribe. They inhabitate in Djong. Dirang, Namsu and Yayung in the Darang circle of west Kameng.

As per 1991 census their population was 5028 of which 2508 were males and 2520 females. They speak Sangla dialect of the Monpa language which belongs to the Bhutia group of the Tibeto Burman language family and use the Tibetan script.

There are many folk beliefs regarding their origin. One popular belief is that they originated from an ancestral monkey. According to the Dirang Monpas, the transformation of the monkey into human being might have taken place somewhere in the north by the power of the *lama* named *Lapan Rimpoche*. They believe themselves to be the original inhabitants of the Dirang Circle of the West Kameng district.

Their sacred place of the Dirang Monpas is the monastery which houses the images of Bodhistavas (different incarnations of Buddha) and Buddha himself in different *mudras*. The lama i.e the priest who is the sacred person of the community is consulted on different occasions like marriages and births and deaths. Simultaneously they retain practices of pre-Buddhistic animism or shamanism. The animistic priest or shaman is known as *phrama*. His duty is to cure diseases and ailments. He is also engaged for the removal or evil spirits and protection of the villagers from the evil actions of the malevolent spirits. They observe number of festivals, such as–Losar, Losarkachot, Ngoh, Sakadawa, Druparasajee, Ganden-nymchot, Nyanpa-gozum, Torgya etc. These festivals have a socio-religious significance.

Previously they had to pay heavy taxes to the Tibetans. Now they have established close religious linkages with other Buddhist groups like the Sherdukpens, Tawang Monpas, Lispas and other Buddhist groups of Arunachal Pradesh. They share the gumpha (religious shrine) with the other Monpa groups. Some of them send their children to acquire a training of Lamaism. (K.S. Singh; 1995: 228-31).

The Sherdukpens

Sherdukpens are also a small Buddhist tribe inhabiting southern part of the Bomdila Range in the valleys of Tengapani river. The main concentration is spread over the village of Kupa, Jigaon and Shergaon. However at present, some of them have settled in Kamengbari areas, a new settlement area under Bhalukpong circle. They are also known as Sanjee or Sainjee i.e the people of the Sain area as well as Thungjee or Jigaonjee i.e the people of the Thung or Jigaon area.

The Sherdukpens trace their origin to Tibetans. Their dialect belongs to the Tibeto Burman linguistic family closely related to the dialect of the But and Lish Monpas and Miji communities. Myth goes that they originated from marriage of a Tibetan prince with a princess of Assam, possibly of Kachari origin. They have three synonyms–Sanjee or Sainjee, Thungjee and Jigaonpee, Sanijee means the people of Sain area, Thungjee means the people of Thung area and Jigaonpee means the people of Jigaon area. Sherdukpens who are also keen traders are a small tribe and are mostly distributed in two villages namely Rupa and Shergaon.

As in the case of other Buddhist tribes of Arunachal , their Buddhism too is blended with local beliefs and shamanism even though monasteries with images of Chenrezig (Dhyani Bodhisatava; Avalokiteshvara), Guru Rimpoche, Lord Buddha and his different incarnations are their main places of worship. Manes (stone shrines) are scattered all over their habitat with the inscription of the sacred formula '*Om Mani Padme Hum*'. Chhorten which are stupa-shaped structures and Kakalingsor high gates are also found at Rupa and Shergaon.

Their regional and village deity is known as *Phu* (the hill deity). They observe a number of festivals, the most important being *Losar* (the beginning of the new year, celebrated in the month of January or February), *Chhakar* (observed in the month of May or June), Wangand Khiksawa (associated with the harvesting of food crops and observed in October). These are Buddhist festivals of Tibetan origin. These are performed by local priests called *Chize* or *sishi* (Singh; 1995: 288-92).

The Sherdukpens perform various religious and social ceremonies. The local priests, Jijis, are inferior to the Lamas. Anyone can become a lama after taking training in any monastery in India or Bhutan. A number of festivals and holidays with no less a number of dances form part and parcel of the social life of the people.

In accordance with the tenets of Buddhist faith there is belief in rebirth, karma, heaven (chungba sangze) and hell (sango thong). The songs and dances of Sherdukpen women have a strong influence by Tibetan-Bhutanese culture. They perform many pantomime dances. Among these, the *Ajilamu* dance is very popular their musical instruments being the same as those of the Buddhist Monpas and Tibetans.

The Khampti

The word 'Khampti' means 'tied to the spot'. They settled in the Tengapani and Noadihing rivers basin during the 18th century and also in the Dibrugarh district of Assam. This area lies to the south of the Lohit river contiguous to the Tirap district of Arunachal Pradesh. They are migrants from the Bor-Khamti area, the mountainous region which interposes the eastern extremity of Assam and the valley of Irrawady. They call themselves *Tai*. Their population was 8462 in the census of 1991. Of them 4344 were males and 4118 females.

The Khamtis are followers of Theravada Buddhism of Tai Burmese tradition. The religious practices of the common people rather conform to a little more than polytheism under a thin veil of a Buddhist pantheon Each village has a Chong or monastery also known as Buddha vihara adorned with images of Lord Buddha.

They celebrate the two great religious festivals of the Buddhists, one to celebrate the birth and the other to mourn the death. To commemorate the birth of the Lord, a lively representation of an accouchement is enacted.

There are two categories of priests- Chowsra or the principal monk (*sthabira/ mahasthabira or bhikhshu* in Sanskrit) and the Chowsang or ordinary monk known as *shramana or grihatyagi* in Pali. Their priesthood is not hereditary. Anyone can become a chowsang but to become a chowsra or principal monk one has to study Buddhist philosophy through Pali literature and have an experience of minimum 10 years. The monks reside in the monasteries and receive *Som* i.e. food from the villagers known as *dana* The monks give religious teachings to the villagers and perform birth, marriage or death rituals for all the families The priests of the Khamptis are well-versed in Buddhist tenets and command greater respect than their chiefs. Nothing is done without first consulting them. Auspicious days are predicted by them. They have shaven heads and amber coloured garments and rosaries. The priests collect offerings from the people every morning in a lacquered box. The women stand waiting at their doors with a portion of their ready cooked food on hearing the tintinnabulation of their bells. The Khampti priests, chowsangs, are not social parasites, as they are good workmen at ivory, bone and wood. Education of the boys are compulsory and traditional learning is imported by the priests in their temples (P.T. Nair, 1985: 58-63).

As in the case of the Mahayan tribes, the religion of this tribe is also tinged with traditional beliefs and practices. They believe in different spirits and usually propitiate the spirit of the dead parents or grandparents known as Phi Hum or Phi Num. They also propitiate the spirit of the founder of the clan. (Phi Num Hum) They believe that each village has its own spirit Phi Moong in whose name a small monument is constructed at the entry of the village. This symbolic monument or hut is known as Lho Phi.

The main festival *Poi Sangken*, is observed three days at the end of a year and the beginning of the new year, which corresponds to the end of the Chaitra and the beginning of the Vaisakh months. *Kartik purnima* or *Kartik Bihu* held in September & October in the full month of Kartik bear a religious significance. The Maiko Chumfai or Palguni purnima is observed by taking grains or rice from the new harvest. This almost resembles the Magh Bihu of the Assamese. The Vaisakhi purnima is observed as a day when Lord Buddha was born and attained Nirvana (K.S. Singh; 1995: 179-84).

The Singphos

The Singphos constitute one of the small endogamous groups inhabiting the Tirap and some of adjoining Lohit district of Arunachal Pradesh.

Before, the introduction of Buddhist religion, the Singphos mainly practiced animism characterized by belief in two sets of benevolent and malevolent supernatural powers. Buddhism was a late introduction.

In support of this view, an observation has been made by Prof. A.R. Das who did his field work among the Singphos in the villages of Bordumra Circle in Tirpa district. His observation is that the Singphos here are mostly Buddhist just for one or two generations, and many of them are converted only in the span of twelve to twenty years back. Earlier, in the pre-Buddhistic stage, they had their own deities images of some of which, it is reported, have been thrown into river while they were being adopted to the doctrines of Buddhism. (A.R. Das, 1986).

An oral history about the origin and migration of the group are many and inconsistent. The most commonly accepted tradition, however claims that they were formerly inhabitants of upper Burma.

The Singphos living in the area have migrated from the Hukang valley some hundred years ago. Dr. Dutta (1990) has mentioned about the date of their migration as "the end of 18th century". Some of them are still there in their original home-land, with whom the present population have got close relations.

The traditional history of their migration says that they have come to their present habitat across the Frontier wall the Patkai, through two routes. One is called Chowkang Iam, along the bank of Upper Noa Acting, and the other, Namjung Iam or Kadak Iam, through Pangchu pass (P. Dutta, 1990: 3-10).

The Singphos are one of the Buddhist Communities of Arunachal Pradesh. They call themselves Jingpho. As per the 1981 census 98.515 of them are Buddhists.

The Singpho religion is an amalgamation of Buddhism and the traditional religion. Though they are Buddhists, they believe in a number of *benevolent* and *malevolent nats* (spirits). The spirits of the house, clan and village are known as Smathi, Natgoon and Mrig Natgoon, respectively. Their traditional priest is known as dumsawa or dumsa. The role of the priest is to cure diseases, protect the villagers from evil spirits and remove the evil spirits. The priest also examines the liver of chicken for prognostication and divination. They also have faith in the *chowsra* (Buddhist priest) who gives religious teachings and performs the birth and death rites. The chowsra resides in the village *Buddha-Vihar* or *Bapu-chong* (monastery) which is adorned with the images of Lord Buddha. The main Buddhist festivals include the spring festival sangken which is held on the last day of Chaitra. The traditional festival is *Sipongyoung Poi or the Singpho* New Year, held sometimes in the month of February. During this festival animistic rituals are performed such as sacrifices of buffaloes. Dancing and singing are parts of this festival.

In the context of religious beliefs and practices the Singphos have developed close links with the Khamptis, Khmiyangs and Donmias neighbours who employ Singpho Buddhist monks. The Singpho community also celebrates some *Tai* festivals in close association and collaboration with the Tai Budhists (K.S. Singh; 1995: 293-97).

Khamba

The Khambas call themselves Kham-Zayu. Their original group was Kham which belonged to Borge, a place in the north. Other similar territorial subgroups were Khan-Jarten, Chungpho, Kham-Traya, Popa, Kham-konjo and Kham-Jarten. Members from all these sub-groups constitute today's Khamba Community. Their habitat in the north was known as Kanam Showa Phodung. At present they are distributed in Nyering, Nuykkang, Yortung, Mankota and Tashigong in the Singa Circle, west Siang district. In 1991 census their population was only 534 of which 261 were males and 273 females.

The community profess the Mahayana sect of Buddhism. Each village has sacred centre called *gomba* or *dhakoho* (the shrine with the image of Buddha). The *lama* is the community's sacred specialist. They preside over births, marriage, and funeral rites, besides propitiating the deities to ensure health and prosperity. In December the community celebrates the *Cungripa Losar* festival signifying the enjoyment after working hard in the fields. The *Tombo Losar* is celebrated in January, in honour of the some spirit as in the *Cungripa Losar* festival. In February they hold the *Mendruk Drua*, a prayer for recovery from stomach troubles; the *Duwa Ripa*, to start cultivation and *Ngungne* (feasting), signifying the purification of the soul. (K.S. Singh; 1995: 167-72).

Their art is highly stylistic having a transHimalayan artistic tradition. It is influenced by Mahayana philosophy–scroll painting (thanka), murals, kakariang or village gate gompa and mane(shrine) as well as painted, wooden household objects and masks.

Membas

As per 1981 census 99.33% of the members of this community are Buddhists. The Membas derived their name from the village Meula.

They belong to the Tsangla group. They migrated from the North eastern side of the country and later crossed the Lusela pass to settle in a number of villages in west Siang district. They are distributed in Mechuka. Opu, Bona, Galling Korfu, Dorgling halung and Tuting villages.

The Membas are divided into a number of sub-groups such as *Umber Cheje, Oksang Ollgel* etc. These sub-groups fall under a class of chiefs, while the Saleng, Tamang, Topta and Brahmi sub-groups constitute the class of commoners. They migrated from the north to the eastern side of the country, and later crossed the Lusela pass to settle in a number of villages in the Tuting and Mechuka circles of the West Siang district.

The Membas practice Buddhism and their sacred place is called *gompa*. The *lama* is the chief of the *gompa*. He looks after the welfare of the community. The major festivals of the community are *Lopar, Druba, Pemasuba, Pemajaleng, Dosipai, Kartholain, Pirathechu* and *Lochoi Towadrupa*. All these are observed for the members of the community. They also perform mask dance.

Their traditional dance is known as *Bro* which is followed by the *Bah* (mark) dance. They use musical instruments like gongs, bells etc.

The Memba handicrafts also bear marks of Tibetan Mahayana philosophy. Scrolls, murals, decorative wooden objects, images and masks are their handicrafts.

SUMMARY AND CONCLUSION

The latest data said that the total population of the state of Arunachal Pradesh is 1,091,117 of which 573,951 are males and 517,166 are females.

The total number of Buddhist population of India is 7955,207 their number in Arunachal Pradesh being143,028. The Buddhist literacy rate of the state is 44.9%.

Arunachal is basically a tribal state where most of the original inhabitants are animists with their belief in numerous spirits both benevolent and malevolent. Buddhism exists side by side with animism. The number of Buddhist tribes are many. The most important Buddhist tribes are Monpa, Sherdukpens, Khamptis, Singphos Membas and Singphos, and Khambas. The Buddhism as practiced by these tribes are of two schools–Mahayana of the Tibetan type and Theravada or the Burmese type. This has been possible due to the location of the state which is a neighbour of Tibet and Bhutan in the North and Burma in the east.

All the Buddhist villages have gompa or the monastery which is the most sacred place where the Buddha images and the holy books are kept. One or more officiating lamas are attached to a gompa. The Mahayana lamas are often trained in the monasteries of Bhutan or India. Their handicrafts too bear the influence of the religion and share the traditional characteristics of the Tibetan handicrafts. The tribes practicing Theravada Buddhism too have monks of various grades such as the *Mahasthabir, Sthabir, Bhikku, Sharmaneya* attached to these monasteries. The sacred books are also kept in these monasteries. For Khamtis the monastery is also an important place of learning where the boys learn their own scripts along with *Pali*.

On the whole Buddhism of this state exhibit some peculiar characteristics which is a result of its amalgamation with the tribal animistic practices in the surroundings. The Buddhist tribes worship Lord Buddha and side by side follow the traditional shamanistic practices which also forms an important role in their life. They believe in witchcrafts and evil spirits and to control these they seek the help of the traditional priests.

In concluding part it may be said that animism existed in Arunachal even before before the introduction of Buddhism. As a result even the Buddhist tribes have been unable to give up all the old practices and beliefs or in other words, to come out of their little tradition. So the final result is the peculiar syncretism of Buddhism and the Animism. Initially the Christian missionaries were not allowed to preach inside Arunachal Pradesh, but of late the Christian missionaries have begun to exert a considerable influence among the Buddhist tribes. Economically backward tribes are converting to Christianity even from among the Buddhists.

REFERENCES

Ahmed, F., *Communities of NE India.*

Baruah, T.K., *The Singphos and their Religion*, The Janabhumi Press, Shilong, 1997.

Census of India, Arunachal Pradesh, Directorate of Arunachal Pradesh, Itanagar, 1991.

Dutta, P.C., 'Development of Traditionl Democratic Institution in Arunachal Pradesh' in *Peoples of NE India* Sarthak Sengupta (ed.), Gyan Publishing House, New Delhi, 1996.

Dutta, P., *The Singphos*, Directorate of Research Govt. of Arunachal Pradesh, Itanagar, 1990.

Das, A.K., 'Religion and Ethnic Dilema: A Case Study of Singphos', Special Lecture C.H.S., N.B.U., 1986.

Das, G., *Tribes of Arunachal Pradesh in Transition.*

Dutta, P.C., *Aspects of Arunachal Pradesh,* Directorate of Research Govt. of AP, Itanagar, 1990.

Nair, P.T., *Tribes of Arunachal Pradesh*, Spectrum; Publication, Guwahati, 1985.

Sarkar Niranjan,Tawang Monastery, Directorate of Research, Government of Arunachal Pradesh, Itanagar, 1996.

Sarkar, S., '*Society and Culture Among the Tribes of AP: Tradition and Change*', in S. Sengupta, (ed.) Tribes of NE India Gyan Publishing House, New Delhi, 2003.

Singh, K.S. (Ed.), *People of India: Arunachal Pradesh*, Seagull Books Calcutta, Vol.-XIV. 1995.

Sen, S., *Arunachal Pradesh and the Tribes: Selected Bibliography*, Gyan Publishing House, Delhi, 1986.

INDEX

H

I

J

E

L

Q

R

U

V

W

Y

Z